THE DEVIL AND THE JEWS

THE MEDIEVAL CONCEPTION OF THE JEW AND
ITS RELATION TO MODERN ANTISEMITISM

PUBLISHED ON THE
MARY CADY TEW MEMORIAL FUND

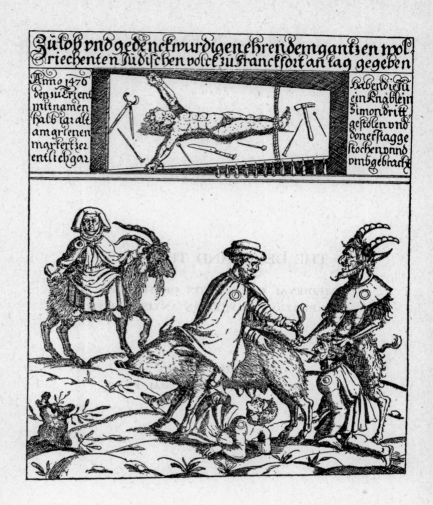

The Judensau

An early seventeenth-century version of a design engraved at
the entrance to a bridge at Frankfort in the fifteenth century,
which was in turn derived from an older and very popular medieval theme

THE DEVIL AND THE JEWS

THE MEDIEVAL CONCEPTION OF THE JEW

AND

ITS RELATION TO MODERN ANTISEMITISM

BY

JOSHUA TRACHTENBERG

NEW HAVEN

YALE UNIVERSITY PRESS

LONDON : HUMPHREY MILFORD : OXFORD UNIVERSITY PRESS

TO THE MEMORY OF

A TRUE SCHOLAR

JACOB MANN

(1888-1940)

CONTENTS

LIST OF ILLUSTRATIONS ix

PREFACE xi

INTRODUCTION. MEDIEVAL SUPERSTITION AND MODERN
ANTISEMITISM 1

PART ONE: THE "DEMONIC" JEW

I. "DEVIL INCARNAL" 11
II. ANTICHRIST 32
III. WITH HORNS AND TAIL 44

PART TWO: THE JEW AS SORCERER

IV. "A JEW IS FULL OF SORCERY" 57
V. EUROPE DISCOVERS THE KABBALAH 76
VI. MAGIC AND MEDICINE 88
VII. THE POISONERS 97
VIII. HOST AND IMAGE DESECRATION 109
IX. RITUAL MURDER 124
X. THE BLOOD ACCUSATION 140

PART THREE: THE JEW AS HERETIC

XI. CHURCH AND JEW 159
XII. INFIDEL OR HERETIC? 170
XIII. THE ATTACK UPON USURY 188
XIV. THE CRUSADE AGAINST SORCERY 196
XV. HERETIC-SORCERER-JEW 207
EPILOGUE. STILL THE DEVIL'S OWN 217
NOTES 221
BIBLIOGRAPHY 256
INDEX 269

40420

ILLUSTRATIONS

The *Judensau*. (Early seventeenth century)   *Frontispiece*

The Wandering Jew. Gustave Doré (1852)   16

"Aaron fil diaboli" (1277)   27

Der Juden Badstub. (Early seventeenth century)   28-29

Satanic figures with Jew badge (1571)   30

Satan attended by Jews (1575)   30

Antichrist. Lucas Cranach (1493)   33

"Youth, Virgin, Jew, and Soldier" (1624)   45

Jew astride a goat. (Fifteenth century)   45

The demon Colbif claims Mosse Mokke and Avegaye (1233)   53

Johann Fischart's *Wunderzeitung* (1574)   53

The demon Belial before Solomon (1473)   62

Demons serving humans (1555)   62

The "Kabbalistic" magic circle   78

The execution of Münzmeister Lippold (1573)   85

Christian girls desecrate the Host (1567)   112

Host desecration at Sternberg (1492)   112

Conjuring the devil (1575)   136

Torture applied to produce a "confession" (1475)   136

Heresy. Anton Eisenhut   172

Satan participates in Jewish financial transactions (about 1620)   195

Sorcerers paying homage to the devil (1626)   209

A witch's departure for the Sabbat. Hans Baldung (1514)   209

PREFACE

NOT so very long ago Archibald MacLeish bitterly castigated the "Irresponsibles" who in our time elect the safe seclusion of "pure" scholarship or art and either disdain or fear to descend into the heart of the conflict. Certainly, at a time when the world is tortured with bloodshed and tyranny, when our culture and perhaps civilization itself are in jeopardy and men by the millions pit their lives to preserve them, I cannot escape a self-conscious twinge of guilt to be caught rummaging in musty medieval texts. If the pen is a weapon, ought I not be wielding mine, feeble though it be, in the thick of the battle?

Yet even medieval texts have a pertinency for today—and what has been brought between the covers of this book is not without meaning for our world. There *is* an abiding value in the discovery and statement of the truth; surely this is the greatest of all the principles for which we fight. Even a world in turmoil needs the truth—perhaps such a world especially. The problem that is treated here has become one of increasing importance to the peace of the world. To elucidate its background is to render it the better understood, and thus perhaps to move it a step nearer solution. I am under no illusion as to the immediate practical utility of such an investigation. But at least for the record, and for those who cherish truth above fancy, the story is here.

I undertook this work with no preconceived notions. Indeed, when I started it I had no idea it would lead in this direction. This book is an outgrowth of my earlier book, *Jewish Magic and Superstition*, in particular of its first chapter. It was my aim to examine more thoroughly than I had been able to the accusation of sorcery against the Jew. But before long I realized that the subject had far deeper implications, that it involved, in fact, not alone this one charge but the entire medieval conception of the Jew, and that this same conception, in another vocabulary, still prevails through much of the world. If the Jew is today despised and feared and hated, it is because we are the heirs of the Middle Ages. If it is possible for demagogues to sow the seeds of disunion and discord, to stir fanatical emotions and set neighbor against neighbor, it is because the figure of the "demonic" Jew, less than human, indeed, antihuman, the creation of the medieval mind, still dominates the folk imagination.

"Out of the mouths of babes and sucklings" we may still learn the unvarnished truth. It came to the father of a friend of mine recently when he parked his car in a small French Canadian town. Two youngsters at play in the street ran over and peered curiously at its occupant. "C'est un Juif," declared the older and wiser, after a moment's consideration. "Mais non," protested the other in his innocence, "ce n'est pas un Juif; c'est un homme." When I repeated this to another friend he told me he had overheard the same exchange in South Africa. "Daar komt een mens," remarked a boy and his companion corrected him, "Dit is geen mens, dit is een Jude."

Obviously, we must at last recognize, the lie is a more potent weapon, skilfully wielded, than the bare and simple truth, as Adolf Hitler once so forcefully declared and has since demonstrated. For the lie can be molded to match the "will to believe"; the truth is made of less malleable stuff. The exaggerated materialist interpretation of history, no less than the demogogic, has fostered its own wilful distortion of truth. That anti-Jewish sentiment is the product of social and economic tensions is true —but yet only half the truth. Maurice Samuel, in his remarkably sensitive and astute book, *The Great Hatred*, has done a superb job of puncturing the exclusively materialist interpretation of *antisemitism*, which is something else again, a psychological-cultural phenomenon altogether outside the ken of materialists. The distinction is crucial. I must emphasize, in order to avoid misunderstanding, that this is not a study of anti-Jewish prejudice in all its aspects, and that this book does not purport to tell the entire story. My concern here is with that element in the complex of anti-Jewish prejudice which renders it different, in expression and intensity, from other manifestations of racial or minority antipathy—the demonological. Samuel's insistence upon the "unique demonological character among group hostilities" of antisemitism, upon its "diabolisation of the Jew," is startlingly apt and correct and basic. (It was from him that I first heard the term "demonic Jew," long before I, and perhaps he too, was aware of its *literal* appropriateness.) Without my intending it so, this book has developed into a chapter-and-verse demonstration of the historic correctness of this thesis.

In acknowledging with gratitude the interest and counsel of a number of friends, I must first offer my thanks to the audience which generously criticized the thesis when it was embodied in a paper presented before the Jewish Academy of Arts and Sciences in New York City in November, 1939. One highly respected reverend gentleman unwittingly encouraged me to continue my research with the contention that this is an inopportune time to revive the unpleasant memories stirred up by the subject matter. Why dig up all this muck at a time when antisemitism has attained such intensity? Just so! Could there be a better time? And it was Professor Morris R. Cohen's suggestion that such a study is incomplete without an indication of origins and causes that produced the final section of this book.

The first draft was read and criticized by Professors Salo W. Baron of Columbia University and Guido Kisch of the Jewish Institute of Religion, and by Dr. Solomon Grayzel of Philadelphia, from whose generous advice I profited greatly. Indeed, it was at the instance of Professor Kisch that I continued the work, and with his graciously proffered assistance that I revised and expanded it to its present shape and size. I have also benefited from the criticism of Professor Roland H. Bainton of Yale University, who read the manuscript before publication. Responsibility for the contents, of course, remains exclusively mine.

I am grateful, too, to the libraries that took the trouble to store up the books without which this work could not have been accomplished. Only one who has hunted in vain through card

catalogue after catalogue for some obscure item can appreciate
the sense of personal favor conferred by the wholly impersonal
institution which has foreseen and provided for his need. They
are too many to name. But to Mrs. Mary Fried of the Jewish
Theological Seminary Library I owe special thanks for her kindness in facilitating my use of that institution's rich collection.

My wife, as always, was an unremitting stimulus and aid,
as only she can be. And to Judith Miriam, too, I am indebted—
for keeping the peace when my work demanded it.

Easton, Pennsylvania   J. T.

INTRODUCTION

MEDIEVAL SUPERSTITION AND MODERN ANTISEMITISM

WHY are Jews so cordially hated—and feared? By what mysterious legerdemain can a weak, defenseless minority be invested in the public eye with the awesome attributes of omnipotence? How is it that men believe of the Jews what common sense would forbid them to believe of anyone else? These are questions that must bother many people. Yet, for all the vast polemical literature that modern antisemitism has produced, they are questions that still await a satisfying reply. Every charge against the Jews, sober or intemperate, has elicited its meticulous and solemn defense. On the basis of cogency of argumentation and sheer weight of statistics, Jew hatred should long since have been exorcised. But it flourishes, a menace not alone to the peace of mind and bodily security of the Jewish people but just as much these days to the inner cohesion and stability of all democratic nations. Jew hatred is hardier than the liberal utopians who placed their trust in reason and knowledge imagined.

All the statistics and arguments that have been advanced to refute antisemitic libels have not succeeded in effectively demolishing a single one of them. They thrive, apparently, in very despite of the fact that they can be and are so easily exploded. No lie is too petty, or too silly, or too big to work its calculated effect. Roosevelt a Jew? The New Deal a "Jew Deal"? Benjamin Franklin the author of a vicious anti-Jewish diatribe? Do Jews control commerce and industry, or the press, or whatever else you please? What about the "Aryan" race and the pariah "non-Aryans"? Historians and sociologists and economists and anthropologists and all the rest, not to mention simple lovers of truth and justice, can argue themselves blue in the face, but those who believe these fables go on believing—and acting as though they were true.

Why in Heaven's name is this? There can be but one answer: people believe such things because they *want* to believe them. They are predisposed to accept any and all accusations, irrespective of objective merit, that fit into their preconceived notion of the Jew. The specific charges are nothing more than rationalizations of an underlying animus. If one is temporarily outmoded a dozen others spring up in its place—and they need but be superficially plausible to be embraced as gospel truth.

Hatred of the Jew is not the result of a rational process. If it were, the absurdity of antisemitic accusations would stifle it stillborn. A casual examination of the stock-in-trade of anti-Jewish agitation reveals a mixture of contradictory and mutually canceling generalizations that no man of any degree of intelligence could credit. How can one believe that all Jews are at the same time Communists and capitalists in the face of the obvious untenability of all such generalizations, in the face of the well-known lower middle class and proletarian economy and general poverty of the Jewish masses, in the face, indeed, of the logical contradiction inherent in the dual characterization? The attempt to *prove* logically and statistically that this is not so can quite apparently make no impression upon minds that are blind *ab initio* to the all-too-evident truth of the matter.

No, hatred of the Jew rests upon no rational base. When everything possible has been said about the psychological xenophobia that rejects "difference" and resents minority cultures, about the economic and social frictions that exacerbate social relations, about the astute and persuasive propaganda techniques of anarchical demagogues, about the need for a "scapegoat" for release of social tension, about the imperfections of the Jews themselves, and their abnormal economic status—and all these are potent *immediate* stimuli of active Jew hatred—the *ultimate* source, buried deep in the mass subconscious, is still untouched. Underneath the present stimuli, and contributing to them their explosive potentiality, lies the powder keg of emotional predisposition, of a conception of the Jew which has nothing to do with facts or logic.

What is the real meaning of the charges leveled against the Jew? Whether as international Communist or international capitalist, and all the more as the two in one, he is the archenemy of Western civilization. He is alien, not to this or that land, but to all Western society, alien in his habits, his pursuits, his interests, his character, his very blood. Wherever he lives he is a creature apart. He is the arch-degenerate of the world, infecting its literature, its art, its music, its politics and economics with the subtle poison of his insidious influence, ripping out its moral foundation stone by stone until it will collapse helpless in his hands. This is his final goal: to conquer the world, to refashion it in his own craven image, enslave it to his own alien ends.

Antisemitic propaganda paints a fantastic Jekyll-Hyde portrait of "the international Jew," ostensibly meek and powerless, impoverished and oppressed, few in number and pitifully disunited, but in reality wielding immense power, dominant everywhere by virtue of his world-embracing secret organization, his iron discipline, his unprincipled methods. Absurd? Yet this is the conception that makes it possible for a large part of the world to believe that the "Elders of Zion" plot world destruction and conquest while Jews in the hundreds of thousands fall victim to Nazi barbarism. The Jews engineered the Bolshevik revolution, and foisted Communism upon an unwilling Russian people; the policy of the Soviet Union has ever since been a Jewish policy, and the Comintern has been manipulated for Jewish ends. Jews "stabbed Germany in the back" and caused her defeat in 1918. The Jews rule, or rather misrule, every state that has not yet seen the light and blasted their power—read: the democratic nations; indeed, "plutocratic democracy" is a sinister Jewish scheme to dominate the earth. Behind the scenes, it was the Jews who made the present war and who successfully conspired to drive America into it. Always the Jews—and always engaged in antisocial, destructive enterprise. "The basis of the Jewish religion," affirms the high priest of modern antisemitism, "comprises a direct criminal assault on all nations of the earth."

Such contentions, it is true, are usually advanced by tyrants and demagogues, who cynically clothe the naked absurdity of their case and the naked depravity of their motives in a plausible veil of racial and economic abracadabra. This is "scientific" antisemitism. But antisemitism is "scientific" only for those few who demand an intellectual camouflage to conceal their aims and prejudices. What does all this add up to for the people, for the inchoate, spellbound mass of men and women, free from all taint of philosophy and science, who provide the grist for the antisemitic mill? To them the Jew represents the mysterious, fearsome evil forces which from time immemorial have menaced the peace and security of mankind. The hypocritical hocus-pocus of the professional antisemite makes its calculated impression: the simple common man may not comprehend its sound but he does understand its meaning. This is simply the new way of expressing his inherited dread.

The mass mind is eminently retentive. Man, in Nietzsche's definition, is the being *with the longest memory*, and José Ortega y Gasset has recently affirmed (in his *Toward a Philosophy of History*) the objective existence of the accumulated past, as a positive element in creative action. But we cannot neglect the reality of the accumulated past as a *negative* influence—a pathological barrier to creative action. Man's inability to forget is the obverse of his faculty of memory. We may please to consider ourselves "moderns," but under our skeptical rationalism and scientific objectivity the conceptions of our forefathers are still potent motivating forces. If we have succeeded in banishing ancient notions from our conscious minds (and it need hardly be pointed out that a vast portion of the Western world has not yet exorcised the spirits and ghosts that preyed upon their ancestors) they have merely receded into the murky depths of the subconscious. Rationalize as it may, the Jew whom the world fears and hates is a heritage from the past—and the not-so-distant past at that. All our wrestling with the rationalizations is pointless effort until we uncover the hidden emotional roots from which illogic and untruth acquire the color of truth and meaning.

It is no sheer accident that Germany has become the motherland of modern antisemitism. The program of National Socialism has simply brought to the surface and intensified the latent hankering of the German people for its romanticized past. Otto D. Tolischus, the distinguished foreign correspondent who has observed Germany at close range throughout its crisis years, offers in his book, *They Wanted War*, a pat characterization of this spiritual regression: the German people, he remarks, "is dominated by Richard Wagner—not the Richard Wagner of the incomparable though still debated melodies, but the Richard Wagner who brought back to life the dismal, pitiless and forgotten world of German antiquity, the world of fighting gods and fighting heroes, of dragons and demons, of destiny and pagan epics, which presents itself to other peoples as mere Wagnerian opera, but which has become subconscious reality to the German masses and has been elevated to the inspirational mythos of the National Socialist movement that rules the Third Reich." We need not quarrel about how far back we must trace Germany's psychic atavism; it is the sober fact that seems unimpeachable. If the Nazi program has sometimes been loosely described as "medieval," in the matter of its Jewish policy it assuredly harks back to the psychology of the Middle Ages.

Modern so-called "scientific" antisemitism is not an invention of Hitler's. But it was born in Germany during the last century, and it has flourished primarily in Central and Eastern Europe, where medieval ideas and conditions have persisted until this day, and where the medieval conception of the Jew which underlies the prevailing emotional antipathy toward him was and still is most deeply rooted. ("Medieval" defines not a chronological but a mental epoch.) Hitler's contribution stemmed from his intuitive awareness of the elemental universality of this conception: call it inspiration or shrewdness, he sprayed the world with the antisemitic virus, knowing that it would everywhere fall upon hospitable ground, breeding the spiritual and social corruption that would open to him the path of conquest.

"The proficiency of the Jews in magic and their kinship with Satan would reveal, if we had the stomach to pursue the subject, the ultimate spring of medieval Jew-hatred," remarks Marvin Lowenthal in his study of *The Jews of Germany*. This is the conception, based upon the crassest superstition and credulity, that has permeated to the lower depths of Western culture, and which we must "have the stomach to pursue" and expose to the light of day if we are to comprehend the ultimate spring not only of medieval Jew hatred but of its modern, occasionally more sophisticated, version. Here, in this region of the mass subconscious we shall uncover the source of many a weird notion—of the horned Jew, of the Jewish thirst for Christian blood, of the Jew who scatters poison and disease broadcast, of the secret parliament of world Jewry, meeting periodically to scheme and plot, of a distinctive Jewish odor, of Jews practicing black magic and blighting their surroundings with the evil eye—notions that still prevail among the people and that have been advanced by official Nazi publications, for all the "scientific" verbiage of current antisemitism. But, more important, here we shall uncover the spring of the general conviction that prompts Jew hatred: of the Jew as an alien, evil, antisocial, and antihuman creature, essentially subhuman, indeed, and therefore answerable for the supreme crime of seeking to destroy by every subversive technique the fruits of that Christian civilization which in his heart of hearts he despises and abhors.

Anti-Jewish prejudice is older and more extensive than Christendom. It would be absurd to attribute its every manifestation to doctrinaire Christian hatred of the "Christ killers." But its unique demonological character is of medieval origin, with premonitions in earlier times of the turn it was destined to take; the "demonic Jew" was born of a combination of cultural and historical factors peculiar to Christian Europe in the later Middle Ages.

It should be unnecessary to point out that this study is not polemical in intent. However, since the material assembled here
emanates from Christian sources it becomes necessary to add a
word about the position of the Church. The facts have been permitted to tell their own story; but it was not easy at times to steer
a clear course between the often contradictory positions taken by
"the Church." Actually there were two Churches: the hierarchy
which laid down and defined general principles, and the lesser
clergy and the laity who translated principle into practice. The
two were not always in agreement. This is notably true insofar
as the Jews were concerned, for the hierarchy was often inclined
to be humane and to extend a degree of protection to them,
whereas the people, inspired usually by the local clergy, were not
equally disposed by a strict interpretation of canon law and
ecclesiastical pronouncement to exercise the restraint demanded
of them. The result was that practice and principle were often
at opposite poles. The people frequently chose to act upon the
implication of a policy which officially excoriated the Jews while
extending them the promise of protection. But the people were
"the Church" just as much as the hierarchy was; both made the
history of Christendom. I have sought, where necessary, to distinguish their attitudes toward the Jew, but it must be said that,
whether they were in agreement or not, the practical consequences of Christian principle are justly attributable to "the
Church."

The medieval conception of the Jew is the subject of this
study. We shall have to consider it at some length, for it is so
foreign to our modern point of view, to many, no doubt, so incredible, that only extended demonstration can persuade us that
it was actually and literally held—and that it must still be reckoned with in our own time. It may bring no comfort to concede
this, but the wealth of evidence at our disposal is too overwhelming in its cumulative effect to permit of any other conclusion.

PART ONE

THE "DEMONIC" JEW

CHAPTER ONE

"DEVIL INCARNAL"

CHRISTENDOM'S hostility toward the Jew reached its apogee in the post-Crusade period. It had been gathering force through many centuries. But the widespread social unrest, the rising menace of Islam, the spread of heresies that marked the eleventh and twelfth centuries and continued unabated for several hundred years while the Reformation and the Renaissance-to-be slowly germinated called forth the greatest energies of the Church, to combat its enemies from within and without. The Crusades and the Inquisition were among its most powerful instruments for preserving the unity of Christendom. It was inevitable that such a period of social and religious stress, especially noteworthy for a marked intensification of Christian fanaticism, should witness also a heightened antagonism toward the Jews—the most notoriously "heretical" and anti-Christian force in Europe, living in the very midst of the citadel whose security was being threatened from every side. The antagonism was not new, but the form and intensity it assumed as a result of the peculiar circumstances of the period were.

The problem of understanding the medieval attitude toward the Jew is necessarily a complex one, for just as today a variety of factors operated during the Middle Ages to complicate and embitter Christian-Jewish relations: the anti-Jewish tradition stemming from the Gospels themselves; the dogmatic enmity of the Church underscored by the religious and cultural nonconformity of the Jewish people within what was essentially a totalitarian civilization; economic rivalry and the sometimes superior, or at any rate strategic, economic position of Jews; the gradual evolution of a new social balance of power and the political struggle it entailed; the emergence of the national spirit.

These all played a part in estranging the two. And we must recognize also the share that universal ignorance and misunderstanding of Judaism and the sense of frustration and exasperation aroused by a people which, against all reason and the saddest of experience, refused to merge with the dominant Christian world played in fostering a psychological antipathy toward them.

Without in any way minimizing the force of these factors, we believe nevertheless that they do not tell the whole story or even the essential part of the story. The most vivid impression to be gained from a reading of medieval allusions to the Jew is of a hatred so vast and abysmal, so intense, that it leaves one gasping for comprehension. The unending piling up of vile epithets and accusations and curses, the consistent representation of the Jew as the epitome of everything evil and abominable, for whom in particular the unbounded scorn and contumely of the Christian world were reserved, must convince the most casual student that we are dealing here with a fanaticism altogether subjective and nonrational. True, Jew hatred, as ever, is often accounted for in the medieval sources on ostensibly objective grounds; but the intensity of the reaction is so disproportionate to the reasons given that we are forced to pry deeper for the source of the emotional bias which made it possible for the Middle Ages to believe anything and everything reprehensible concerning the Jew, no matter how wild and fantastic the charge, and which led to such passionate outbursts of violence against him.

It is no wonder that the word "Jew" has become a term of abuse. It was invariably so used in medieval literature[1] and is still so used to this day. The popular literature produced during the Middle Ages was almost entirely dominated by a single point of view, that of orthodox Christianity; mystery, miracle, and morality plays, chronicles and legends, poems, folk tales, and folk songs, all painted the Jew as the fount of evil, deliberately guilty of unspeakable crimes against the founder of the Christian faith and the Christian Church, and against its adherents as individuals. No sin was too foul to be adduced against him—but the most heinous offense of all was his imputed intention to destroy

Christianity and Christendom. The Jew was the inveterate enemy of mankind. This was the gravamen of the charge against him. And under this head every accusation found an easy acceptance. The secular literature that emerged toward the end of the Middle Ages followed this lead, depicting the Jew in the same terms, though the motivation was no longer religious. The secular drama, for instance, touching upon social matters, presented the Jew in a social role but possessed of the same vicious character, still the personification of evil—still the archenemy of society.[2] The pattern was preserved for posterity. Where another note was permitted to intrude, it was only extremely rarely one of kindliness and commiseration; more usually it was one of scorn and derision—the Jew was a comic as well as a vile creature.

To the masses the Jew who appeared upon the stage and in the tales and chronicles and moralized anecdotes, or *exempla* of the preachers, was not an individual but a type—the pattern after which the entire people was modeled. This Jew often lacked a name; rarely did he own personal characteristics. But more noteworthy still is the fact that a conscious effort was often made to represent him, even in material dealing with past events, such as Biblical drama and legend, not as a historical figure but as the contemporary Jew with whom the audience was more or less familiar. The sins of Jesus' contemporaries were deliberately piled upon the collective head of medieval Jewry. In more than one German and French mystery play, for instance, we find such stage directions as that the Jews are to be *jüdisch gekleidet* ("clothed in Jewish garb") or *avec rouelle et bonnet cornu* ("with Jew badge and peaked cap"), the distinctive dress of the medieval merchants and peddlers. In the Frankfort Passion Play the Jews who mock and strike Jesus bear names current in that vicinity until today.[3] When we consider that these plays, though primarily religious in theme, often embodied a social commentary and criticism as well, serving as the foremost medium of folk expression of the time, so that the audience tended to interpret the scene before them as applying to their own time and their own lot,[4] we can appreciate the direct impact of this picture of the

Jew. The manner in which the Jews treated Jesus and the saints in this literature was presented, and understood, as illustrative of the character of the contemporary Jew. Nor were these legends and dramas devoted exclusively to ancient history. The manifold crimes attributed to the contemporary Jew also found a prominent place in them, and served to substantiate and to fill out the detail in the portrait drawn by the older material.

The historical authenticity of these tales was of no importance. The Christian cherished them as his primary source of entertainment and instruction and would have rejected out of hand (had this occurred to him, which it did not) any suggestion of a critical examination of their veracity. He could no more question them than he could the religious authority which proffered them wrapped in the aura of highest truth. "Whether what I am relating is true or not is no concern of mine," wrote a twelfth-century chronicler; [5] "it is told thus, and thus must it be accepted." From a careful student of the documents relating to alleged Jewish criminal acts of the sort we are interested in comes this statement: "If we today must conclude that there is scarcely a vestige of objective truth in these accusations, it is nonetheless quite certain that the common people *in toto,* and indeed the greatest part of the more educated laity . . . was firmly convinced of the guilt of the Jews." [6] It is this attribute of unimpeachability that renders the legends and charges so powerful an instrument in shaping public opinion. "The medieval mind was ready to believe anything and everything—especially if there were any kind of written evidence for it," says E. B. Osborn. [7]

Supported by the official policy of the Church, actively propagated by all its organs of popular instruction, given added weight by the legislative enactments of secular and ecclesiastical authorities, the conception of the Jew which emerges from this literature became one of the basic convictions of the Middle Ages—a conviction that aroused deep-seated and unreasoning hatred, and from which all the individual specific charges derived their capacity to evoke the venom of the masses.

Medieval Christendom was so firmly convinced of the incontestable truth of its own tradition and teaching that it could conceive of no rival truth. Curious as this may seem, there is overwhelming evidence that the Catholic world believed that the Jew himself recognized the truth of Christian doctrine!

According to this view, the Jews knew that the coming of Jesus was foretold in Scripture, even though they stubbornly denied this. To the Christian the conventional interpretation of Scripture was the only possible and sensible one; the Jewish interpretation could not therefore fail to seem the product either of wilful misunderstanding or falsification. Jerome and other early Church Fathers frequently complained that the Jewish teachers consciously and deliberately perverted the meaning of the original text, and Justinian went so far as to embody this complaint in law, requiring the reading of the *Torah* in the synagogues in a language comprehensible to the hearers, and forbidding the customary explanation that followed the reading: "Thus there shall be no opportunity to their interpreters, who make use only of the Hebrew, to corrupt it in any way they like, since the ignorance of the public conceals their depravity." [8] Medieval scholars did not hesitate to impute to Jews even the crime of tampering with the text of the Bible in an effort to destroy its Christological meaning. One fifteenth-century writer adopted the conspiratorial theme and told how the rabbis "assembled in great multitudes at the Babylon of Egypt, which is called Cairo, where they, with as much secrecy as possible, falsified and corrupted the Scriptures. . . ." [9] Martin Luther frequently exploded in bitter and even foul denunciation of the Jews for what he considered their wilful refusal to acknowledge the plain sense of the text.[10]

The Jews, moreover, had actually witnessed the events attendant upon the Passion of Christ, and if they perversely denied what their own eyes had beheld, at least one of the eyewitnesses had been providentially preserved to give them the lie direct with his living testimony of the correctness of the Christian tradition, and of the truth and power of the word of Christ. It was in the

The Wandering Jew

GUSTAVE DORÉ (1852)

thirteenth century that news of the Wandering Jew, who had taunted Jesus on the way to the crucifixion and had been told by him to "go on forever till I return," first reached Europe. In 1228 an Armenian archbishop, who was visiting St. Albans in England, reported that this character, Joseph Cartaphilus by name, lived and was widely renowned in the Orient; and in 1252 this statement was confirmed by other Armenian pilgrims to the same monastery.[11] This information was promptly recognized and hailed as a most weighty proof of the truth of Christianity, and continental writers did not fail to apply its full apologetic force against Jews and heretics. Stories of his odd experience multiplied. In most of the accounts the Wandering Jew had forsaken his false faith and adopted the true faith of Jesus, in contrast to the obduracy of his fellow Jews; several versions, however, have him remain a Jew, refusing to acknowledge through baptism the truth to which his own unique career testified, and thus typifying the attitude of all Jews.[12]

Christians were convinced that the later Jewish literature contained proofs and admissions of the truth of Christianity. The Jews, it was widely believed, had attempted to disguise or delete such passages—an open confession, of course, of their damaging existence![13] Nor was this all. The charge of mutilation of the host by Jews rested upon the belief that they too accepted the dogma of transubstantiation, the most peculiarly sectarian of Christian dogmas. Marlowe's Jew of Malta even swears by the *Corpo di Dio!* The plenitude of miracles that accompanied alleged Jewish criminal acts against Christianity, such as the mutilation of the host and of images of Jesus and the saints, as well as the so-called ritual murders, were constant and inescapable evidence which the Jews presumably could not deny (though they did). Several times, indeed, pious Jews are represented in the miracle dramas as acknowledging the miracle-working powers of St. Nicholas and revering his image.

Obviously, then, the refusal of the Jew to identify himself with Christendom in the face of such apparently conclusive evidence that he was aware of the truth of its religious position perplexed and enraged the pious Christian. As Cecil Roth points out in his recent study of the problem,[14] "the medieval mind was as keen, as logical and as eminently reasonable as is ours." It demanded—and found—an explanation of this seemingly inexplicable behavior, an explanation which accounts for the intense emotional antipathy that has ever since characterized Christian-Jewish relations.

What was this answer? Roth's too-ready acceptance of the usual view that Catholic Europe ascribed the bigotry of the Jew to sheer perversity and stubbornness leaves something to be desired. If his postulate of the reasonableness of the medieval mind is correct, as undoubtedly it is, then it is strange indeed that "such a mind should ascribe to a group of people a type of psychology which is contrary to all human experience." [15] It is an explanation which cannot satisfy us, and therefore we may assume that it did not satisfy medieval Europe either.

We must seek further. That Jews were possessed of the spirit of perversity and stubbornness the medieval mind did not doubt. But whence came that spirit? How was it that the psychology of the Jews should be contrary to all human experience? The answer was that the Jew was *not* human—not in the sense that the Christian was. He was a creature of an altogether different nature, of whom normal human reactions could not be expected. "Really I doubt whether a Jew can be human for he will neither yield to human reasoning, nor find satisfaction in authoritative utterances, alike divine and Jewish," protested Peter the Venerable of Cluny.[16] What then? He was the devil's creature! Not a human being but a demonic, a diabolic beast fighting the forces of truth and salvation with Satan's weapons, was the Jew as medieval Europe saw him. One might as soon expect the devil himself to submit of his own free will to Christ, as the Jew. And against such a foe no well of hatred was too deep, no war of extermination effective enough until the world was rid of his menace.

This answer is so grotesque that it must require a little reflection before we can accept it in all its literalness. If our minds refuse at first blush to countenance such a proposition it is because Satan has been banished from our mental purview. Yet, in considering the medieval world we must revert to the premises upon which the medieval *Weltanschauung* rested. We can follow its logic only by recognizing its underlying axioms.

The devil has never played a very prominent role in Jewish thought as a distinct personality; during the Middle Ages in particular the figure of Satan "was little more than an allegory, whose moral was the prevalence of sin." [17] But to the medieval Christian he was a very real personage indeed, as real, at one end of the moral scale and the world scheme, as Jesus was at the other. The Christian was constantly oppressed by his omnipresence, incessantly subjected to his temptations and blandishments, tormented by his machinations and those of his agents, the demons. Christian laymen and clerics, learned or unlettered, paid him the homage of belief and reverence, in the fear and trembling with which they regarded his nefarious activities.

Satan was the archenemy of mankind, seeking to destroy it, as Jesus had come to save it. This, too, was an axiom of medieval belief. While in the Synoptic Gospels the episode of Jesus' temptation [18] is incidental to his preparation for his active ministry, little more than a preliminary test, so to speak, the tendency became increasingly pronounced to describe Jesus' ministry in terms of a struggle between him and the devil for control of the world. Jesus became ever more the god in Christian belief and thus came to represent the principle of good in its eternal struggle with the evil principle, as it had been personified in ancient legends and theologies. The earliest Christian Anglo-Saxon poetry (eighth century) depicts Jesus as a mighty warrior pitted against the forces of Satan; we may see in this perhaps the influence of older pagan models. But some centuries later this conception of the mission of Jesus was quite common, and it is basic to the theme of most of the mystery plays. One of the oldest English ballads, "The Harrowing of Hell" (early fourteenth century), based on the apocryphal gospel of Nicodemus, opens with the lines: "Alle herkneth to me nou, a strif will I tellen ou, of

Jesu and of Satan." [19] Indeed, this elemental feud actually antedated the birth of Christ. For no other reason than to trick the
devil into taking him for an ordinary man did Jesus suffer the
"penaunce" of circumcision. And it was for the infant redeemer's
protection that he was born of a married virgin, the medieval
preachers reassured their congregations: Satan, whose study of
the Prophets had apprised him of the virginal birth of the Messiah,
would not think to seek him out among the offspring of a married
woman.[20]

The New Testament accounts, which are polemical writings,
already display the animus of the early Church toward the Jews,
in portraying them as the implacable enemies of Jesus. Indeed
Luke, who emphasizes throughout the universal appeal of Jesus
and is clearly anxious to present the Romans in as favorable a light
as possible, has Pilate make *two* attempts to free Jesus, and even
introduces Herod to support him. The desire of Pilate to release
Jesus is still more strongly emphasized in the apocryphal gospels.
Thus gradually the Roman participants in the Passion drama
receded altogether into the background, Pontius Pilate was completely exonerated of guilt, and all the blame for the suffering and
death of Jesus was put upon his fellow Jews. In some of the mysteries we find Pilate fervently pleading Jesus' cause, only to be
overridden by the merciless Jews.[21]

The two inexorable enemies of Jesus, then, in Christian legend,
were the devil and the Jew, and it was inevitable that the legend
should establish a causal relation between them. In fact, the association of the two in Christian polemic appears quite early:
John, definitely hostile to the Jews, says of them that they are of
their "father the devil" (8.44), while Revelation (2.9 and 3.9)
curtly calls a Jewish house of worship a "synagogue of Satan,"
an epithet made trite in later usage by constant repetition. During
the fourth and fifth centuries, when the Church had finally established itself and felt free to lash out at its foes, abuse of this sort
was liberally showered upon Judaism and all its works.

The very first law of Constantine which dealt with the synagogue referred to it by a term never used of a religious building,

and which in Roman slang meant a brothel. Chrysostom of Antioch maintained that "the synagogues of the Jews are the homes of idolatry and devils, even though they have no images in them," and again he insisted that "the Jews do not worship God but devils, so that all their feasts are unclean." On the strength of Ps. 96.37 he asserted that the Jews "sacrificed their sons and daughters to devils. . . . They are become worse than the wild beasts, and for no reason at all, with their own hands they murder their own offspring to worship the avenging devils who are the foes of our life." His contemporary, Hilary of Poitiers, believed that "before the Law was given the Jews were possessed of an unclean devil, which the Law for a time drove out, but which returned immediately after their rejection of Christ." An early disputation, dating from the seventh century, depicts the Church rejoicing while the devil repines when his Jews are vanquished and converted. Jew and devil were often coupled by later Byzantine writers and preachers; in the sermons of Eusebius of Alexandria, for example, the devil refers quite casually from time to time to "his old friends, the Jews." [22]

Thus, the tradition of a union between the two archopponents of Christ seeped deeply into Christian thought. If it originated purely as vilification, it was yet calculated to assume the proportions of actuality in the mind of the uncritical. The struggle against the forces of evil in the spiritual realm, exemplified by the devil and his cohorts, and against the enemies of the Church in the material world, prosecuted with unparalleled vigor during the later medieval age, impressed this subtle amalgamation of the two aspects of the Christ legend indelibly upon the public mind: the devil and the Jew joined forces, in Christian belief, not only in the war against Jesus during his life on earth but also in the contemporaneous war against the Church and its civilization. All the power of Christian propaganda was exerted to arouse fear and hatred of the Jews, for while Jesus fought the devil on his ground, his followers must destroy the agents of the devil on theirs, lest Satan inherit the earth and truth and salvation be lost. Christendom was summoned to a holy war of extermination, of which the Jews were only incidentally the objects. It was Satan whom Christian Europe sought to crush.

An examination of the available material demonstrates how deeply this conception of the intimate relations between Satan and the Jews was implicit in the medieval point of view.

The mystery plays dramatized the events connected with the Passion of Jesus. It was here that the basic charge of satanism was hurled against the Jews. "Some of the characters," we find noted in a fourteenth-century French mystery, "represent the Jews, who have deserted God, while the others are the people of God." [23] Behind this desertion of God lurked the fine hand of Satan. It was not merely that, as one French mystery, *La Vengence et destruction du Hierusalem*,[24] portrayed the sequence of events, the Jews were stricken with blindness and stubbornness by Satan *after* the crucifixion and refused to accept the evidence of miracles and signs manifesting God's wrath, which they therefore condemned as illusions. Other such plays present the devil in person, and his legions, inciting the Jews against Jesus and plotting his destruction with them. In the famous French drama, *Le Mystère de la Passion*, the devils take the initiative, but once they have successfully carried out their design

> To invest the Jews with courage
> To kill him by their outrage
> And to hate him just as we do,[25]

it is the Jews who occupy the center of the stage, as the villains of the piece, with the devils hovering solicitously in the background. This mystery succeeds in playing up very effectively the joint conspiracy of Jews and devils; in the big scene they work hand in hand instigating Judas to betray his master, and howl with demoniacal glee when their efforts are successful. Around the cross on which Jesus hangs the Jews whirl in a dance of abandon and joy, mocking their victim and exulting in their achievement. This telling detail climaxes the crucifixion scene in a number of mysteries coming from England, France, and Germany.[26]

This same theme is pursued, with many variations, in the miracles, plays which portrayed the lives of the saints and the miraculous deeds accredited to them. When a Jew is apprehended and condemned for mutilating a host, it is to the devil that he cries out for succor; while the Jew expires in agony at the stake, and this occurs in several of the plays, devils rush in upon the stage to carry off his soul.[27] Time and again the Jews are described in these plays as "devils from Hell, enemies of the human race."[28] In the Chaumont Christmas play Jews are introduced upon the stage in the guise of devils, strenuously exerting themselves to prevent the entrance of the religious procession into the city.[29]

The earliest German version of the Faust legend pits a Jew against the devil, to whose wiles, of course, the Jew succumbs. The author does not fail to point his moral: "Thus can the devil lead into error the minds of those whose hearts do not cleave to God's word."[30] Here it is the Jew's refusal to accept the true doctrine that renders him defenseless against Satan. But the Theophilus legend, one of the most popular in the Middle Ages, which occurs in every language and in every literary form, and which strongly influenced the Faust legend if it did not indeed serve as its model and source, puts the matter in another light.

There are several dramatic versions of this tale, each presenting the situation with a somewhat different emphasis but all agreeing on the essential point: the intimate relations joining devil and Jews. If one, the Low German version, appears to offer a surprisingly favorable picture of the Jew, this may be ascribed to its anticlerical motivation. Here the pious archdeacon, Theophilus, who has suffered disgrace, turns for help to a magician with the plea that he direct him to the devil; instead the magician sends him to the Jews. But when he enters a synagogue and expresses a desire to join them, they decline to accept him, with the double-edged contention that a bad Christian makes a bad Jew and is no gain for Judaism. He insists, however, and offers to sell his soul to any Jew (as to the devil!) who will have him. Finally one of the Jews gives in and shows him the way to the devil, but only after his strenuous efforts to dissuade the cleric from this course have been brushed aside with disdain. The Jew's parting shot as Theophilus enters the devil's abode is that not for all the money in the world would he become one of Satan's men. Of course the inconsistency in this account is only too apparent: the Jews who profess to abhor the devil are known by the magician to be in touch with him and in the course of events prove this to be so. But the author is not bothered about consistency; his seeming defense of the Jews, itself a comic touch whose implausibility will not escape his audience, is a foil to his primary satire on the Christian clergy, which is readier to serve the devil than even the Jews are.[31]

The approach of the other German version is less circuitous. Theophilus repairs directly to a Jew, who introduces him without much ado to the devil, to whom the archdeacon renders over his soul in return for restoration of his position and reputation.[32]

The French version, not content with so simple a statement, emphasizes the relationship between Jew and devil far more sharply. Theophilus has already lost his soul to the devil when he appeals to the Jew for help. But instead of freeing him from Satan's clutches the Jew, all the while Satan's ally though posing as the friend and protector of the tormented cleric, actually is the instrument of his final delivery into the devil's hands. "I have such great power in his court," the Jew reassures Theophilus, and when Satan appears in response to his call, the Jew greets him as "my king and my lord," "my master and my companion." Yet the Jew does not hesitate to command Satan, to display his own power and authority over the lord of the underworld; the Jew is even Satan's master, just as intent as he is upon the destruction of Christian souls. (Indeed, we read of the "Jewish devil," as though the devil were himself a Jew.) "Many Christians has he thus conquered," chants one writer; "through his counsel has many a soul descended to the fire and flame of Hell," laments another as Theophilus is enmeshed in the devil-Jew's net.[33]

This legend, so popular throughout Europe, exerted a great influence in shaping the conviction that the Jew and the devil are close allies. Master, companion, or servant, what matter? The incontestable fact was that the interests of devil and Jew were one, that both made common cause. And this not as a result of Jewish refusal to acknowledge the truth, the Christian truth, but *ab initio*, because the nature and character of the two are alike.

Another cycle of legends, almost equally popular and widespread during the Middle Ages, was that centering around the figure of Solomon. His dominion over the demons was a main feature of these legends. As early as the sixth century Leontius of Byzantium utilized this tradition in a disputation, when he charged the Jews with having subjected themselves to these same demons, or at least with being on a par with them, as the mutual subjects of the Jewish king and—quite logically—in rejecting Christ. The point was often made again. Here we have an excellent instance of the medieval propensity to ascribe a legendary element associated with a biblical character to the contemporary Jew. During the Middle Ages these legends, constantly retold in every form and tongue, must have had just the effect demonstrated by Leontius on public opinion: Solomon is a Jew, and his control over the demons is unchallenged; certainly, therefore, all Jews are at the very least in intimate contact with these creatures.[34]

There are other legends, less widespread but equally effective in making this same point. In one of them, when an impoverished Christian in desperation calls to the devil for help a Jew suddenly appears and offers to aid him if he will deny Jesus. Other versions of this popular tale concern a man who, having lost his wealth, is introduced by a Jew to the devil and agrees (in some accounts at the Jew's request, in others, at the devil's) to renounce Christ and the saints in return for his possessions but balks when he is told he must deny Mary too. The purely incidental introduction of the devil-Jew element is eloquent evidence of its traditional quality, for the story is aimed in another direction altogether: the hero is rewarded for his constancy when the Virgin miraculously restores his wealth. Quite frequently in these tales the Jew is the devil's associate, accepting his counsel and leadership, actively co-operating with him as his terrestrial agent.[35]

We find the same conception in the graphic arts, as may be expected. One of the earliest dated sketches of a medieval Jew, from the Forest Roll of Essex (1277), bears the superscription *Aaron fil[ius] diaboli*, "Aaron, son of the devil." The sixteenth-century series of prints entitled "Juden Badstub" shows the devil assisting the Jews in the functions of the bathhouse, drawing water with them, building up the fires, etc. A seventeenth-century print, "Der Juden Synagog," depicts the devil as a participant in the Jewish ritual. The notorious figure of the *Judensau*, portraying the sow as the mother feeding her Jewish offspring, one of the commonest caricatures of the Jew in the Middle Ages, occurs also with the devil represented as supervising the operation. Satan's semitic features are often emphasized with grotesque exaggeration (Mephistopheles is usually swarthy, hook-nosed, curly-headed); when he is portrayed with a Jew badge on his cloak, as we find him several times, the allusion is clear enough. And with a little ingenuity the Jew badge may be explained altogether as a sign of the Jews' allegiance to the devil, as medieval versifiers ultimately get around to doing. In fact, on the island of Crete Jews were obliged to proclaim that allegiance with a novel variation of the Jew badge—a wooden figure of the devil affixed to their doors.[36]

It must be noted finally, in this connection, that even the Jewish ritual was represented as satanic. Not only was Satan a member of the congregation. There have come down from the Middle Ages several parodies, still current as children's play songs, which purport to be Jewish prayers directed to him, mimicking the Hebrew words.[37] (The belief current quite recently in some German provinces that a toad or a cat is to be found ensconced on the "altar" of synagogues would accord the devil, whom

"Aaron fil diaboli"

Forest Roll of Essex (1277)

1. Ja blieh dich wol vnd eben fast /
   Vielleicht der Badstub nötig hast.

2. Nun geh hin ein du armer Schweiß /
   Was gilts die Zween machen dir heiß.

3. Ihr liebe Freund mein gbrechen ich /
   Euch hab gesagt / verlast mich nicht.

4. So wollen wir nun wasser schöpffen /
   Mein gspan / zu baden disen Tropffe.

5. Zeuch du / ich blas daß ich schwitz /
   Mein Sohn daß wird geben groß hitz.

6. Wir beyde vnser best auch thun /
   Machen den Offen heiß vnd schön.

7. So machen wir die stuben rein /
   Was gilts es wird sich schicken fein.

8. Kraw du den Rucken / ich die Fus /
   Mein GOLM ist das Bad nicht süß.

9. Wolan kom iettund her zu mir /
   Auff das ich lustig schreyffe dir.

Der Juden Badstub

An early seventeenth-century satire on Jewish cleanliness: since the devil helps prepare the bath it serves only to produce blindness.

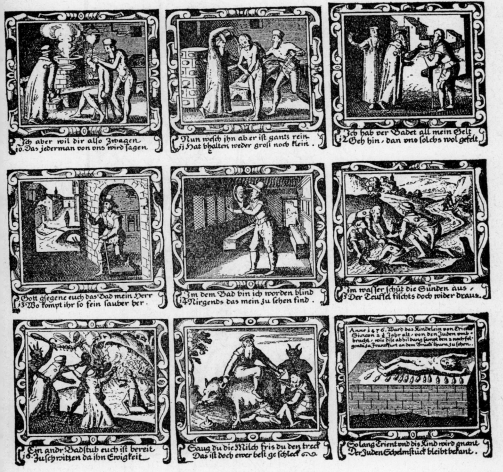

Der Juden Badstub

When the Jew seeks to wash himself clean of sin in the river, the devil, down-stream, gathers up his sins and has a hotter bath awaiting him in Hell. The last two pictures reproduce the *Judensau*-Simon of Trent theme from the Frankfort bridge

Satanic figures identified with the Jew badge
From title page of *Der Juden Erbarkeit* (1571)

Satan attended by Jews
Pierre Boaistuau, *Histoires prodigieuses* (Paris, 1575)

these creatures represent, a position analogous to that of Christ in the church.[38]) Many innocent ritual practices, as we shall see, were interpreted as of sinister anti-Christian import. When the Jews prayed, it was said, their most fervent prayers were for the destruction of the Christians. Very few doubted that Jewish ceremonial required the use of Christian blood, during the Passover service, on Purim, at circumcisions, at weddings. Even the Jewish inability, or rather refusal, to read into the Bible what Christians found there, was in the end attributed to "the spite of the devil, who puts such absurd nonsense into men's minds." Only the *verzweifelten Teufelslügenmäuler der Juden* could refuse to acknowledge what all right-thinking men could plainly read in Scripture.[39]

What more authentic reflection of the prevailing opinion can we hope to find than Shakespeare's lines from *The Merchant of Venice* (III, i, 22), "Let me say 'Amen' betimes lest the devil cross my prayer, for here he comes in the likeness of a Jew." And, as succinctly and finally as the proposition may be put (II, ii, 27), "Certainly the Jew is the very devil incarnal"!

It is undoubtedly true that often the ascription of a satanic nature and allegiance to the Jew must have been intended merely as invective, the cuss words of a bygone age. Yet the charge could not have been so frequently and insistently iterated, even in mockery or as abuse, without leaving its impression upon the suggestible mind of the masses. Moreover, it is inescapable that t⸍ accusation was only too often leveled in all seriousness. O⸍ other supposition can we understand how it was that the m⸍tual and not only the masses were guilty here, but their i⸍ vilest and spiritual mentors as well—could be led to cred⸍eatedly charges on the flimsiest of evidence and to rise ⸍nce. against the Jews with such overwhelming fury a⸍

ANTICHRIST

THE most vivid, and no doubt impressive, statement of this attitude is to be found in the numerous versions of the Antichrist legend, which was universally known and accredited in Christian Europe. According to common belief, Christendom faced an imminent war with the embattled forces of Satan, which would engulf all the world and at whose successful conclusion Christ would reappear to usher in the millennial era of peace under the banner of his catholic church. Not only the masses but many outstanding thinkers anticipated the speedy coming of Antichrist, the grand marshal of Satan's hosts, and the embodiment of all evil, who, as Hildegard of Bingen (twelfth century) voiced the prevailing view, will excel "in all diabolical arts" and in "the magic art." [1]

There is evidence in the records of the Spanish Inquisition that the messianic expectations widely held among the harassed Marranos, or crypto-Jews, during the fifteenth century were interpreted as relating to the Antichrist. The two themes were intimately associated by Church dialecticians. Early in the Christian era it was pointed out that "if Jesus was the Messiah, the only person for whom the Jews could be waiting would be, by their own method of arguing also, the Antichrist." An eleventh-century emancipation of renunciation of Judaism requires the convert to anathematize all those who hope for the coming of the Messiah, or rather with the Antichrist"; the context links this declaration definitely with the Jewish tradition concerning the Messiah. [2]

The Antichrist legend, however, as distinct from the simple belief in this figure, is of comparatively late origin —a reference in a ninth-century source to "that nun [sic!] who is expected by the Hebrews to give birth to the Antichrist" indicates that it was shape by that time. [3] A popular legend

Antichris

LUCAS CRA

Schedel, *Nürnbe*

illustrates the process of its formation quite graphically: it relates that after the destruction of Jerusalem Satan appeared to the Jewish exiles and offered to restore them to their homeland; but when they accepted his offer he caused them to drown by thousands in the sea. The purport of the legend—to present Satan as the expected Jewish Messiah—is unmistakable. But this is not legend, only feeble parody of a historic event. Such an incident actually occurred. In the fifth century a certain messianic pretender, calling himself Moses, appeared in Crete and persuaded thousands that he would lead them across the sea to Palestine. In this belief they leaped from the cliffs and many were drowned. Christian legend simply identified the Messiah of this incident more specifically.[4]

The legend blossomed forth as a fully developed popular theme only in the later Middle Ages. Leading scholastics, such as Thomas Aquinas and Albertus Magnus, devoted considerable attention to it, holding in general that Antichrist will be born in Babylon, of the tribe of Dan, will proceed to Jerusalem, where he will be circumcised, and will easily persuade the Jews that he is their long-awaited Messiah. He will then rebuild the temple, establish his throne there, and proclaim himself god. By means of miraculous deeds, bribes, and sheer force he will rapidly accumulate a vast army of adherents, but his power is destined to endure only three and a half years. God will then send Enoch and Elijah to raise an opposition against him, but he will overcome and slay them. Thereupon Christ will dispatch the archangel Michael to destroy him on the Mount of Olives. The millennium, however, will not necessarily begin immediately thereafter.[5]

The popular view tended to follow that of the schoolmen, with the difference, however, as might be expected, that it embellished this general outline of the Antichrist's career with lush detail. Of especial interest to a good many people, it would seem, was his origin, which was expounded in increasingly extravagant terms, only the minority holding that he would be a natural man, legitimately born. For most he was to be at the least a bastard, or the of a whore, or of an incubus and a whore. The scholastics were willing to permit him a prostitute mother, but when the devil was brought into the picture as his father, they rebelled, though they were prepared to agree that his birth would in some way be influenced by the latter. The tendency to accord the devil and his Jews leading roles in the piece was not, however, to be downed. It was climaxed, to the distaste of the more critical, by the antithetical parallel between the Antichrist and the Christ, making the first the child of a union between the devil and a *Jewish* harlot—in deliberate contrast to that other son of God and a Jewish virgin.[6] Though born in Babylon (or Persia), this popular parallel proceeded, he would be raised in Galilee, and trained by sorcerers and witches in their black art, until, at the age of thirty, he would reveal himself to the Jews in Jerusalem as their Messiah. His apparent triumph, made possible by his assumed personal probity and saintliness, by his vast erudition and persuasive preachments, which unite all preceding heresies, by his miraculous (but really magical) feats, his great wealth derived from the hidden treasures that the devil discloses to him, and the force and terror unleashed by his armies, is brought to an end after only three and a half years (the duration of Jesus' ministry), when he tries to ape Jesus' final achievement and ascend to heaven borne by demons. Michael is dispatched to destroy him, his followers are annihilated after a period variously given as of twenty-five to forty days during which they continue in the delusion of victory, the world comes to an end, and Christ makes his second appearance. This was the biography of the Antichrist as the masses knew him.

The relation between the Jews and the Antichrist was particularly stressed in these accounts of his career. Not alone was his parentage Jewish—on both sides, it might be said—but so was his earliest and most effective support. Even the artists who designed the manuscript illuminations, and later the woodcuts and engravings, and painted the pictures that adorned the churches went out of their way to emphasize this point. "When it is a matter of depicting them [the Jews] in an odious role," remarked Ulysse Robert in a study of the medieval Jew badge,[7] "such as the agents of the Antichrist, the executioners of Enoch and Elijah, for example, or the enemies of Christ, then the circles are deliberately exaggerated; one must not be left in doubt that these are Jews."

Besides the pamphlets and tracts in prose and verse which presented the legend in full and terrifying detail, and the homiletical disquisitions that pounded home its moral, the stage also seized upon the theme and lavished upon it its capacity for incitation.

The Latin original of the medieval Antichrist plays, *ludus paschalis de adventu et interitu Antichristi* (thirteenth century), accords the Jews a somewhat incidental role in that only after the Antichrist has made wide conquests do they accept him as their redeemer. But the later French and German versions, following the popular disposition, display the Jews as prime movers in the drama. In the French play of Besançon a Jewish prostitute eagerly offers herself to her satanic paramour in order that she may bear a child who will wield the greatest power among men, and through whom "Christendom will be destroyed, and Jewry raised up again" (*yert crestienté mort et juif seront relevé*). The Maurienne version of this drama has a Jewish voluptuary deliver his daughter into Satan's hands for the express purpose of mothering the Antichrist.

The child, in both plays, is reared for his mission by Satan, and when he is finally ready to go forth he appears first among the Jews, who instantly flock to his standard and acknowledge him as their true Messiah and Redeemer. Throughout this action an acute contrast is drawn between the Jews' rejection of God's son and their acclamation of Satan's. With the aid of the Jews Antichrist conquers the world, until through a series of miracles God reveals his real character: Antichrist and Jews fall dead, and the millennium is ushered in with great rejoicing, as much over the eternal damnation of the Jews as over the final victory of the Church.

The German Lenten play *Herzog von Burgund*, by Hans Folz (fifteenth century), also based upon the Antichrist theme, omits the reference to Antichrist's Jewish parentage but places the eager adherence of the Jews to him in sharp relief by playing up

their contemporaneous situation, referring especially to the
recent expulsion of Jewish communities along the Rhine and the
Danube. The Jews are his protagonists on the stage, extolling
before their Christian audience the "new order" he is about to
inaugurate, which will be dominated by their own *Jüdischheit*,
for, they exult, as the *Entcrist* his mission is "to put an end to the
Christians." When a "sign" is demanded to prove Antichrist's
right to the Messiahship the Jews indignantly reject the imputa-
tion of fraud and brazenly offer to become prisoners of the Duke
of Burgundy should their champion be shown up as a liar. Antichrist, of course, fails to pass the test, while the Jews wail and
curse in comic hyperbole. Finally the impostor is forced to show
his true colors. For fourteen hundred years, he says in response to
the Duke's demand that he explain why he proclaimed himself
Messiah, we have suffered the gravest injuries from the Christians; and we would have suffered much more did you but know
the intense hatred we feel for you, how we have robbed you and
our physicians have poisoned you, how many of your children
we have stolen and killed, etc. Now the Antichrist himself speaks
as a Jew, the long-awaited Messiah come to redeem his people.
This false-Messiah act, he admits, was a deliberate attempt to con-
fuse and subdue the Christians; if it miscarried this time, it will yet
succeed another. But that hope is vain. The Duke's men unceremoniously fall upon the Jews, subject them to extreme and even
fantastic tortures, and the drama concludes with a dance of glee
around their corpses.[8]

The effect of these plays upon the passions of the mob may be
gauged from the action of the Frankfort City Council, in 1469,
establishing special regulations for the protection of the Jewish
quarter during the period when such a play was being presented.[9]

To appreciate fully the peculiar impact of the legend we must
set it against the prevailing psychological mood. It may be too
easily dismissed as pure fantasy, merely another of the fabulous
motifs that entertained the Middle Ages, without exerting any
momentous influence upon the thought and action of the common people. But the Antichrist was no legendary dragon spout-

ing imaginary fire; he was a terrifying reality, even in those ages
when his appearance was not imminently awaited. What an abysmal shudder of dread rocked all Europe when it came to anticipate his appearance with every rising sun! A religious current of
guilt, fear, desperation, and disillusion seems to have overwhelmed the continent in the fifteenth century. The end of the
world was at hand! The witchcraft madness swept into full
swing. The Hussites broke away from the Church after a fierce
struggle, and everywhere heretical views, brazenly voiced, became increasingly prevalent. The Turks overran the Balkan peninsula and advanced toward the heart of Europe. Mass hysteria of
epidemic proportions produced physical as well as psychic manifestations in many communities. These phenomena were seen as
nothing less than warnings of the approaching end of days. Even
the expansion of scientific knowledge and the invention of mov-
able type (at the beginning of the sixteenth century the Sorbonne
petitioned the King to suppress "the diabolical art of printing" [10]), and particularly the increasing number of editions of the
Bible in the vernacular, were singled out with dismay as signs of
the time.

Die zit, die kumt! es kumt die zit!
ich vörcht der endkrist si nit wit!

gloomily chanted Sebastian Brant:[11]

The time is coming! The time is here!
I fear the Antichrist is near!

One can hardly exaggerate the impression made upon the common people by the Antichrist theme, which both summed up and
dramatically expressed all their overbrimming black discontent
and foreboding. We can recognize the characteristic hysterical
outbreaks as a product of the unbearable tension induced by the
fear of Antichrist's arrival with a good deal more assurance than
they distinguished them as a "sign" of his coming. A favorite
homiletical text dinned into their ears by the preachers, constantly presented under churchly auspices and in the tract and
creative literature, in poetry and drama and art, freely and frequently debated in open disputations, often at the express request

of the laity, the Antichrist was no mere creature of scholarly dispute but the deeply disturbing concern of everyone. Matthias of Janow, who died in 1394, before the public apprehensiveness had attained its greatest intensity, could already write that this theme was so universally and thoroughly discussed that at Antichrist's appearance even the little children would instantly know him. We may well believe the plaint of Hieronymus de Villavitis, about half a century later: "So much is being said of the day of the last judgment and the Antichrist, that our heart trembles greatly." In the last years of the Middle Ages no less a person than John Calvin testified: "Among the Catholics nothing is more discussed or well known than the anticipated coming of the Antichrist." He was in error if he meant to imply that the reformers were innocent of this superstition. Martin Luther, for one, played the universally popular game of checking off the "signs" of his advent.[12]

True, the Antichrist legend bore assurance that the Adversary would ultimately be defeated. Why despair? But his coming meant the end of the world and the Last Judgment. Who could anticipate this event with anything but fear and trembling? And suppose the legend was wrong. The devil was a mighty antagonist. His full strength was as yet untested. Suppose in the end he did win!

The Jews once again played a sinister role in world history.

Their association with this awful figure, as we have noted, goes back to the earliest Christian period, but it assumed really frightening proportions only toward the end of the Middle Ages, when Antichrist's Jewish parentage became definitely established, and the Jews were expected to form the spearhead of his legions. They were not quite so weak, in the medieval imagination (aside from their satanic backing), as we may suppose, judging alone from their numbers and social position. For a terrible, mysterious Jewish horde hidden somewhere in the East awaited the signal to pour out upon Christendom and annihilate it. The rumors of the birth of Antichrist, which became increasingly frequent and circumstantial after the thirteenth century, kept Europe on edge, awaiting the bloody outbreak of the "red Jews" from their secret mountain retreat in the vicinity of the Caspian Sea, where, according to legend, Alexander the Great had long ago confined them.[13] This is one of the most curious features of the entire Antichrist complex, for it harked back to the old Jewish tradition that the "lost" ten tribes of Israel still maintained an independent and glorious existence somewhere in the Orient and would one day rejoin their brethren at a critical moment. Indeed, the belief that the Antichrist would be born to the tribe of Dan in Babylon or Persia was of a piece with this notion, for Dan was one of the "lost" tribes which were supposedly in this region.

When news of the Mongol incursion in the thirteenth century reached Western Europe, a number of reports assure us the Jews were overjoyed at the prospect that their "brothers, the long-shut-up tribes of Israel," were at last moving to deliver them; the Jews of Germany, in particular, were accused of undertaking traitorous measures to aid the invading hordes, and suffered severe persecutions.[14] Such rumors kept cropping up from time to time, and as late as 1596 several "true news reports" were published in pamphlet form recounting that these "red Jews" (constituting an army ranging from 196,000 to 900,000 men, according to different statements, with a virgin at their head) had already begun an attack upon the Turks, to regain the Holy Land.[15]

Moreover, another ominous figure made his appearance on the European scene at about this time. The Wandering Jew, reports of whose existence in the Orient had reached England some three centuries before but of whom little new had been reported since, suddenly undertook a personal tour of Europe in the sixteenth century, visiting with startling rapidity all its foremost cities. The significance of this apparition, now known by the name of Ahasuerus, lay in the "fact" that he was to die at last when Christ returned to earth.[16]

These reports must be considered in conjunction with the recurrent rumors of the birth of Antichrist if we are to appreciate fully their effect upon the masses. In 1599, while stories of the eruption of the "red Jews" were still circulating widely, according to Canon Moreau, a contemporary historian, "a rumor spread with prodigious rapidity through Europe, that Antichrist had been born at Babylon, and that already the Jews of that part were hurrying to receive and recognize him as their Messiah." One can understand that the advent of every pretended Jewish Messiah was heralded among Christians in this fashion, though the announcement of the *birth* of Antichrist is an obvious reflection of the parallelism between the Christ and the Antichrist myths and indicates that the reference is to no historic pseudo-Messiah, of whom there were not a few in this period. The very next year we are provided with conclusive proof that the legend operated without benefit of the Jewish messianic expectation and had, in fact, no relation to it: the announcement was broadcast that Antichrist had been born that year in the neighborhood of Paris, of a Jewess named Blanchefleure, who had conceived by Satan. A witch, under torture, acknowledged that she had rocked the infant Antichrist on her knees, and she testified that he had claws on his feet, wore no shoes, and spoke all languages.[17]

Medieval Christendom was in no position to assay such rumors critically, since the constant repetition of the legend, with the assent and indeed under the auspices of the Church, had prepared it for just such an eventuality, which it believed foredoomed. Satan and the Jews *must* one day descend upon the Christian world in a final mad effort to destroy it.

The theologians held that there were two realms on earth: the Kingdom of Christ and the Kingdom of the devil. All men belonged to one or the other. "This belief was not simply a pious thought, not merely a symbolic figure for good and evil, but stark reality" for the common people as surely as for the school-men. And, writing on the "Jewish question," a member of the Pope's household reminded Duke Henry of Bavaria, in 1449: "wer nit an Got gelaubt, der ist des teufels"—whoever does not believe in (the Christian) God belongs to the devil.[18] Thus the common phrase "their [the Jews'] father, the devil," was no mere aspersion but a statement of bare fact, so far as Christian belief was concerned. The noted Spanish theologian Alfonso de Spina went so far as to prove *from Jewish sources,* in a chapter of his famous *Fortalitium fidei* devoted to "the parentage of the Jews according to the doctrine of the Talmud," that the Jews are the children of the devil. Quite plausibly Christians who were seduced into joining "the synagogue of Satan" entered it "at the instigation of the devil," and there found themselves, in company with the devil's offspring, "invoking demons, and giving to them the honor that is due to God." When Christians suffered they did so "to the great joy of the devil and the Jews." When Jews remained steadfast in their faith and refused to submit to the blandishments or threats of their would-be Christian saviors, "preferring to let themselves be burned alive, rather than yield a needle-point of their belief," the source of their obstinacy was easily discernible—they were "damned devil's martyrs." [19]

Small wonder, then, that in view of this attitude the conscience of Christendom was little burdened by the unexampled persecution to which the Jews were subjected. They had it coming to them, the average Christian could contend, for Christian treatment of the Jew was mild compared to what *they* would suffer were the world in Jewish hands. "The children of God, that we are, poisonous worms, that you are; if we were by you controlled, as you in our power are enrolled, no Christian would survive the year," [20] wrote a medieval rhymester, a sentiment strongly echoed by Luther. And Abraham a Santa Clara, writing in the seventeenth century, could say of the Jews, "those mad fiends," as he called them: "After Satan Christians have no greater enemies than the Jews. . . . They pray many times each day that God may destroy us through pestilence, famine and war, aye, that all beings and creatures may rise up with them against the Christians. Can greater scoundrels than these Jews be found anywhere in the whole world?"

Little wonder, too, that Jews were accused of the foulest crimes, since Satan was their instigator. Chaucer, in his "Prioresses Tale," placed the ultimate blame for the alleged slaughter of a Christian child by a Jew upon "our firste fo, the Serpent Sathanas, that hath in Iewes herte his waspes nest." [21] Gregory of Tours took pains to note that when a certain Jew vented his displeasure upon another, who had permitted himself to be baptized, by dumping a pot of rancid oil on his head, Satan was behind the deed.[22] But such tautologies were hardly required; everyone knew that the devil and the Jews worked together. This explains why it was so easy to condemn the Jews a priori for every conceivable misdeed, even if it made no sense. They were just as likely to invade a church and desecrate its sacred images in the presence of a large and hostile audience, to deride sacred Christian beliefs publicly, to shower abuse and filth on religious processions, or refuse to acknowledge the veracity of miracles which trustworthy Christian witnesses had observed, thus deliberately, madly (if they might be judged by purely human standards) inviting disaster, as to murder Christian infants in secret, despoil the host, spread poison with the wind, practice infamous sexual immoralities. The catalogue of alleged Jewish crimes is long and varied indeed, and wholly unreasonable, unless we accept the self-evident fact, in medieval eyes, that as Satan's agents nothing was beyond the depraved and evil nature of the Jews.[23]

CHAPTER THREE

WITH HORNS AND TAIL

THE story is not yet complete. The Jew was also believed to possess certain physical characteristics which definitely set him apart from other men and identified him with the devil—corroborative evidence that points up the literalness of this conception in the medieval mind.

The figure of the horned Jew was not uncommon during the Middle Ages. We know it best through Michelangelo's magnificent "Moses," which reproduced a traditional feature of the Lawgiver's countenance, on display in many a medieval church and manuscript. The customary explanation of those curious horns protruding from Moses' brow is that they are the products of a misinterpretation of Exod. 34.29, 35: "And behold the skin of his face sent forth beams." [1] The old translations render the Hebrew root *karan* correctly as "shine"; Aquila and the Vulgate, the standard text followed by the Church, read however: "His face had *horns*." This misunderstanding may have been favored by the Babylonian and Egyptian conception of horned deities (Sin, Ammon), by the Greek use of horns as symbolic of might (e.g., the horned figures of Jupiter), and by the legend of the two-horned Alexander the Great, referred to in the Koran (sura 18.82, 85). It is quite likely that this misinterpretation was at the bottom of Michelangelo's conception of the two-horned Moses. But when we find ordinary Jews, medieval Jews in typical medieval garb, crowned with horns, we may reasonably suspect that something more lies behind this than a faulty translation.

Indeed, this matter of horns went considerably further than pictorial representation. Jews were actually obliged to appear in public with the distinguishing horn somewhere on their garb. In 1267 the Vienna Council decreed that Jews must wear a "horned hat" (*pileum cornutum*), a provision which later councils sought

Der Jüngling dantzt und ſpringt laher | *Der Jüd thut nichts als betrügen wil:*
Ihrs Krantzs frewt ſich die Jungfraw ſehr | *Der Kriegsman abr frewt ſich zum ſpiel.*

"Youth, Virgin, Jew, and Soldier"

(Frankfort, 1624)

Jew astride a goat

Wood carving on choir stool in the Church of Notre Dame,
Aerschot, Belgium (fifteenth century)

strenuously to enforce; and Philip III required the Jews of France to attach a horn-shaped figure to the customary Jew badge.[2]

Talk of the devil and his horns appear, says the proverb. In an age so familiar with Satan's least feature as the medieval, the portrayer of the horned Jew need not have felt called upon to make his allusion more specific—yet an occasional hyperliteralist, not content with sketching the horned Jew alone, scratches a devil alongside him, for good measure. And in one instance at least, that horned Jew is identified with the legend, in bold face, "This is the Jew Devil." [3]

Nor were his horns the Jew's sole physical token of his satanism. The devil's tail is as characteristic as his horns, and consequently only the least stretch of the imagination was required to perceive the Jew's diabolic dorsal appendage, even though he managed cunningly to hide it from common view.[4] And in the event we find it difficult to believe that these notions were accepted in all seriousness, it must be pointed out that such beliefs are still prevalent, not only among benighted European peasantries but even in our own enlightened land.[5]

A supposedly characteristic feature of the Jewish physiognomy, which is constantly stressed in the prints and particularly in the folk tales, is the so-called *Ziegenbart* (goat's beard, or goatee). This otherwise obscure detail assumes meaning when we consider it in conjunction with the common representation of the Jew in association with the he-goat, either as his favorite domestic animal or as his favorite mount (which he prefers to ride facing backward, to judge from the prints).[6] Or the goat is offered as the symbol of Judaism and the Jewish God.

> When Ikey came a-riding
> On a billygoat
> He had the Jews believing
> It was their precious God,[7]

runs a widely current bit of doggerel whose origin is placed in the late Middle Ages. Evidently the intent is to single out the goat as the Jews' beast, or perhaps the *Ziegenbart* emphasis is intended to identify the Jew as the human goat. Indeed, a carved relief of the *Judensau* with her Jewish brood, once to be seen on the tower of a bridge in Frankfort, included the figure of a Jew with two unmistakable goat's horns on his head. To make certain that the origin of those horns was not missed, the artist cut a billy goat with identical horns into the stone, interestedly watching the proceedings.[8]

The *Bock* or billy goat, as the Middle Ages knew full well, is the devil's favorite animal, frequently represented as symbolic of satanic lechery. According to popular legend, the devil created the goat,[9] which appears in picture and story as the riding animal of every conceivable sort of hobgoblin, as well as of witches and sorcerers. In the witch craze that swept Europe toward the end of the Middle Ages the devil's most usual disguise was said to be that of a goat, which the devotees worshiped and adored, and it was the animal most commonly offered to him as a sacrifice. So close was the relation between them that an early fifteenth-century illustration picturing four Jews being led by him represents Satan himself as having goat's horns.[10] The purport of this association of Jew and goat is quite unmistakable. A fifteenth-century sculptured figure in a Flemish church shows a Jew astride a goat, facing its rear; the animal's hind hoofs are cloven, and its forefeet end in claws.[11]

The ascription to the Jew of a distinctive and unpleasant odor has often been commented upon. Many peoples, of course, have at various times had this libel leveled against them, not only in popular belief but even in pseudoscientific works. We may interpret it as an effort by one group to stigmatize another, socially inferior, group as being physically inferior as well, a sort of extra prop to bolster up the former's sense of superiority. It is probable that when an offensive odor was charged against the Jews by ancient writers, such as Martial and Ammianus Marcellinus, it was more as an expression of contempt for the barbarians than with any more subtle intent.[12]

But the notion of the so-called *foetor judaicus*, so prevalent in the Middle Ages,[13] though undoubtedly reflecting something of the same motivation (and perhaps at the outset little more than an echo of the classical charge), carried a deeper meaning to the medieval Christian. "There was never a state so large that a mere thirty Jews would not saturate it with stench and unbelief," declaimed the thirteenth-century Austrian poet Seifried Helbling.[14] "Stench and unbelief" were characteristic Jewish attributes, *in combination*. The measured sobriety of legal prose buckled under the necessity of legislating for Jews: in 1421 the city of Ofen (Buda) ordered "the Jews, the mean, stiff-necked, stinking betrayers of God"[15] to—anticlimactically—pay a tax on their wine. The combination holds. And its meaning is clearly indicated when we read that the Jew emits a foul odor as punishment for his crime against Jesus.[16] Yet this is only a partial explanation. Why a foul odor as punishment?

The answer is apparent when we consider that according to common Christian belief during the Middle Ages good spirits emit a marked fragrance, while evil spirits, and in particular, of course, Satan, are distinguished by an offensive stench. Myrrh gushes forth like fountains from the graves of the martyrs, we are told, and when the coffin of the martyred St. Stephen was opened his body filled the air with fragrance. The "odor of sanctity" indeed. On the other hand, when the devil is caught masquerading as an astrologer he vanishes in a whirlwind, with a stench (*cum turbine et fetore recedens disparuit*).[17] Brimstone and sulphur.

The *foetor judaicus*, then, is another distinctive sign of the "demonic" Jew. Nowhere is this special significance of the Jewish odor specifically stated, except perhaps in the comment that Jews stink like the he-goat.[18] But it is certainly implied in the frequently expressed belief that the Jew loses his odor after he is baptized. We have direct testimony that "the water of baptism carried off the Jews' odor," leaving them with a fragrance "sweeter than that of ambrosia floating upon the heads touched by the sanctified oil."[19]

A number of popular legends illustrate this conviction. According to one, when a Jew approached his daughter who had just been baptized she suddenly became aware of an exceedingly foul stench emanating from him (which she had formerly, as a Jewess, not noticed). Another legend relates that when a recently baptized Jewish boy came home one day emitting a very pleasant odor his parents imagined that he stank. Still another legend brings the point home beyond any doubt. To undo the effect of baptism a Jewish mother purposes to immerse her erring daughter three times in the waters of a sewer (but is, of course, frustrated by outraged Christians). The point of this legend is that it reproduces another popular fable, according to which, when the devil accidentally fell into some consecrated water, his grandmother freed him from its effects by dipping him three times into the sewer of Hell.[20]

It should be observed that more recently some writers have admitted a pinch of skepticism into their discussion of the *foetor judaicus*. Tovey[21] records that "the author of *Roma Sancta* takes notice, upon such an occasion [baptism], that whereas Jews naturally stink, they constantly lose that ill savour after baptism. But Misson [*Voyage into Italy*] accounts for the miracle, by answering, that before such sort of people intend to appear in publick, they take care to wash themselves well; and that their ill smell before baptism, which prejudic'd men think natural, arises from the sordidness of their habits, occasion'd by poverty." Bravo for Misson! The age of reason has dawned! But how faintly it glimmers still. If it has been somewhat difficult for the *foetor judaicus* to stand up in recent times (though not among the Nazi theoreticians, who have now proclaimed it as a profound "scientifically" verified fact that the "faint-sweet" racial odor of the Jews is one of their distinctive physical characteristics[22]), it is still prominent in the folk literature in a "refined" version, namely, that the Jews are guilty en masse of the egregious sin of "garlic eating." [23] This is "modern" antisemitism, as distinguished from the medieval variety.

That medieval idea is but another instance of the conviction that the Church was engaged in a holy war against the forces of Satan; the Jew could shed his demonic attributes only by sloughing off his former demonic self and being reborn through Christ. Such is the moral of these legends; yet, as we shall see, Christians came to doubt whether even baptism could effect a real change in the Jew. Not even his peculiar odor remained permanently effaced, to judge from the plaint heard in fifteenth-century Spain that Conversos smell bad. Whether this was the result of backsliding or of culinary habit remains an open question even after the statement of the contemporary chronicler Andrés Bernáldez: they "never lost their Jewish tastes in eating . . . stews of onion and garlic, and fried in oil, and the meat cooked in oil . . . to avoid lard; and oil with meat is a thing which gives an ill smell to the breath . . . and they themselves had the same smell as the Jews owing to their stews and *to their not being baptized*." [24]

In still another way did the Middle Ages proclaim its belief that the Jew was not quite human. All men are subject to disease, the Jew among them. But the Jew suffered also from certain peculiar and secret afflictions that were especially characteristic of him, and which did not normally trouble Christians. Indeed, it was this belief that helped to account for the Jewish need of Christian blood, the sole effective therapeutic available to them. Most often mentioned among these ailments was that of menstruation, which the men as well as the women among the Jews were supposed to experience; close seconds, in point of frequency of mention, were copious hemorrhages and hemorrhoids (all involving loss of blood). Among the great variety of these maladies were included quinsy, scrofula, a marked pallor, various mysterious skin diseases, and sores that gave forth a malodorous flux.[25] (Here we have another explanation of the *foetor judaicus*.) A number of late medieval sources affirm also that Jewish children are born with their right hands, blood stained, resting on their foreheads "as though they were attached to the skin," so that it requires something of an operation to release them. And quite recently the belief was expressed that "the Jews are always born blind." [26]

These infirmities were generally believed to afflict all Jews, though they usually managed to conceal them—or to heal them by magical means or through the use of Christian blood. For the accepted explanation of these ailments connected them with the persecution and murder of Jesus.[27] What more natural than that the devil's brood, having brought about the death of the Saviour of men, should forever after bear the signs of their iniquity? Indeed, in the seventeenth century (that late) there began an exercise in tabulating and classifying these fancied ailments, according to the twelve tribes of Israel (despite the fact that ten tribes had disappeared long before the crucifixion and tribal distinctions had long since vanished among Jews) and the alleged crimes of these tribes against Jesus. Thus, in 1602, the converted Jew Franciscus of Piacenza published the following catalogue of secret Jewish ailments and disabilities, which reappeared subsequently in several versions and languages: [28]

The members of the tribe of Reuben, who seized and beat Jesus in the garden, cause all vegetation which they touch to wither within three days; during four days annually bloody wounds appear on the hands and feet of descendants of the tribe of Simeon, because their ancestors struck Jesus while he hung on the cross; Levi struck Jesus in the face and spat on him, therefore the members of this tribe have difficulty in spitting and cannot bring up phlegm; because Zebulon threw lots for Jesus' cloak, annually on March 25 they suffer from open wounds in the mouth and spit blood; the tribe of Issachar, who bound Jesus to the post and whipped him, break out with bloody weals and incurable wounds all over the body on the same day; Dan it was that cried out "Let his blood be on us and on our children," and therefore every month bloody sores open on their bodies, and they stink so badly they must hide (only smearing themselves with Christian blood can remedy this); Gad wove the crown of thorns from fifteen branches and pressed it on Jesus' head until it penetrated the flesh, therefore annually fifteen painful bleeding bruises appear on their heads and necks; Asher slapped Jesus in the face, and so their right arms are a hand's-breadth shorter than their left; Naphtali, according to this imaginative account, hid their children in pigpens, with instructions to grunt and squeal when Jesus passed by, and when they asked him what these were, and he replied, "They are your children," they denied it, insisting these were pigs; whereupon Jesus said, "If they are swine, then swine let them be, and swine let them remain," and thus the tribe of Naphtali have four large pig teeth, pigs' ears, and stink like swine; Joseph (there was no such tribe), who forged the nails for the crucifixion and dulled their points, on the advice of a Jewess named Ventria, in order to increase Jesus' suffering, was punished in that the women of this tribe, after their thirty-third year, have live worms in their mouths while they sleep; and, finally, the tribe of Benjamin, who offered Jesus a sponge saturated with vinegar and gall, cannot raise their heads, always suffer from thirst, and when they try to speak live worms jump from their mouths.[29]

It can readily be seen, then, that Johann Fischart's illustrated *Wunderzeitung* of the year 1575, announcing the birth to a Jewish woman of Binzwangen, near Augsburg, of two little pigs, need not have unduly strained Christian credulity.[30] Nothing was too monstrous to be told about the Jew.

*The demon Colbif claims Mosse Mokke and Avegaye,
agents of Isaac of Norwich, for the devil*

Tallage Roll (1233)

Ain Gewisse Wunderzeitung von ainer Schwange-
ren Judin zu Binzwangen/vir meil von Augspurg/welche kurzlich den 12.Septem-
bris/des nächstverschinenen 74. Jars/an statt zwaier Kinder zwai leibhafte Schweinlin
oder Fürslin gebracht hat.

Johann Fischart's Wunderzeitung *announcing the birth of
two pigs to a Jewish woman*

(Strasbourg, 1574)

PART TWO

THE JEW AS SORCERER

CHAPTER FOUR

"A JEW IS FULL OF SORCERY"

W HEN Johann Fischart, writing in 1591, attested that "in our time the Jews produce many sorcerers," [1] he was revealing no startling discovery; the statement was a time-hallowed cliché, a fact that was taken for granted. Early in the eighteenth century the Frankfort theologian and anti-quarian Johann Jakob Schudt [2] heartily endorsed Luther's verdict that "a Jew is as full of idolatry and sorcery as nine cows have hair on their backs, that is: without number and without end." It is an opinion that time has not yet completely extinguished. To this day in backward regions of Europe the Jew's black magic is dreaded by the peasantry, and he continues to figure as the sorcerer in fables and nursery rhymes. [3] Describing his child-hood in a by-no-means-primitive Dutch village, Pierre van Paassen writes: "There was current among our people a vague belief which was always mentioned in mysterious tones. It at-tributed to the Jews some secret magic power which enabled them to suspend, or at least effectively intervene in, the normal processes of nature."

The Middle Ages inherited a tradition of Jewish sorcery from the ancient world. The Hellenistic magical papyri lean heavily upon Jewish elements, particularly the mystical names that have always been preëminent in Jewish practice, and in popular belief the Jews were held to be adroit in all the skills of the magician. [4] Juvenal's famous quip, "The Jews sell at cut prices as many dreams as you may wish," is the typical overstatement of the satirist, but we have evidence that it did not outdistance the pre-vailing opinion. Joseph, who had learned the secrets of magic in Egypt, was "the first to interpret dreams," and his descendants reputedly retained his precedence in the art.

But the Jewish addiction to magic was traced back generally

to Moses himself (not without biblical warrant, be it admitted), who was included among the most famous magicians of all time. The lawgiver had embodied in his code the vast store of occult learning that was his, so the theory ran, and in consequence Judaism was considered a repository of magic, which its adherents learned from childhood. So great was his repute as both legislator and sorcerer that the standard magicians' code, containing a complicated ceremonial for the induction of a candidate into the fraternity, was ascribed to him and bore his name—the "Book of Moses"; a share of his renown glorified even the name of his sister, for Maria or Miriam the Jewess, who was said to have been instructed by none other than God himself, was one of the most famous sorceresses of ancient times, with many important works attributed to her.

Lucius of Samosate (second century) chides "the fool who submits himself to the incantations of a Jew" to cure his gout.[5] Procopius reports that both a Byzantine general and the Emperor Justinian himself resorted to Jewish diviners.[6] Origen, the great theologian of the third century, who boasted a wide knowledge of Hebrew literature, did not hesitate to single out magic as a specifically Jewish pursuit.[7] And Chrysostom of Antioch, a bitter enemy of the Jews, incensed by members of his flock who attended Jewish services, participated in Jewish fasts and festivals, and even considered an oath taken in a synagogue more binding than one made in a church, angrily charged that Christians were attracted to the synagogue by the offer of charms and amulets.[8]

This tradition penetrated deeply into Christian thought, as we may see from the action of the Council of Narbonne (589) which brusquely prohibited Jews from harboring or consulting sorcerers.[9] Yet the tradition alone does not explain the virulence of the medieval charge of magic, nor its wide-flung ramifications. It found expression in so many forms and aroused such a violent reaction that we must seek its source in more immediate and compelling reasons. Certainly it was not aroused by the culpability of the Jews, for though they did own and practice a highly developed magic of their own, this was not generally accessible or even evident to Christian Europe. Contemporaneous Jewish magic was entirely free of the satanic element that figured so prominently in the familiar sorcery of the Middle Ages; the demons appeared in it almost exclusively as evil influences to be fought off, rarely indeed as agents of the magician. Its primary principle was an implicit reliance upon the powers of good: the angels and the manifold differentiated and personalized attributes of God, which were invoked by a complicated technique of permutation and combination of the letters of the Hebrew alphabet.[10] By virtue of this principle, which involved a close acquaintance with Hebrew mystical lore, this essentially beneficent magic remained distinctively Jewish, until it was appropriated and perverted by non-Jewish circles in the sixteenth century under the erroneous designation of Kabbalah. Prior to that time it was a closed book which very few non-Jews indeed succeeded in prying open.

The accusation of sorcery did not derive from observed acts of Jews, except perhaps in isolated instances, but was rather an integral part of the medieval conception of the Jew, embracing the entire people. In fact, the magic which Christendom laid at the door of the Jew had very little relation to the magic current in Jewish circles; it was a reflection of beliefs and practices current among Christians.

At a time when change and progress were already in the air, when Reformation and Renaissance were noticeably gathering strength, the vast mass of Europe's inhabitants was still steeped in an abysmal ignorance and superstition, breathing an atmosphere polluted by dark spirits and demons, constantly oppressed by a sense of its inadequacy and defenselessness against the forces of evil. Unseen, the devil and his hordes strove tirelessly to destroy them, while on earth sorcerers and witches, privy to the secret powers of the underworld, aided and abetted them. The revival of classical learning and of humanistic studies in the twelfth and thirteenth centuries was accompanied by an unparalleled and almost universal addiction to magic; Satan attained the peak of his notoriety, and the seeds of witchcraft thrust forth their first shoots. While the intellectual élite shared the general superstition, the common people were completely blocked off from the potentially liberating force of the new learning. It is ironic indeed that just in the fifteenth and sixteenth centuries, when both Reformation and Renaissance burst into full flower, this superstition assumed the proportions of a mass mania: it seems as though half of Europe was enrolled in the endemic witch-cults which adored and served Satan, while the other half cowered in dread of these representatives of the devil and hunted and slaughtered them with a fanatical ferocity.

In such an atmosphere the reputed allegiance of the Jew to Satan could not but have borne its full sinister implication. The devil was the ultimate source of magic, which operated only by his diabolic will and connivance. Indeed, magic was the technique whereby Satan promoted the designs of those evil humans who fought with him to overthrow and destroy Christendom. The widely heralded collusion between Satan and the Jews in bringing about the death of Jesus lent itself perfectly to the elaboration of this theme. Several medieval dramatic versions of the Passion exhibit the Jews, instigated by Satan, working their most potent charms against Jesus, mixing a typical witches' potion with all the lurid ceremonial of the well-known witch-cults, while the devil solicitously supervises the operation.[11] What more natural, in these circumstances, than that the Jews should be feared and hated as Europe's peerless sorcerers? Not only did medieval Europe interpret every innocent Jewish act as a devilish anti-Christian device but it invented or gave new prominence to a number of supposedly characteristic Jewish crimes against Christendom, essentially magical in their import. The blanket charge of sorcery against the Jews was the product of that peculiar combination of ignorance, superstition, and fanaticism which so strongly marked the common people of the period.

It is difficult to say how important a factor the ancient tradition of Jewish magical superiority was in the development of this medieval conception; if we find few direct allusions in medieval literature to the aspersions of classical writers, the tradition as such was preserved by the Church, which did not neglect any weapon of attack against the Jews. Whatever significance it may have had as a starting point, certain other traditional elements which remained prominent in medieval belief and folklore served to drive it home as an indisputable truth.

The Hebrew language, the tongue in which the sacred Scriptures were written, had achieved the status of an especially effective magical medium in ancient times; among Jews it was believed to be the sole language understood by the angels, and the syncretistic magic of the Hellenistic period favored words and names from the Hebrew. This same tradition penetrated the usage of Mohammedan magicians, and is apparent also in medieval European sources, where as an exotic and unintelligible tongue it lent special effectiveness to magical formulas. Hebrew names and terms occupied an important place in incantations and books of magic; they "appear to have been the most potent constituent" of such works. Benvenuto Cellini's account of the incantation scene in the Coliseum at Rome records that the necromancer uttered his "awful invocations, calling by name on multitudes of demons . . . in phrases of the Hebrew." Indeed, a number of late medieval amulets which were formerly thought to be of Jewish origin because of their Hebrew inscriptions are now known to have been made by and for Christians exclusively.[12]

Thus the popularity of Hebrew among sorcerers would tend to stamp the masters of that tongue as adepts. Christian Europe, having branded the Jew as Satan's creature, could not but see in this magic language the means of inviting and securing the devil's aid, and so when Jews are represented in the mystery plays as summoning their demonic confederates their charms are uttered in a gibberish that is intended to simulate Hebrew; even when the magician is not a Jew (for example, Saladin, the sorcerer in *Le Miracle de Théophile* by Rutebeuf, one of the most celebrated *trouvères* of the thirteenth century), his incantations are couched in a similar unintelligible abracadabra. As G. Schiavo has observed in this connection, the medieval au-

*The demon Belial presenting his credentials
to Solomon*

Jacobus de Teramo, *Das Buch Belial* (Augsburg,
1473)

*Demons performing various services for
humans*

Olaus Magnus, *Historia de gentibus septentrio-
nalibus* (Rome, 1555)

dience was not often composed of philologists; the tradition of Hebrew as the sorcerer's tongue was enough to identify both the language and the sorcerer as Jewish.[13]

There were also a number of very popular legends, part and parcel of medieval culture, which strengthened the conviction that Jews were, by definition, master magicians. As we have already had occasion to comment, the Middle Ages was not particularly distinguished for a critical historical sense. Legends were freely incorporated into the chronicles and accepted as indubitable fact.[14] The prominence of miraculous or supernatural elements in these tales by no means discredited them. Fantasy had for so long simulated fact in the intellectual diet of Europe that the presence of such elements only lent these fables a higher degree of credibility.

The Solomon cycle of legends merits special attention since it seems to have made a particularly strong impression upon the medieval imagination. These legends possessed two main elements: the wise monarch's dominion over devil and demons and his utilization of this power for magical ends. This latter theme was developed with all kinds of variations, so that Solomon came to be regarded both as the type of the sorcerer and the original source of occult science. So deeply did the belief in his magical supremacy enter into medieval thought that nothing more was required to authenticate the worth of a formula or an amulet than to trace it to him, and the most popular magical works drew their authority from his reputation. Even Aristotle was dragged into the picture. As teacher of the legend-encircled Alexander he was accredited throughout the Middle Ages with the authorship of the widely circulated *Secreta Secretorum*, in which were revealed all the mysteries of nature. According to vulgar opinion he was a Jew; nor was this enough, but he must also be a pupil of Solomon's and have learned how to command the spirits and to imprison them like flies in glass or rubies through studying the vast library of the master of all magic.[15] The number of Solomonic pseudepigrapha devoted to magic runs into scores, and their contents cover every aspect of magical activity. Petrus

Comestor, in his *Historia Scholastica*, written about 1170, ascribed all the magic books and paraphernalia current in his time to Solomon.[16]

The inference from Solomon to his people, the Jews, was an easy and obvious one, not alone with respect to the demon association which we have already noted but with respect to the complementary proficiency in magic as well. Already in the third century Origen, describing the Jews as a nation gifted in sorcery, based his opinion upon Solomon's fame as an exorcist and invoker of demons. The equation demons-magic-Jews did not have to be pressed upon the medieval mind, which eagerly seized upon it, not doubting that Solomon's skill had been bequeathed to his people. John Trithemius, Abbot of Sponheim toward the end of the fifteenth century, listed in his library of works on magic books attributed to or citing as authorities Solomon, Adam, Seth, Noah, Abraham, Moses, David, Ezekiel, Daniel, Job, Raziel, Joseph, Reuben, Enoch.[17] The ancient Jews had written all the important literature, and the contemporary Jews had mastered it.

Another popular figure in medieval legend was the Jewish magician Zebulon, who appears in conjunction with the Virgil cycle. (Virgil himself was an outstanding magician in these tales.) The three books of magic sometimes ascribed to Solomon and said to have been suppressed by King Hezekiah are also attributed to Zebulon. The anti-Christian function of Jewish magic received special emphasis in these legends. According to the version preserved in the *Wartburgkrieg* (second half of the thirteenth century) and in the adventures of Reinfrid of Braunschweig (after 1291), Zebulon, the son of a Jewish mother and a heathen father, wrote these books to prevent the birth of Jesus, for he had seen in the stars that through Christ "all Jews would be deprived of honor" (*alle juden gar von êren gestozen wurden*). The failure of these books to effect their purpose did not lessen the popular estimation of this magician's power—or of the power of Jewish magic in general. Indeed, they continued to circulate in Christian circles as especially noteworthy and reliable sources of magical knowledge. The impact of Zebulon upon the popular imagination is attested by the fact that the magician (Jewish in name only) who provides the love potion which brings the lovers together in Beaumont and Fletcher's *The Custom of the Country* (written in 1619 or 1622) bears his name, Zabulon.[18]

The famous disputation reputedly held before Emperor Constantine between Pope Sylvester I (314–335) and a group of Jews, which assumed great importance in Church history and was widely recounted to substantiate certain juridical rights supposedly arising out of the conversion of Constantine to Christianity, provided medieval Christendom with the figure of another memorable Jewish magician—Zambri. This incident was a popular subject for medieval chronicles and miracle plays. The details vary from one version to another, though all agree that a considerable number of Jews was required to combat the redoubtable champion of Christ; the figures range from 4 to 161. While some versions make Sylvester triumph over his Jewish adversaries by force of argument alone, the most popular conclusion brings the contest down to a direct trial of power between the Pope and the Jewish champion, "Zambri the magician, of Hebrew race and a sorcerer, in whom the Jews had the greatest confidence," as the earliest account of the disputation describes him. Zambri undertakes to kill a fierce bull simply by whispering the holy and omnipotent name of God into the beast's ear. Pressed to tell how he came to know this secret name he finally discloses that he had fasted seven days, then poured water into a new silver vessel and pronounced certain mystical charms over it, whereupon the letters of God's name appeared on the surface of the water. The Pope accepts the challenge, and when Zambri succeeds in putting the bull to death, as he promised, Sylvester promptly restores it to life with the name of Jesus, thus proving the superiority of Christianity over Judaism.[19] Here again Jewish magic fails, but only because Christ is mightier than the Jewish god (read: the devil).

Zedekiah, the Jewish physician of Emperor Charles the Bald

toward the end of the ninth century, was another such renowned figure in medieval folklore. His fame increased with the centuries, until in the later years of the Middle Ages he was credited with knowing how to fly and with having not only once swallowed a man whole but consumed an entire wagonload of hay, with horses and driver for good measure. His most astounding performance, however, was to chop off the hands, feet, and head of a man and then set them back on their owner without the least harm to him; or, as Johannes, Abbot of Trittenheim, described it in 1378: "he threw a man into the air, tore him there into pieces, piled his organs in a heap, and then joined them together again," which sounds even more remarkable.[20]

The Theophilus legend set the capstone on this representation of the Jew as sorcerer, for it depicted the Jewish magician explicitly as operating through the agency of Satan. "Master of the diabolical art," he is called, and the many versions, though differing in detail, all make it plain that his skill is deliberately directed against the pious and unsuspecting Christian.[21]

The theme of this legend is duplicated in the report of a certain Heliodorus, a native of Sicily in the eighth century, "who was full of all kinds of sorcery and jugglery," which he had learned through a "certain Hebrew who was famed for his magic and witchcraft," and who had given him a paper by means of which he was enabled to force the devil to do his bidding.[22] Enemies of the renowned scholar Photios, Patriarch of Constantinople in the latter part of the ninth century, went so far as to explain his great learning and wisdom as the products of his relations with "a Hebrew magician" who offered him "a strange charm" that would bring him "prosperity and wealth, great wisdom and joy." In return he was called upon to "deny the cross on which we nailed Jesus." Photios' detractors did not hesitate to imply that the Patriarch willingly complied with this characteristic demand.[23] Thus Guibert, Abbot of Nogent (eleventh century), who was much concerned about clerical immorality and especially the prevalence of sorcery among the clergy of his time, felt himself on completely safe ground when he laid the blame for this condition upon the Jews who, he asserted, introduced the clergy to the company of the "villainous Prince" and taught them to serve him.[24]

So convincing was the tradition that it found expression—or substantiation—even in matters not directly affecting Jews. Indeed we can find no more striking evidence of the popular equation of Jew and sorcerer than in certain regulations affecting sorcerers—*non-Jewish* sorcerers. Thus, in a German code dating from the end of the fourteenth century (an alphabetical register of existing laws arranged according to subject matter), under the rubric *Juden* and in the midst of the usual legal provisions covering testimony of Jews, the Jewry oath, usury, etc., there appears a paragraph on the punishment of *sorcerers,* not Jewish sorcerers but just sorcerers. And then the code proceeds, as though nothing extraordinary had just been permitted to intrude, with the usual run of Jewry-law.[25] The apparent divagation can only be accounted for on the assumption that the compiler believed that a paragraph headed "Concerning sorcerers" belonged under the general heading "Jews." Furthermore the Buda (Hungary) code of 1421, provided that anyone apprehended for the first time as a "conjuror, sorcerer, or witch" should be obliged to appear in public "with a peaked Jew's hat on his head, with the holy angels painted on it." [26] No more appropriate index was available than this distinctive and well-known Jewish headgear. It must have been easy indeed to see in the yellow felt patches which monks and priests condemned for sorcery were required to wear on the breast and shoulder[27] nothing other than the familiar Jew badge —if indeed such signs were not actually meant to be just that.

This sort of reputation obviously did not ease the position of the Jews, for, aside from the public reactions, the juridical and executive organs of both Church and state took stern cognizance of it. In Byzantium, in the eleventh century, a Jew who desired to be admitted into the Church was obliged first to anathematize, *inter alia,* "all their [the Jews'] witchcraft, incantations, sorcery, soothsaying, amulets and phylacteries." [28] The context of this official formula of renunciation makes it plain that such practices were considered integral and essential elements of Judaism. But not until the thirteenth century did the sorcery charge produce really oppressive results. The attacks upon the Talmud at that time were caused perhaps as much by the suspicion that it concealed the secrets of Jewish magic as by its reputedly anti-Christian teachings. Agobard of Lyons, in his work *De judaicis superstitionibus*, assailed the Talmud as containing magical elements which he took to be the true expression of the Jewish religion.[29] The "ordinance for the reformation of morals" issued in December, 1254, by Louis IX of France, who a few years earlier had ordered the burning of the Talmud, leaves room to suppose a similar opinion on his part.[30] There can be no doubt that this notion was widely held in later years. A satirical attack upon the Bishop of Würzburg and his followers in 1397 condemned them all roundly as students of the Talmud, since "the holy Scriptures seemed to them not good": "they had all learned its lessons well, its teaching is called necromancy; Satan was also with them while they pursued their study." [31] And in 1553 a committee of experts appointed in Venice to examine the Talmud supported the decision to ban its use by Jews "since primarily the majority of their Talmudists are sorcerers, heretics and vicious persons." [32] It was in part due to this conception that the Inquisition assumed authority to censor and proscribe Hebrew works.

On July 26, 1240, the Synod of Worcester, in England, decreed that "when men and women magicians shall be found, and also such as consult Jews for the purpose of finding out by magic about their life or actions, they shall be brought before the bishop to be punished. . . ." The Jew, who is apparently by definition a magician, it is to be noted, is here not subjected to the bishop's jurisdiction. The Provincial Council of Béziers, on May 6, 1255, however, ordered Jews directly to "desist from usury, blasphemy, and magic," while the action of Philip the Fair, who in 1293 and again in 1302 expressly forbade the Inquisition to proceed against Jews on the ground of usury or sorcery, indicates that the Inquisition had already seized upon this pretext to extend its jurisdiction over them. In Spain, at a later date, a common charge against Conversos was that they had reverted to the practice of Jewish magic, and unconverted Jews were also occasionally brought before a tribunal to answer for the crime of sorcery. Pope Alexander V in 1409 ordered the Inquisitor of Avignon, Dauphiné, Provence, and Comtat Venaissin to proceed against several categories of persons, including Jews who practiced magic, invokers of demons, and augurs.[33]

The very oath *more judaico* which juridical procedure obliged the Jew to take during the Middle Ages, and which was permeated with religious sanctions that the Church believed would bear with special force upon the Jew, expressed this same attitude. An oath was essentially a magically coercive formula, binding upon the maker and *upon God and His agents*, in the European view, and the *more judaico* was therefore designed by Christians to incorporate what they conceived to be magically binding Jewish components. Thus the Jew was required quite generally to swear by the Hebrew name of God, *Adonay*, and not by this one name alone but by "the seventy names of God," as in the Narbonne oath formula. The Navarre oath included the recital of the names of seventy angels, and of other epithets, bizarre and clearly magical in import; in Tortosa the subject was instructed to swear by such "saints" as Tuobe, Trach, Bucisma, Mucrenti, Azdd, etc., and was then charged: "I conjure you, Jew, by all the saints who are in heaven and in the sea and in the earth and under the earth. . . ." These formulas also commonly included the recital of a variety of attributes of God, such as "who created heaven and earth," "who led us through the Red Sea," etc., which were characteristic of medieval incantations. In addition the Jew was obliged to call down upon his head, in the event that he should be perjuring himself, an assortment of imprecations and curses drawn from biblical examples and amplified by local invention: fever, loss of sight, loss of property, wild animals, plague, starvation, death of children, etc., etc. The intent of such formulas was not only to frighten the Jew but actually to subject him automatically to the prescribed heaven-sent penalties if he swore falsely. Finally a culminating magical test (in the nature of the ordeal) was appended in some instances to the act of oath taking: in France, in the eleventh century, a necklace of thorns was clasped around the Jew's neck and a twig five ells long, full of thorns, was drawn forcefully across his hips; if he came out of this experience unharmed, his oath was considered acceptable and he was cleared. A similar provision is found in the Silesian *Landrecht* of the fourteenth century: the oath was to be taken while standing barefoot on a three-legged stool; if the swearer fell off he was subjected to a fine; the fourth fall lost him the case.[34]

If we turn now to the specific charges of magical activity which the records disclose, we find them to be surprisingly few and unvaried, despite the sweeping accusation leveled against the Jews. It will not require much space to run through them.

Jews were supposedly possessed of the evil eye. The famous canon 49 of the Council of Elvira, adopted in 320, forbidding Jews to bless standing crops in the field, was intended to frighten the peasants by arousing the suspicion that the harm thus done could not subsequently be undone by the benediction of the priest.[35] This same suspicion may have prompted the exclusion of a Jewish delegation bearing gifts and pledges of allegiance to the coronation of Richard I of England, in 1189. A Hebrew account of the incident informs us that "there came also the leading and wealthiest Jews to bring an offering to the King, and evil men began to say that it was not right for Jews to look on the King's crown when the monks and priests crowned him." This sounds very much as though it was the evil eye that the "evil men" dreaded. However, other contemporary evidence leaves the matter in doubt. Matthew Paris attests simply that they were expelled "because of the magic arts, which used to be practiced at royal coronations, for which the Jews . . . are infamous," and which they allegedly planned to work against the King. According to William of Newbury Richard ordered their expulsion "either because he was less favorable to them than his father, or had some premonition, a certain superstitious foreboding about the plans of certain persons." Whatever the specific nature of the charge, it is clear that it had to do with some sort of magic. This incident provided the signal for a bloody outbreak against the Jews which continued into the following year and overwhelmed every community in the land—the earliest instance of a mass attack upon the Jews as sorcerers.[36]

Fortunetelling was another *forte* of the Jews, we must conclude from the persistent attribution to them of this skill. How great their reputation was may be judged from the generally accepted story that Leo the Isaurian was influenced to initiate the destruction of Christian images by the prediction of "two enemies of God . . . Hebrews addicted to fortunetelling, casting of lots, mixing of poisons and augury," that he would become emperor if he undertook such a campaign.[37] (One is reminded of the similar prophecy tendered to Vespasian by Josephus.) Likewise the thirteenth-century chronicle popularly known as *Philomena* attributed the fall of Narbonne to Charlemagne (it was Pepin who took the city in 759) in part to the Jewish prediction that the city was doomed.[38] Schudt, who repeats many tales of Jewish essays in divination, advances as partial proof of the theory that the gypsies are descended from or in some way related to the Jews the fact that gypsies also excel in the art of prophecy, though to tell the truth his opinion of Jewish proficiency is not very high: "The Jews are pretty poor soothsayers, and quite unlucky in prophesying things to come," he remarks in one place, after a few stories of unsuccessful ventures in this field.[39]

Legends concerning buried treasures also have a close Jewish connection, for it was generally believed that the devil was privy to their whereabouts, if he had not himself planted them in their hiding places. This left ample room for the Jews to enter the picture. They appear in these legends as guardians of the secret hoards, or as their discoverers, often by magical means or through imprisoned spirits. Jewish synagogues were regarded as likely repositories. In Hamburg, in 1783, the opinion was expressed that the sacrifice of a Jewish girl was necessary to the successful unearthing of a treasure.[40]

From Spain we learn that the Jews were credited with the power to bring rain in time of drought, when Christian prayers failed to produce results; [41] and that they were considered unusually adept in the interpretation of dreams, a distinction which they modestly disclaimed.[42] Invoking demons by magic chants was charged against the Jews of Avignon during the reign of Pope Martin V (1417–31),[43] and a report published in Vienna in 1599 had it that two Jews, by magic, had caused the sudden death of thousands of head of cattle.[44] Luther was warned by friends against a certain Jewish physician who possessed the magical power to render himself invisible at will; [45] the Town Hall of Kissingen houses (or did until recently) a statue commemorating a Jew who, during the siege of the city by the Swedes in the Thirty Years' War, cast bullets that never failed to hit their mark; [46] nursery rhymes current several centuries ago preserve the tradition that Jews could and often did turn themselves into cats.[47]

Astrology, "the fundamental doctrine of the medieval *Weltanschauung*," in the words of Lynn Thorndike, and alchemy, its sister pseudo science—part magic, part true science, both of them —had captured the interest of everyone with the intellectual capacity to dabble in them. It is therefore not surprising to encounter a good many references to Jewish astrologers, many of them undoubtedly trustworthy since Jews are known to have practiced this "science" quite extensively, especially in Southern Europe, where they were often to be found serving as professional stargazers in the courts of high-ranking prelates and noblemen. Yet, for all the undoubted repute of some Jews in this field, the Jewish people hardly merited the tribute that, like the Arabs, they were "the successors of the Chaldeans and the legitimate heirs of their skill in reading the stars." [48]

Alchemy, too, was regarded as a Jewish specialty, despite the fact that the number of Jewish alchemists known to us is small and that among the thousands of alchemical works in world literature "Jewish literature cannot boast a single original and comprehensive work" on the subject. There was, of course, some acquaintance with alchemy among Jews but not more than generally in Europe. What facilitated the association was the fact that alchemy was a department of magic: *magnus experimentator et nigromanticus* is the description of a Jewish alchemist of Mallorca in 1345.[49] The Jewish community of Southern Europe produced a few experts; in the North almost none are known. The founder of a heretical Judeo-Christian sect at Novgorod, Russia, in 1470, which spread to Moscow and won many adherents until it was violently suppressed in 1504, was a Jew named Zachariah, said to have possessed unusual alchemical skill—the Muscovites attributed his success in perverting Christians to black magic.[50] About the middle of the sixteenth century we learn of three Jewish alchemists in Germany, none of any importance.[51] Rabbi Judah Löw of Prague is also counted by tradition among the alchemists, and his famous audience on February 16, 1592, with Emperor Rudolph II, who was intensely interested in alchemy, was said to have dealt with this subject. There is no proof of this, however, and Löw's biographer, Nathan Grün, has shown that he had no interest in or knowledge of the field.[52]

It is ironic that Luther should have warned the elector Joachim II of Brandenburg not to place too much trust in his court Jews lest they prove more expert in alchemy than in the conduct of his affairs. For Joachim, who was constantly in need of money and therefore desirous of advancing the science of gold making, had established at his court an alchemical laboratory, in which he set up some of the leading exponents of the science. Not only was there no Jew among them but the only share Jews had in the business was when his financial agent Lippold was called upon periodically to cover the expense of the experiments.[53]

Luther, like the medieval community in general, equated alchemists with Jews. After all, were not the leading source books ascribed to Abraham, Adam, Moses, and Solomon? Did not the contemporary alchemists trot out, besides these, such names as Bezaleel, David, Elijah, Isaiah, Elisha, Ezekiel, Zechariah, Malachi, Daniel, Ezra, Job—to mention only a few—as authorities? Was not Maria the Jewess renowned as one of the most important exponents of magic alchemy? As early as the eleventh century the Kabbalah was credited by Christian alchemists with being the source of their knowledge; by the sixteenth century the two were so closely associated in the common view that alchemy and Kabbalah were thereafter practically synonymous. Who could remain unaware of this association? Even the symbol of the philosopher's stone often displayed the Star of David and a Hebrew inscription. In the face of these considerations it mattered not at all that Jews provided so little direct evidence of expertness. Luther stood on the sure ground of unassailable tradition.

The reputation of the Jews as experts in the magic virtues of precious and semiprecious stones was equally far wide of the mark. Medieval Europe devoted a good deal of speculation to the supposed superior occult powers of gems; they were even the subject of a heated theological debate centering about the question whether their peculiar virtues were divinely implanted or merely part of their nature. Jews, who were the leading importers of and dealers in gems during the early Middle Ages, were commonly accredited with a certain specialization in their magic properties. Konrad von Megenberg based his account of the peculiar virtues of these stones, in his *Buch der Natur,* on a work which he attributed to "the great Jewish master," Tethel. *Christianos fidem in verbis, Judaeos in lapidibus pretiosis, et Paganos in herbis ponere,* ran the adage, which Goethe echoed in the tenth ballad of *Reineke Fuchs: Und auf Kräuter und Steine versteht sich der Jude besonders.* Yet, as Steinschneider remarks, "Hardly a single dissertation on this subject is to be found in Hebrew literature . . . and the little that does exist is very insignificant and recent, derived mainly from non-Jewish sources." [54]

Finally, there are a number of allusions to the Jewish proclivity for dispensing amulets. The nature of these objects is indicated by a tale in Schudt [55] about an amulet which a Jew had provided to quiet a restless horse; after having done its work well and faithfully for many years, the amulet was opened and was found to contain this inscription in Hebrew characters: "The master of the horse shall belong to the devil so long as the horse stands still when it is struck"! In Castille a legend arose that Pedro I (1350–69) had been victimized by a jealous mistress, Doña Maria de Padilla, who presented him with a waistband that his Jewish treasurer, Simuel Halevi, had bewitched; when Pedro wore it at a court reception, "it turned into a great serpent in the sight of all the court, and coiled itself around his body, to the great terror of all present and also of the King himself." [56] Interestingly, testimony before the Spanish Inquisitorial courts relative to the reversion of Marranos to Judaism often hinged on their possession of Hebrew amulets, as though this were the one essential Jewish practice these converts could not dispense with.[57]

The reputation of Jews as manufacturers and peddlers of amulets is satirized in an anecdote recounted by Luther. A Jew proffered to Count Albrecht of Saxony an amulet which would make him immune to all weapons of attack; Albrecht forced the Jew to take his own medicine: to test the efficacy of the amulet he hung it about its donor's neck—and ran him through with his sword.[58]

A striking Hebrew parallel to this tale illustrates the tragic use to which this reputation could be put and the tragic necessity which prompted such a use. During the Chmielnicki pogroms of 1648–49 a young Jewish girl of the city of Nemirov was abducted by a Cossack. Preferring to elect her own fate, she offered him a similar amulet. " 'If you have no faith in me,' she assured him, 'test it by shooting at me. You cannot harm me.' Her credulous captor, not doubting her word, fired straight at her and she fell dead, for the sanctification of the Holy Name, and to preserve her purity. May God have mercy on her soul!" concludes the pious chronicler of one of the bloodiest pages of Jewish history.[59]

CHAPTER FIVE

EUROPE DISCOVERS THE KABBALAH

A S the Middle Ages expired, by an ironic paradox the medieval conception of the Jew experienced a lusty rejuvenation. Out of the birthplace of the Renaissance, at the moment of its most brilliant flowering, came the most authoritative statement of this attitude.

"The worst of it is that they seduce a great many imprudent and weak persons with their satanic illusions, their fortune-telling, their charms and magic tricks and witcheries, and make them believe that the future can be foretold, that stolen goods and hidden treasures can be recovered, and much else can be revealed." These were the words with which Pope Pius V explained his expulsion of the Jews from the Papal States, with the exception of Rome and Ancona, in 1569.[1]

The Pope's declaration was supported by a curious concentration of interest in Italy at this time on the purported magical activities of the Jews. One wonders how much this was influenced by renewed acquaintance with the classical writers—it was on Rome's Appian Way that Juvenal's Jewish fortunetellers plied their trade—and by the local preoccupation with sorcery, which naturally accented the tradition of Jewish excellence in the field; or in how far it reflected a true state of affairs. Undoubtedly Jews must have capitalized on their reputation—the temptation was only too great in a society which paid high prices for charms and love potions and occult poisons, and often esteemed its citizens in the degree in which they inspired fear and hate. Only a little peddling of enchantments would have sufficed to underscore the tradition. Jewesses were outstanding "beauticians" in sixteenth-century Rome, much in demand for their private concoctions guaranteed to enhance the charm of young ladies and restore that of old ones—a specialty not unconnected with magic, for it employed fantastic ingredients, utilized the mystic phrase, and promised remarkable results. Pietro Aretino expressed the opinion that the Roman prostitutes, who "tried to enhance their personal attractions by charms of another description," learned their arts from certain Jewish women who were in possession of magical appurtenances (*malie*). It was in such comments that Ferdinand Gregorovius, the historian of Rome, found warrant to remark on the "Jewish women [who] told fortunes in the homes of the nobility and brewed love philters in the clandestine night for languishing ladies." [2]

But the tales of Jewish sorcery outdistanced plausibility. Ludovico Ariosto selected as the hero of his comedy of the necromancers a Jewish exile from Spain, whose pretensions as a sorcerer he held up to ridicule. This man claims that "his incantations can darken the day and illumine the night, that he can move the earth, make himself invisible, and turn men into beasts," and he persuades people that he can conjure up ghosts and make a corpse talk. Among the fabulous inventions of Ortensio Landi we read of the activities of two magicians, a Sicilian and a Jew, of magic mirrors, of a conversation with a death's-head, and of birds stopped short in their flight.[3] When the plot required a sorcerer, as often as not a Jew filled the bill. Pius V's decree bespoke the prevailing view. And not of Italy alone but of all Europe.

For this was the century that uncovered the mysteries of the Kabbalah to Christian eyes. Until that time Europe had been aware that the Jews possessed a mystic doctrine, and Christians had pretended to draw much magical inspiration from it, though few were familiar enough with Hebrew to gain more than the most casual acquaintance with it. The growing interest in Hebrew studies that was a feature of the Renaissance gradually opened the pages of this theosophical system to the curious. Pico della Mirandola and Johann Reuchlin were the first to popularize their Kabbalistic gleanings in Christian circles; in their opinion they had discovered not only the supreme "science of nature," but, *among Jews*, final proof of the divinity of Christ! These were

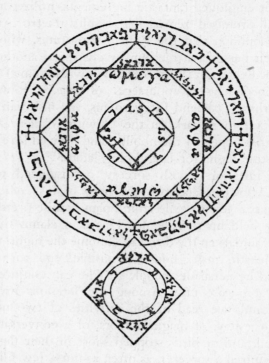

The "Kabbalistic" magic circle employed among non-Jews, with its characteristic Hebrew inscription

Clavicule de Salomon, Bibliothèque de l'Arsenal, Ms. 2350

the dual interests that led them to introduce the Kabbalah in full dress to a new and eager audience. But the Kabbalah as Christian Europe finally embraced it was not the Kabbalah of the Jews.

On the fringe of the Jewish theosophy was the magical lore that non-Jews had heretofore but dimly perceived. This had little enough to do with Kabbalah proper, and was, in fact, denominated in Jewish circles the "practical Kabbalah" as distinct from the authentic "theoretical Kabbalah." It was the practical Kabbalah in a theosophical dress that Christians found the easier and the more desirable to assimilate. It became a prized adjunct of astrology and alchemy, a marvelous magic apparatus, in the general view. Jewish elements were soon absorbed and so transposed as to remain Jewish in name only. Since the sixteenth century there has grown up a vast library of Kabbalistic texts, so-called—a new, Christian Kabbalah, that speedily parted company with its ostensible parent and ventured off in other directions wholly on its own. The term Kabbalah became synonymous with magic, under this new dispensation.[4]

Physical attack upon Jews specifically as sorcerers was quite rare in the earlier centuries—the subsidiary charges, such as poisoning, the host and blood accusations, and the rest which we shall shortly consider, were then still persuasive enough to serve as sufficient pretext. But when the Reformation destroyed the effectiveness of some of the more popular earlier accusations coincidentally with the startling revelation of the Kabbalah, the sorcery accusation came into its very own.

In 1551, Schudt informs us,[5] Duke Christopher of Württemberg unleashed a savage assault against the Jews, peremptorily ordering them out of his state because "they were overt sorcerers." This charge was evidently leveled thereafter with sufficient frequency to constitute a major danger to Jewish communities, for we find the *Vaad*, or Council of Lithuanian Jewry (which first convened in 1623), decreeing in 1637, and again in 1647, that the expense of combating it, and the damage resulting from it, must be shared by the entire Jewry and not left for the community directly involved to bear alone. In 1681, when the accusations did not let up and the burden of contending with them grew too heavy for the impoverished and decimated Jewry, exhausted after the devastating Chmielnicki outbreak, the Lithuanian *Vaad* turned to the Council of Polish Jewry (the famous "Council of the Four Lands") with the plea that it too bear a share of such expenses.[6] This action is poignant evidence of the effect of the renewed and reinforced sorcery propaganda upon the attitude of the Christian masses.

When Luther excoriated Jewish superstition and magic, his real target was this newfangled Kabbalah.[7] When a host of works on magic appeared boasting Jewish inspiration, it was this they really meant.[8] When the attack on Jews as sorcerers increased in intensity and the Pope gave it official expression, the Christian version of Kabbalah was the cause. Only an unbalanced Judeophile could have doubted the veracity of the report that Charles V's naval excursion against Algiers in 1542 had been frustrated by a Jewish magician who raised a terrific storm and did so much damage to the imperial fleet that it was obliged to retire in utter confusion.[9] Paracelsus went about elaborating a scheme to create a homunculus by alchemical means with supreme assurance of its ultimate success—for had he not learned the secret from the Kabbalah?—and Schudt could proclaim confidently: "The present-day Polish Jews are notoriously masters of this art, and often make the *golem* (a homunculus), which they employ in their homes, like kobolds or house spirits, for all sorts of housework." [10]

Down to the present century Kabbalah has been a favorite of Christian pseudo mystics and amateur magicians. And because Kabbalah is the name of a Jewish theosophical discipline, the Jews were irrevocably branded as master magicians: the ancient tradition had at last received its final vindication.

One should imagine, in view of all this, that the records of judicial proceedings—secular and ecclesiastic—would be our richest source of information. Sorcery was a crime severely prosecuted by both Church and state, and there are countless reports of court proceedings in such cases during the Middle Ages, particularly with the inception of the witch trials. If Jews were such notorious magicians as the record indicates they were commonly held to be, then Jewish names ought to predominate— well, at least they ought to be fairly prominent—among the sorcerers apprehended by the authorities. If it seem reasonable to make such a supposition, the facts belie reason in this instance. I have done no more than make a sampling of the pertinent literature, a fairly extensive sampling, at that. If I cannot pretend that the following is a complete listing of sorcery cases in which Jews were involved, I am confident that no matter how industriously others hunt up more, the sum total will still remain astonishingly insignificant.[11]

The earliest report that has come to my attention dates from the year 637 or thereabouts, when a Jewish sorcerer of Salamis, Daniel by name, was burnt at the stake for plying his trade; [12] we have no further information as to the specific act or acts for which he was punished. There follows a period of five centuries without a single case to record. Our next item is dated 1131, when the Jews of London were fined £2,000 "for the sick man whom they killed." This was an enormous sum, probably more than £125,000 at present value, and so strikingly disproportionate to the customary exactions for such an offense (e.g., twenty shillings "for a slain Jew") that we must agree with Joseph Jacobs that it is quite possible "some charge of magic was involved." [13] If this seems a rather dubious exhibit, our catalogue is not so long that we should cavil about including it.

We are indebted to the diligence of the Spanish Inquisition for a few cases. In 1352 Mosse Porpoler of Valencia was fined by the Inquisitor because he and some other Jews had tried to recover stolen property by magic; part of the fine was remitted by King Pedro IV of Aragon. A quarter of a century later his successor, Juan I, fully reversed the verdict of the Inquisition and absolved three Jewesses of Teruel of a similar offense. The magic by which they were accused of endeavoring to recover their property comprised these mysterious activities: reeling off thread through the streets of the Jewish quarter, abducting a Jew, offering specially prepared dishes to various prisoners, and concealing their threads at the entrance to the synagogue and in the Jewish slaughterhouse.[14] Whatever may have inspired the King's action —a private feud with the Inquisitor, cold cash, sheer chivalry?— the ladies were probably guilty as charged. Our verdict fortunately can do them no harm. The circumstantial detail of the charge rings authentic, and the entire operation fits the pattern of similar devices we know to have been widely employed by Jews and non-Jews.

At about the same time, in 1393, Jacob Façan, a Jew of Murviedro, was haled before the Inquisition charged with aiding Conversos to revert to Judaism; a subsidiary count was to the effect that he had sought, with the help of (presumably Jewish) magicians, to ascertain the cause of his daughter's illness.[15] In 1451, in the city of Messina, Sicily, we hear of the conviction of a Jewess named Gemma on "several charges of a magical nature" (*nonnullis criminibus artis magice*);[16] and in 1485 a Jew, Juan de Talavera, was accused before the Inquisitorial Court of Segovia, in Spain, of practicing sorcery.[17] A few years later a Marrano, Guillermus Raymundus Esplugues, confessed to the Inquisitorial court at Valencia that he had practiced *Negromancia*, though it is difficult to tell whether his guilt went beyond accepting an amulet from a Jewish physician to ease his wife's labor pains, and later passing it on to another woman. However, works on alchemy were found in his possession, which seems to have been pretty damning evidence against him.[18]

A strange case is that of the converted Jew, Johann Pfefferkorn (not identical with the convert of the same name whose debate with Reuchlin over the Talmud made history), executed in Halle in 1514 or 1515.[19] He is reported to have confessed stealing an "imprisoned devil" from a priest (!) in Franconia, with which he performed much magic before he finally sold it for five gulden. Nor was this the full measure of his crime. He had also gone in for poisoning on a large scale, stole several consecrated hosts, and kidnaped two children, one of whom he sold to

Jews that they might extract its blood, the other he let go free "because it had red hair"! Besides all this, he seems to have been a fairly common type of criminal—and a little demented in the bargain, to judge from the scanty information available.

And this is all. All except for the *cause célèbre* of Münzmeister Lippold, which provides a keyhole through which to watch the unpopular Jew being beaten with the convenient big stick of the sorcery charge.[20] Lippold was the mintmaster and financier of Elector Joachim II of Brandenburg for many years, his trusted confidant as well as treasurer, who underwrote not only his experiments in alchemy but his more fruitful essays in love as well. Lippold's influence with his liege was too much for him, and for the court, and he succeeded in making himself thoroughly hated among his coreligionists as well as among the members of the Elector's official family. If his overweening self-esteem merited a just measure of retribution, his terrible end was assuredly greater punishment than he had earned.

No sooner did Joachim die, on January 3, 1571, than his successor had Lippold arrested on a charge of embezzlement and theft, which was soon enlarged to include the murder of the late Elector by poisoning. Diligent investigation, however, could uncover no evidence of any offense, and he was freed. But he was carefully shadowed until, almost two years later, the "magic book" showed up, and his persecution took a fatal turn. Spies overheard his wife, in the course of a family quarrel in which she rehearsed all his sins (of omission, no doubt, as well as of commission), mention a "magic book" that he owned. That innocent, if barbed, allusion was his undoing: the instant the suspicion of sorcery fell upon him he was lost. The house was ransacked, the book was found—a Kabbalistic booklet in Hebrew, of the sort then popular among Jews. Whether it was a "magic" book or not is immaterial now, as it was then (the title is not preserved in the record); enough that it was Kabbalistic. Lippold was given "the works"; for a time he remained obdurate. Then, finally, on January 16, 1573, he "confessed"—voluntarily (*in der guthe*), the record states, though a little further on we learn that "he also requested that he be spared the torture, he would say freely what he knew."

The details of his confession[21] are typical of contemporary magical practice; he evidently knew what his inquisitors were after and was prepared to give full satisfaction. He admitted having successfully performed a variety of magic crimes against specified persons: he had conjured the devil, who put in an appearance once as a black dog and again in human shape, had entered into a pact with him and had made him offerings "from his body, his head, and his nails"; he had set the devil against several people, causing them ill luck, injury, and death; he had induced sexual incompatibility between a married couple, had aroused illicit passion in an unmarried couple, and had dispensed recipes for love philters; and he had manufactured a magic key that opened all locks and even defeated bolts and bars.

"Further interrogated: since he was a Jew and by nature neither faithful nor pleasing to a Christian, and on the other hand, since Christians could not be friendly to Jews, he should state whether there was not also in this book a means of winning the favor of people; to which he replied yes, there was in it such a technique whereby one could gain the goodwill of others." And he confessed, as was demanded, that he had used this magic to get into the good graces of the Elector. Obviously, Joachim could not possibly have befriended a Jew and reposed so much trust in him without some supernatural compulsion.[22]

The final item in this confession was to the effect that he had with the aid of magic poisoned his patron.

At the close of the inquisition[23] he was severely tortured to test his veracity, and when he failed to retract any part of his confession his guilt was adjudged proven. With this document as basis, he was formally placed on trial, January 28; evidently offered a commutation of death sentence if he would become a Christian, he redeemed himself at the very end by choosing to die "a pious Jew in his faith." In accordance with medieval procedure he was again requested to make confession. This time, stiff-necked Jew that he was, he denied everything: "He had

The execution of Münzmeister Lippold at Berlin, 1573 (contemporary engraving) admitted all this only for suffering and pain." But he had not reckoned with the rack. So savagely tortured that "blood spurted from his neck," his resistance broke and he acknowledged everything once more as before. He was executed in Berlin in a manner, even for that time, unusually barbarous, and when his bowels were burned together with the unlucky "magic book" and a large mouse jumped out of the fire, the audience recognized in it the devil and accepted this as the culminating evidence of his guilt.

The Jews of the Electorate then paid their penalty for his "crime"—they were attacked, their property was confiscated, and in the end they were driven out. Lippold's sin, to have been the Elector's favorite, was amply expiated.

These few cases exhaust the official record of Jewish implication in crimes of magic. What of the witch trials? Does Jewish sorcery make a better showing there? Poor Johann Schudt! How he squirmed when he came face to face with this question. All the fables he had assembled to bolster the contention that Jews are the world's master magicians must have brought little comfort when he finally had to ask himself (for he was, after all, an honest scholar), what about the witch trials? "One will not easily find in the works of those who have written about witches," he was obliged to admit ruefully, " . . . that Jews or Jewesses are among the accused in witch trials, that they appear in gatherings of sorcerers, or have entered into a pact with Satan." So. The fact could not be denied. But honest scholarship can be carried too far. Having done his duty, he proceeded to explain the fact away: "The Jews have no need to ally themselves with the evil spirits by means of the usual pact, like other sorcerers; their Kabbalistic magic arts are already sufficiently the work of Satan." [24]

Be this as it may, Schudt's scholarship is supported by modern research. Among the thousands of witch trials on record, spanning several centuries, there is one case—"in all probability the only one"—involving a Jewess; and the sequel cleared even her of guilt. [25] In Hesse, in the year 1669, a certain Golda, daughter of

Kaiphas of the town of Kell and wife of Reuben of Treis a.d. Lumde, set fire to her house with the aim of razing the whole village of Treis. Haled to court, she admitted not only this intention but also that she had covenanted her soul to the devil, had whored in her youth with a baker's man, indeed, that her mother had cursed her while she was yet in the womb, and that she had in turn visited a fatal curse upon her mother. This is certainly one of the least sensational of the witch trials. She was incarcerated in the tower of Marburg but was there acknowledged to be deranged and was discharged. The effect of the widely current tales of witchcraft upon such poor wretches is only too apparent.

CHAPTER SIX

MAGIC AND MEDICINE

SUCH specific charges of magical activity as we have been reviewing, rare as they were, seem to have been wholly incidental, and probably derived from the general conception of the Jew far more than they influenced it. The essential feature of the Christian fear of Jewish sorcery, it must be emphasized, is that it adhered not to certain individual Jews who had aroused it by their actions but rather to the entire people. That it was so poorly supported by the facts, as we have noticed, in no way diminished the tenacity with which it persisted. The Jew was, by definition, a sorcerer, and all his works were suspect.

The Hebrew sources of the period offer striking testimony to supplement the wealth of evidence from non-Jewish sources. In their ignorance of the Jewish religion, people were quick to perceive a diabolical scheme for working magic against Christians in actually inoffensive ritual acts which by their strangeness laid themselves open to suspicion. The custom of throwing a clod of earth behind one after a funeral (a practice, incidentally, borrowed from Christian usage) brought a charge of sorcery (with intent "to cast a magic spell over the Gentiles, to kill them") in Paris in the early years of the thirteenth century, which might have had serious consequences if a certain Rabbi Moses ben Yehiel had not succeeded in persuading the king of its utterly harmless character. The practice of washing the hands on returning from the cemetery aroused the same suspicion of sorcery and provoked some bloody scenes.[1]

So onerous did these recurrent accusations become that the rabbis of the Middle Ages found it necessary—under the pressure, no doubt, of an apprehensive Jewish public opinion—to suspend some of these customs, or at least to counsel caution in their observance. "Since Gentiles are to be found among us, and there are Gentile servants in our homes, we must be on guard lest they say it is magic," warned a thirteenth-century writer in terms so often repeated by others as to indicate that such misinterpretation was far from uncommon. In the case of the clod throwing, though "many were obliged to disregard the usage for fear that the Gentiles would accuse them of sorcery," custom was proof against fear and the rabbinic authorities refused to sanction its abrogation. But in other instances fear triumphed. The mourning rites of "binding the head" and "overturning the bed" lapsed during the Middle Ages for this reason.[2]

In Talmudic times fear of the same accusation had led Jewish authorities to excuse the head of the household from the rite of "searching out the leaven" on the eve of the Passover in places owned in common with a non-Jew; during the Middle Ages there was a strong but unsuccessful agitation to suspend this rite altogether, even indoors, "because we have Gentile serving-girls in our homes" who might spread the alarm. In Provence, however, the ritual cleansing of the public oven in preparation for Passover baking was widely neglected "because of the Gentiles' suspicion of sorcery."[3] We read also of a lamb slaughtered in fulfillment of a ritual obligation, which was cut up and buried secretly in sections, "so that the matter may not become known and they say it was done for magical ends."[4] To such measures were Jews driven by fear of arousing the suspicions of their neighbors.

When a fire broke out in a Jewish house its owner dared expect no sympathy, and indeed little mercy, from the mob, for he was a sorcerer seeking to destroy Christendom, and his punishment was commonly simultaneous with his crime. Fire swept rapidly through the tinderbox towns of those days, and the populace was justifiedly in dread of a conflagration. But the responsibility was so consistently laid upon the Jews—entire communities were time after time ravaged and expelled, even when the fire did not first break out in the Jewish quarter—that we cannot ascribe this circumstance solely to the cupidity or passion of the mob. If, as was often the case, it was asserted that the guilty arsonists were witches in league with the devil, then the Jews could not escape the taint of complicity, supported as this suspicion was by their purported intention to destroy Christendom by whatever means. The rabbis of the time were therefore unusually tolerant about violations of the prohibition to extinguish fires on the Sabbath and the Day of Atonement, "for this is a matter of life and death, since they accuse us and persecute us."[5]

The ease with which crimes of arson could be pinned on the Jews is excellently illustrated by an incident that occurred in Deggendorf, Bavaria, in 1337. As the result of a charge of host desecration the Jewish quarter was attacked and set on fire; in no time at all the whole town was ablaze. But when some time later a church was erected to commemorate the event and a suitable inscription was placed at its entrance, this was how it read:

> Anno 1337, the day following Michaelmas Day
> here were the Jews slain:
> they had set the city afire![6]

It need occasion no surprise, then, if the Jews, as Schudt maintains,[7] tried to perfect a magical technique to extinguish fires. His painstaking effort to tear down their repute as magic fire fighters indicates that it was fairly well entrenched, though it could not have been any more welcome than their fame as fire makers. It was a perverse fate that exacted a penalty for both, as Rabbi Naphtali ben Isaac had ample occasion to reflect in his Frankfort prison cell. It was generally believed in that city that he possessed a magic formula against fire, but, as luck would have it, a fire broke out in his own house and destroyed a considerable section of the Jewish quarter. He went to jail for having started a fire with his magic experiments to prevent fires.[8]

Jews were stoned as sorcerers. But it needs little knowledge of human nature to believe that the very vice became a virtue when Christians themselves had need of a little expert magic on the side. If Jews were magicians, their every act a charm, then their magic devices could aid as well as harm. We have already seen how the masses turned to Jews to bless their crops or to pray for rain, despite the displeasure of the clergy. Rabbi Isaac ben Moses of Vienna,[9] in the thirteenth century, reports that once when he was in Regensburg over a holiday, "a Gentile who had much power in the city fell dangerously ill, and ordered a Jew to let him have some of his wine, or he would surely die; and I gave this Jew permission to send him the wine in order to prevent trouble, though there were some who disagreed and forbade this." Apparently Jewish wine possessed occult healing powers; perhaps this Gentile had in mind wine that had been blessed by Jews. It would be interesting to know how effective the cure was, but Rabbi Isaac carries his anecdote no further.

The *mezuzah* (a biblical inscription attached to the doorpost) was also an object of suspicion and, at the same time, of desire. The Jews of the Rhineland had to cover over their mezuzot, for, as a thirteenth-century author complained, "the Christians, out of malice, and to annoy us, stick knives into the mezuzah openings and cut up the parchment." Out of malice, no doubt, but the magical repute of the mezuzah must have lent special force to their vindictiveness. That it was regarded as a magical device by Christians we know, for a fifteenth-century writer admonished his readers to affix a mezuzah to their doors even when they occupied a house owned by a non-Jew, despite the danger that their landlord might accuse them of sorcery. Even Gentiles in high places were not averse to using these magical instruments themselves. Toward the end of the fourteenth century the Archbishop of Salzburg asked a Jew to give him a mezuzah to attach to the gate of his castle, but the rabbinic authority to whom this Jew turned for advice refused to countenance such use of a distinctively religious symbol.[10]

In the field of medicine in particular the reputed Jewish magical skill was called upon to perform miracles. According to the popular view demons and sorcery were often responsible for disease and medicine was therefore the legitimate province of the sorcerer or, to put it the other way around, a supply of charms and amulets was a legitimate part of the physician's pharmacopoeia.

> Through superstition without end
> One seeks today his health to mend;
> Did I it all together fit,
> A heresy book I'd make of it,

wrote Sebastian Brant[11] with excellent reason. Jacques de Vitry tells a characteristic story: when the Pope falls ill, Satan appears *in speciem medici* and offers to cure him, but the Pope rebuffs the devil doctor with the affirmation that he trusts less in drugs than in the prayers of pious widows.[12] The medicine man has only just yesterday evolved into the man of medicine.

The tradition of Jewish medical proficiency was so deeply rooted in the Middle Ages that the *Sachsenspiegel*, one of the great German codes, granted the Jews the privileges of the King's Peace on the ground that "it was Josephus who gained this peace for them from King Vespasian when he cured his son Titus of the gout."[13] This legend was quite widespread and recurs in a number of German lawbooks as the explanation of the favor and protection extended to the Jews by the German rulers, who considered themselves the successors of the Roman emperors and therefore bound by the obligations they had supposedly assumed.

There was a fairly substantial basis for the tradition. Jewish physicians, though by no means altogether free from the general superstitious attitude, were among the foremost representatives of a scientific medicine in medieval Europe. Their wide knowledge of languages, the availability of Arabic-Greek medical texts in Hebrew translation, their propensity for travel and study abroad, their freedom from the Church-fostered belief in miraculous cures, relics, and the like, and perhaps not least the tradition that associated the practice of medicine with the best minds and the highest scholarship often conspired to make them more effective practitioners than their non-Jewish competitors.

Paradoxically, their scientific training, such as it was, made them also superior magicians in the popular view, and every triumph of medical science enhanced the Jew's reputation for sorcery. His putative sorcery probably made a deeper impression than his scientific skill. It is no surprise to learn that his proficiency depended upon his ability to interpret dreams, or that he practiced mainly with the aid of "characters and occult names" and similar charms. When someone at his table pointed to the acknowledged ability of Jewish physicians, Luther put him off with the rejoinder, "The devil can do much"![14]

This accounts for the undoubted popularity of Jewish doctors in Europe throughout this period, despite stringent Church prohibitions constantly reiterated by popes and synods,[15] and the caveat of the clergy that these Jews would turn their magic against their patients. In the effort to keep Christians away from Jewish physicians calumnious tales were widely circulated. Gregory of Tours reported, for instance, that after Leonast, Archdeacon of Bourges, had been miraculously healed, he turned to a Jewish doctor for further treatment and his ailment immediately returned. "He would have remained healed," said Gregory, "had he not, after God's miraculous cure, turned to the Jews."[16] (Note how the plural implicates all Jews as accessories to the act.)

By the fifteenth and sixteenth centuries the campaign against Jewish physicians, spurred by motives of economic competition[17] as well as of superstition and piety, attained a high pitch of virulence. No slander was too mean to be turned to account. Not only were they "black satanic sorcerers, godless, accursed, Christian-hating Jews," but they knew nothing of medicine anyway and often caused the death of their patients through ignorance—or through malice, for their primary aim was to injure Christians. "When they come together at their festivals, each boasts of the number of Christians he has killed with his medicine; and the one who has killed the most is honored," runs Johann Eck's variation upon an inexhaustible theme.[18]

The notorious Jewish sorcerer-physician found a part on the stage too. Hans Sachs serves him up as a burlesque fortuneteller who, when he can't make a go of that, sets up shop as a physician, though he knows nothing of either profession. Unabashed, this charlatan declaims: "I have studied neither black magic nor medicine; I know nothing about healing matters, except to make a vile purgation guaranteed to rack the peasant with bellyache; it helps one, the other dies of it, but that makes no difference to me."[19]

This attitude found more frequent and more violent expression in the north of Europe than in the south, where a greater tolerance and a higher degree of scientific learning prevailed, but it was by no means lacking in the south too. A tale of Franco Sacchetti, the friend of Boccaccio, about two women who are swindled by a Jew who sells them a drug to help them conceive, winds up with the fretful exclamation: "It is remarkable that Christians, men and women, will put more trust in one Jew than in one hundred Christians, yet will repose no trust at all in a single Christian." And after another similar story he complains again: "It is something new, to seek healing in Jewish machinations. It happens quite often nowadays that one trusts a single Jew more than a thousand Christians"![20]

Nonetheless, for all the hysterics of the Jew baiters, which were not without their effect upon the masses, Jewish doctors continued in demand. In 1652 the clergy of Frankfort complained to the City Council about their unabated popularity and remarked: "Sooner sick at God's will than healed through the devil and through forbidden means [i.e., magic]. To employ Jewish doctors means nothing else than to cuddle serpents in our bosom and to raise wolves in our home."[21] When a Jewish physician was granted permission to practice in the city of Hall, in Swabia, in 1657, the clergy epitomized the clerical position as it prevailed throughout the Middle Ages in a succinct public statement: "It is better to die with Christ than to be healed by a Jew doctor with Satan"![22] But who would risk his life in the hands of an inferior Christian physician for the sake of theological scruple when a powerful Jewish doctor-magician could be called in? The popularity of these same "Jew doctors" permits us to surmise that this pious preference was reserved for whole moments; when the issue was joined the ministrations of Satan were not rejected. Or was there something to the story two women told of being bewitched by a Jewish doctor so that they could use no other?[23]

A good share of responsibility for the continued dependence upon Jewish medical skill, despite the popular agitation and the increasing obstacles erected by clerical and secular legislation, must be laid to the example set by the nobility and hierarchy: princes and even ecclesiastics right up to the pope held themselves above the restriction they thus imposed upon the masses. The Hebrew account of the Statutes of Valladolid, adopted in 1412, reads significantly: "It was decreed that there should not be among them [the Jews] . . . a physician, except a physician to the king. . . . "![24] The last phrase, which does not occur in the original decree, points to the frequency with which the nobility disregarded the prohibition. Indeed, Pope Martin V, in a bull issued September 20, 1421, granted to Spanish royalty the express privilege of employing Jewish physicians. Even the brother of Louis IX, Alphonse of Poitiers, the most rabidly anti-Jewish prince of the time, pleaded for the aid of a Jewish physician to save him from blindness.[25] Jews were forbidden to reside in England after 1290; but in 1310 Edward II granted a Jewish physician the right to enter the country, and a century later we find Henry IV summoning two Jewish physicians from Italy, Elia di Sabbato and David di Nigarelli of Lucca, and a third, Sampson of Mirabeau, from France, to treat him, and giving them permission for an extended stay.[26] Indeed, everywhere in Europe physicians were often exempted from the restrictions and disabilities imposed upon the rest of the Jewish populace.

For those who are interested there are lists of Jewish physicians practicing during the Middle Ages.[27] We know of many of them only because their names have been preserved in Christian documents, recording their services to Christian rulers and prelates, their receipt or loss of privileges, or the occasional tragic rewards of their efforts. For if the patient risked his life when he called in a Jewish doctor, the doctor risked his too when he rolled up his sleeves and set to work. If his ministrations were successful he was likely to be considered a magician and could expect to be treated as such, with fear and respect and active animosity. If he failed he was all the more a sorcerer and deserved nothing better than to pay promptly for his crime.

CHAPTER SEVEN

THE POISONERS

"IF a king had a Jewish physician," comments Parkes,[1] "and did not actually perish on the battlefield . . . there is nothing surprising in his unfortunate doctor being accused of poisoning him. This happened to the doctors of Carloman and Hugh Capet, though in the former case the historian who recorded the event is honest enough to add *as it is said* to his account." "As it is said," however, was enough to convict, and the honest historian's reservation is a futile appendix to his account of the doctor's sudden and violent demise. Among the first Jewish physicians we hear of in the West was Zedekiah, Emperor Charles the Bald's court physician, whose repute as a magician undoubtedly far outranked his skill as a doctor. He too was accused of poisoning his emperor in 877, and though the sources do not consider it worth mentioning, he no doubt suffered a similar fate.

Poisoning speedily became a trite charge against Jewish physicians, who were of course powerless to refute it. In 1161, in Bohemia, a mass execution occurred when eighty-six Jews were burned as accomplices in an alleged plot of Jewish physicians to poison the populace. Bernardin of Siena is reported to have said that a Jewish physician of Avignon had confessed to him the murder of thousands of Christians by poisoning.[2] The records are full to overflowing with instances of such accusations, and the prohibition against the use of Jewish doctors was often predicated upon just this suspicion. The *Siete Partidas* provided that a Christian might take medicine prescribed by a Jew only if a Christian physician was acquainted with the contents. In 1610 the medical faculty of Vienna solemnly "confirmed" that Jewish physicians were bound by their laws to kill every tenth Christian patient by means of drugs.[3] So strong was the belief that Jewish doctors were poisoners that it easily outweighed lack of proof. Queen Elizabeth felt constrained to order the execution of her physician, the converted Jew Rodrigo Lopez, on the charge of conspiring to poison her, even though she evidently put no credence in the charge and showed it openly by granting certain property to the unfortunate man's widow and children.[4]

The accusation was, however, by no means restricted to physicians. Jews in general were considered especially adept in this art. In the Rhineland, in 1090, we learn of Jews dealing in various drugs and salves, and since the exotic elements of the medieval pharmacopoeia were imported from the East, we may surmise that during this period such items were part of the regular stock-in-trade of Jewish merchants. From the eleventh to the thirteenth centuries a number of rulers expressly accorded them the privilege of selling drugs and medicines; in the succeeding centuries this policy was reversed and the secular and religious authorities made repeated attempts to halt this trade.[5]

But drugs and poisons were practically synonymous to the medieval mind—and to the equation we may add sorcery as well. "Poisoning was for a long time closely associated with sorcery and magic. Mysterious deaths might be attributed to the one or the other, and both purported to employ occult and sensational forces of nature. The same word was used in the Greek and in the Latin languages for poison and sorcery, for a drug and a philter or magical potion. The fact that men actually were poisoned supported the belief in the possibility of sorcery, and this belief in its turn stimulated excessive credulity in poisons which were thought to act at a distance or after a long lapse of time." A good many prominent Christians, laymen and churchmen, were brought to trial during the Middle Ages as sorcerers and poisoners, and the Jew naturally suffered from the coupling of the two concepts.[6] The association is strikingly illustrated in the case of Elector Joachim's court Jew, Lippold, whose conviction as a poisoner was secured only through a successful prosecution as sorcerer.

In 1550 the Polish king Sigismund Augustus demanded of Ivan

IV (the Terrible) that he admit Lithuanian Jews into Russia for business purposes, by virtue of former commercial treaties between the two countries. Ivan curtly replied, "It is not convenient to allow Jews to come with their goods to Russia, since many evils result from them. For they import poisonous herbs into our realms, and lead astray the Russians from Christianity." Luther wrote, "If they [the Jews] could kill us all, they would gladly do so, aye, and often do it, especially those who profess to be physicians. They know all that is known about medicine in Germany; they can give poison to a man of which he will die in an hour, or in ten or twenty years; they thoroughly understand this art." If there is high praise hidden in these words it was wholly unintended. Luther himself seems to have been particularly in dread of being poisoned by Jews.[7]

Small wonder, then, that the Jew plays the stock role of poisoner in legend and literature; the Elizabethan drama was afflicted with a rash of Jewish poisoners, who appeared in at least nine plays written within a few years at the turn of the seventeenth century.[8] Barabas, the main character of Marlowe's *Jew of Malta* (written about 1592), thus lightly expatiates on his budding career:

> Being young, I studied Physicke and began
> To practice first upon the Italian;
> There I enrich'd the Priests with burials,
> And always kept the Sexton's arms in ure
> With digging graves and ringing dead men's knells;

and in the course of the drama as serenely poisons first a thief, then a whore, and finally his faithful slave Ithamore for whose benefit he had been reminiscing in the quoted lines. John Marston's *Malcontent* (1604) attests the high repute of the Jew—and of his rivals—in this bit of dialogue:

Mendoza: Canst thou impoyson? Canst thou impoyson?
Malevole: Excellently—no Jew, pothecary or polititian better.

The frequently repeated legislation, embodied in secular and ecclesiastical codes, forbidding Christians to purchase meat and other foodstuffs from Jews was often motivated by the suspicion that they might have been poisoned, as the Vienna and Breslau Councils of 1267 and the Statutes of Valladolid (1412) expressly stated (though Christian annoyance over the fact that Jews sold them those parts of the slaughtered animal which they themselves could not eat because of ritual restrictions was probably equally responsible for the prohibition).[9] A popular superstition held that before selling meat to Christians, Jews had their children urinate on it, or otherwise rendered it unfit for consumption; if they did not actually poison it then they at least loaded it down with curses, so that it might bring sickness and death to Christians who ate it.[10] Agobard and Amulo, ninth-century contemporaries, accused the Jews of putting filth into the wine they sold to Christians, a suspicion often reiterated.[11] A fifteenth-century Sicilian ordinance forbade the sale of Jewish-made wine, "because it is not fitting that the Christian should drink the grapes trodden out by the feet of Jews, and also because of other deceptions which might be practiced by the admixture of filthy things." This proscription covered not only wine but also "oils, honey, and similar liquids, or anything pulverized, like ground spices and meal and other such things, and in general anything from which can be made a harmful mixture of an evil nature, which enters through the mouth and in which secret deceptions may be made."[12]

Fear of Jewish contamination of foodstuffs produced rather extreme restrictions. A provision from the fourteenth-century statutes of the city of Bozen (Tyrol) which further implements this suspicion reads: "When the Jews wish to purchase anything in the market place they must point it out; what they touch they must buy at the seller's price."[13] Another provision requires that meat that had been touched or stabbed by a Jew could be sold to a Christian only after he had been warned of that fact, so that he bought it on his own responsibility. Similar ordinances were in force in a number of cities.

Popular belief in the possibility of wholesale poisoning was so strong that the rumors of Jewish plots to murder a large part of Christendom, which began to circulate widely early in the four-teenth century, won immediate acceptance. The charge of well poisoning was not altogether unprecedented; it had already cropped up in three places (1308 in the Vaud; 1316 in the Eulen-burg region; and 1319 in Franconia) prior to the first really serious incident.[14] In 1321 the lepers of France were accused of harboring the same design and suffered widespread persecution, but it shortly appeared that they were little more than agents and that the Jews had been the responsible entrepreneurs behind the scheme. One report has it that a Hebrew letter found in Par-thenay in 1321 and "translated" by a converted Jew was said to reveal a huge plot of the Jews, the lepers, and the Saracens of Spain to destroy the whole Christian population of Europe by poisoning the wells. In Teruel (Aragon) a Christian, arrested and tortured for having thrown poison into the local wells, at first placed the responsibility upon a Breton, but when this evidently did not satisfy his interrogators, who continued the torture, he recalled that it was really the Jews who had put him up to it.

The chronicler of St. Denis recounts that "a great and rich Jew" had hired the lepers to do this and had given them the recipe for the poison, which contained "human blood and urine, three kinds of herbs the names of which he did not know or did not wish to disclose," and also "the body of Jesus Christ." This purports to be the confession of a leper "of great renown." An-other account would have the poison include "adders' heads, toads' legs, and women's hair."

Many lepers were cross-examined and abundant testimony elicited as to the complicity of the Jews. According to this testi-mony the plot had originated with the King of Granada, who sought the aid of the Jews; they declined to carry out his plan themselves but with the help of the devil induced the lepers to betray their Christian faith and to procure consecrated hosts for the manufacture of the poison. Some of the lepers went even fur-ther in their confessions and told of four meetings attended by delegates from the various leproseries, at which, following the counsel of the devil supported by the promise of the Jews to apportion the land among the lepers after they had taken it over, this nefarious scheme was agreed upon.

Evidently little credence was placed in these tales, for an edict issued June 21, 1321, directed the arrest and punishment of the lepers involved, without mentioning Jews. However, the incident could not be left wholly unexploited: it would appear that the Parlement of Paris, the King's highest court, exacted a large fine from the Jews of France in consequence of these reports, and the following year Charles IV, having mulcted them of most of their possessions, expelled them from France for their alleged complicity in the plot.[15] This incident became a popular theme for later poets and chroniclers and thus developed into a recurrent motif in European folklore.

If the accusations of 1321 passed without bloody repercussions, it was perhaps only because the immediate resentment of the masses spent itself upon the doubly unfortunate lepers. Apparently the implication of the Jews in the plot came after these wretches had already been victimized by popular credulity, and the Jews escaped comparatively unscathed.[16] But the Black Death which broke out in 1348—in April it had reached Florence; by August it was devastating France and Germany, and a short while later it attacked England; during this and the next year all of Europe was ravaged, from one-half to two-thirds of the population in many places perishing from the scourge—revived the rumors of well poisoning by Jews. This time these rumors did not fail to evoke a swift reaction. To the horrors of the plague itself were added the wholesale massacre of thousands of Jews and the expulsion of thousands more from their homes.[17]

The impression that Jews were intent on the destruction of Christendom was deeply rooted. The leper incident in France had brought it out into the open and Europe could now entertain itself with speculating on the form the plot would next assume. That it was a real conspiracy few doubted, then or later. A sixteenth-century chronicler, Johannes Aventin, records that in

1337 the Jews had planned to poison the entire Christian population of Germany but their plan had miscarried. Another sixteenth-century tradition has it that the Jews of Provence, in revenge for the edict of the Second Council of St. Ruf, in 1337, forbidding intermarriage and the use of Jewish physicians and apothecaries, had brought the pest from India and caused it to destroy entire villages in that region, whence it spread through Europe. Still another sixteenth-century report has it that in 1348 the Jews held a meeting at Benfeld in Alsace, "as they later confessed," and there hatched a plot to poison all the wells in Germany "from the German Sea to the Italian (*welsch*) mountains." [18] Whether these identical stories were current during the Black Death is immaterial. They testify to the undiminished belief of Europe in the nefarious plans of the Jews, a belief which is amply documented at the time in the widely circulated reports holding Jews responsible for the plague.

Rumors of Jewish well poisoning began to circulate in Southern France, where, as early as May, 1348, the Jews of a Provençal town were burned on this charge. [19] From there the wave of persecutions moved southward over the Pyrenees. Pope Clement VI sought to stem the tide with a renewal, on July 4 of that year, of the old bull forbidding violence against Jews, and again, on September 26, with a bull denying that the Jews were guilty of spreading the disease. But his solicitude hardly made an impression outside Avignon, the seat of the Papacy, where the Jews suffered no harm (there the plague was ascribed to astrological causes, or to the wrath of God, or to natural causes—but not to the Jews). Elsewhere the rumors received ready credence. In the Dauphiné large numbers of Jews were imprisoned, their property seized—and only thereafter was an investigation instituted which evidently exonerated the suspects, for there is no report of any further punishment being meted out to them. In Savoy not a few Christians suffered along with Jews, who supposedly had dragged them into the plot.

The attacks thus spread regardless of the result of investigations, which indeed occasionally turned up the "confession" of a Jew to strengthen the rumor, as was the case at Chillon, on Lake Geneva. A Jewish surgeon there, Balavignus, revealed that several Jews in a town in the south of France—he even named them: Jacob à Paskate of Toledo, Peyret of Chambéry, and one Aboget—had compounded a poison out of Christians' hearts, spiders, frogs, lizards, human flesh, and sacred hosts, and had distributed the resultant powder to be deposited in wells and streams which supplied Christians with water. This tale, in one form or other, spread on the heels of the plague and was eagerly seized upon by the terror-stricken populace as an adequate explanation of its origin. By November the plague and its accompanying myth had penetrated German territory. The mayors and councils of a number of German and Swiss towns exchanged official reports containing alleged confessions exacted under torture. At Breisach in Breisgau it was "discovered" that all the Jews of Strasbourg, Basel, Freiburg, and Breisach were in league and had jointly hired agents to deposit the poison, which the Jews of Basel supplied, in the wells. According to a later report the zeal of the Basel Jews drove them also to poison the wine, butter, and other foodstuffs of the local populace.[20] On the island of Gotland the most arrant "poisoners" uncovered and convicted were two clerics, one of whom, before his execution, warned that priests and monks were the worst enemies of Christianity and that the Church was lost unless God intervened directly to save it. Yet a convicted criminal there declared that the Jews, swearing a fearful oath to destroy all Christendom, had hired him to distribute the poison from Dassel in Westphalia to Lübeck and still farther in Prussia and Livonia, as well as in Stockholm and elsewhere in Sweden. (Jews were then very sparsely settled along the Baltic coast, and were altogether unknown in Scandinavia.) The idea was not difficult to comprehend; confessions piled up, from Jews under pressure, and from criminals eager to divert attention from their own misdeeds. In some places the plague was attributed to the incantations as well as to the poisons of the Jews.

These reports, in fact, quickly outdistanced the plague and led Christians to make provision for such Jewish acts even before they occurred. In the spring of 1349, when rumors of the Black Death, but not yet the plague itself, had reached Perleberg, in Brandenburg, the city fathers included in a generally favorable privilege granted the Jews of the city this provision: "Should it become evident and proved by reliable men, however, that the aforementioned Jews have caused or will cause in the future the death of Christians, they shall suffer the penalties prescribed by law, as it is said that the Jews have elsewhere dispatched many persons through poisoning." [21] Actually this was a notice to the Jews that when and if the plague invaded the city they would have to shoulder the blame for it. Indeed, instead of trying to prevent the outbreaks the German Emperor, Charles IV, gave practical immunity to the rioters *in advance*, by making arrangements for the disposal of Jewish property in the event of a riot. This occurred at Nuremberg, Regensburg, Augsburg, and Frankfort and probably elsewhere too.

There was no limit, after this, to the crimes saddled upon the Jews. Concurrently with the Black Death another "epidemic" broke out—of fanatical asceticism, expressed in the cult of the Flagellants, who hoped to assuage God's wrath and stay the pest by penitential and ascetic practice (thus unconsciously rejecting the well poisoning theory of its origin). It won many recruits, particularly in Germany, and undoubtedly helped whip up mob passions against the Jews, for in not a few towns anti-Jewish riots followed upon the visit of members of the order. This spontaneous mass movement, however, shortly displayed anti-clerical potentialities and aroused the displeasure of the clergy, so that on October 20, 1349, the Pope intervened and strongly denounced it, prohibiting Christians from participating in it. Within a month the attacks upon Jewish communities abated, in large measure as a result of its suppression. But the chronicler Jean d'Outremeuse ascribes responsibility for the rise of the Flagellants *to the Jews!* Their poisoning of the wells and water sources had infected Christendom with this madness. [22]

The practice of laying every calamity at the door of the Jews reached such proportions in these years that the representatives of the Jewish communities of Aragon, meeting in Barcelona in December, 1354, felt constrained to petition the Pope, with the support of the King, to forbid by decree the accusation that the Jews had caused whatever plague or famine or other misfortune befell the people, and the consequent bloody attacks upon them. As though the pope's decree could abate the now feverish animosity against them. In such an atmosphere the rare note of skepticism voiced by the contemporary Cyriacus Spangenberg in the *Mannsfeldischen Chronik* certainly went unheard. "In the year 1349," he wrote, "God visited His punishment upon the unbelieving obstinate Jews. Whether they poisoned the wells everywhere, however, I do not know, except that it is incredible that the pestilence should in this manner have spread through Europe, for poison causes not pestilence but certain death." Yet he did not question the justice of the divinely ordained attacks upon the Jews. It was the irrational justification that offended him.[23]

(It may be mentioned, parenthetically, that an incidental by-product of the calumnies heaped upon the Jews during the Black Death was Shakespeare's Shylock. The usurer who demands his pound of flesh in payment of a debt was a quite familiar figure in early medieval tales on the continent, where he had been imported from Oriental sources. In these early versions he is a Christian or a heathen; in several instances a Jew is the unfortunate victim of a bloodthirsty Christian creditor. He appears as a Jew for the first time in Giovanni Fiorentino's collection of tales, *Pecorone*, in 1378. This transformation, it is generally agreed, probably occurred under the influence of the hysterical abuse which was the Jew's daily portion since the calamitous events of a quarter of a century earlier. Thereafter he remained a Jew in the succeeding accounts—and thus Shakespeare found and immortalized him.[24])

The habit of blaming Jews for such calamities, once formed, continued to assert itself. As Schudt[25] found himself remarking with unwonted sympathy: "It had become almost the fashion to ascribe all pestilences to the poor Jews, for when in 1357 a plague again struck Franconia, it was laid to the Jews, whose poisons had caused it." "The fashion" wore a long time. In 1382 the Jews of Halle suffered an attack on suspicion of having poisoned the wells and thus starting an epidemic; the charge was repeated in 1397 in the towns of Rappoltsweiler, Dürkheim, and Colmar.[26] In 1401 the Jews of Freiburg in Breisgau were charged with "planning to exterminate Christendom by poisoning the air"[27]—without doubt the earliest reference to the use of poison gas. These rumors were still in sufficient currency to lead Pope Martin V to issue a bull (February 20, 1422) forbidding the dissemination of the well poisoning accusation as unjustified ("all clerical and lay preachers of whatever rank, degree, order, religion or circumstance," were instructed to cease preaching such fables[28]); yet it was one of the reasons advanced for expelling the Jews from Cologne only two years later.[29] This was a hardy myth indeed: it cropped up in 1448 and 1453 in Schweidnitz[30] and in 1472 in the city of Regensburg[31]; in 1475, during a brief outbreak of endemic disease, the Jews of Germany were again accused of seeking to poison all the wells in the land[32]; early in the 1500's Johann Pfefferkorn laid the same intent to his former coreligionists in Halle[33]; in 1541 it made an appearance in Brieg[34]; and in 1543 in Schweidnitz again.[35] And this list can hardly be said to be complete.

In 1580 there was an epidemic in Aix, the ancient capital of Provence. Thomas Flud, an English physician who was then living in Avignon, is said to have diagnosed its cause as: "poison which the Jews rubbed on the knockers of doors."[36] The method allegedly used to obtain this poison is so curious that I cannot resist describing it (for whatever use it may still have): the Jews enticed a redheaded Englishman, so Flud says, into one of their homes, tied him to a cross during the heat of the dog days, inserted a piece of wood in his mouth to keep it open, and had some adders sting him in the back. The poor man soon died, and the Jews collected the slaver dripping from his mouth, out of which they manufactured the disease-bringing unguent. Other Jews used a redheaded woman (the color of the hair was evidently crucial) for this purpose, burying her alive up to her breasts, which they had adders sting until she drooled. This was the product of the good doctor's private research in epidemiology.

The pestilence of 1679 in Vienna, which first appeared in the Jewish quarter of Leopoldstadt, was likewise ascribed to the Jews by Abraham a Santa Clara, at first somewhat hesitantly: the pestilence broke out because of the bad living conditions in the ghetto, he surmised. But this explanation seemed too simple, and he later made the direct charge that they had maliciously started it, for "it is well known that such pestilential epidemics are caused by evil spirits, by Jews, by gravediggers, and by witches." [37]

It is worth recording too, that, in the opinion of Johann Jakob Schudt and other worthies, the "French disease" was unknown in Africa until the Jews brought it with them after their expulsion from Spain and transmitted it to the natives. [38]

CHAPTER EIGHT

HOST AND IMAGE DESECRATION

IT must be evident from the foregoing that the suspicion of sorcery was born of Christian distrust of the Jew; and that distrust was sired by the conviction that no other course was open to the allies of Christendom's archenemy, the devil, than to seek the destruction of Christian civilization by every foul stratagem. So it was that the Jewish people, and not individual Jews, came to be branded "sorcerer," and that the greatest number of accusations and attacks, by far, were occasioned by alleged activities of a specifically anti-Christian character, rather than by the more individualistic black magic sorcerers have practiced from time immemorial.

One of the commonest charges against the Jews, and the one that must seem to us most unreasonable, had to do with the desecration of the host. During the early Christian centuries the Church had been deeply agitated by the controversial issue of transubstantiation. But the popular mind, disregarding subtleties, had driven straight to the main point, accepting that belief in its furthest literalness. The role which the host, the body of Christ, played in popular superstition and magic throughout the Middle Ages was already evident as early as the fourth century;[1] what more natural than that the Jews, magicians and enemies of Christ, should be charged with utilizing the wafer of the Eucharist in their own diabolic schemes? The doctrine of transubstantiation was ecclesiastically established at the Fourth Lateran Council in 1215, and the consecrated host was thereafter publicly worshiped. This action seems to have precipitated the birth of the legend of Jewish profanation of the host, which soon made its appearance and persisted obstinately until the Reformation broke the hold of Catholic doctrine upon large masses of the European peoples.

Orthodox theology insisted that Christ was bodily present in the wafer, and the masses believed as directed, though not without some naïve and fairly obvious qualms. Berthold of Regensburg, the great popular preacher of the thirteenth century, found it necessary, for instance, to explain why Christ, though present in the wafer, does not let himself be seen in it: "Who would like to bite off the little head, or the little hands, or the little feet of a little child?" [2] he parried, and his simple auditors were apparently content.

The absurdity of attributing to Jews an acceptance and utilization of this most un-Jewish of dogmas never occurred to their accusers. Transubstantiation had been proclaimed a true belief by the Church, therefore it must be true and *must be believed* by all men; how they responded to that belief was something else. In 1205 Innocent III, who was to sponsor the transubstantiation dogma before the Fourth Lateran Council, in a letter to the Archbishop of Sens and the Bishop of Paris asserted that "whenever it happens that on the day of the Lord's Resurrection [Easter] the Christian women who are nurses for the children of Jews, take in the body and blood of Christ, the Jews make these women pour their milk into the latrines for three days before they again give suck to the children." Wherefore Christian women should not enter service in Jewish homes. Prior to this statement, the effort to prevent Christians from serving Jews in the home had been based upon the impropriety of accepting inferior positions relative to Jews, or upon the danger of succumbing to Jewish influence in such an intimate relationship. The statement of Innocent was a characteristic move in the introduction of superstitious barriers between the two groups which became so pronounced during the century.

This notion prevailed for several hundred years and received repeated official support; as late as 1581 Gregory XIII, in his bull *Antiqua Judaeorum*, sanctioned it anew as sufficient reason for forbidding the employment of Christian nurses by Jews. In this instance the Jews were evidently held to be "more Catholic than the Pope," for, as a glossator explained, it must be their belief that "the body of Christ, descending into the stomach, is incorporated in the milk" and thus passed on to their children, which he thereupon proceeded to prove impossible by "several learned arguments." [3]

But the supposed Jewish recognition of the truth of this dogma was believed to involve them in far more reprehensible excesses. The record is replete with accounts of host mutilation by Jews, the alleged motive behind these acts being apparently to vent their anti-Christian spleen once more upon the body of the Christ. Such tales were current even before the rise of the myth of profanation of the host. A tenth-century story told of a Jew who, wishing to insult Christ, went to mass, communicated, and received the wafer on his tongue. But just as he was about to transfer it to his pocket he was seized with fearful pains and was unable to shut his mouth. This Jew and many others were converted as a sequel to this incident, the tale concludes.[4] The purpose of these early tales was simply to illustrate the power of the host in miraculously effecting the conversion of Jews. During the thirteenth century the nature and intent of the fable underwent a marked change.

The typical later version does not let the wafer or the Jews off quite so easily. The plot may be outlined in this wise: a Jew bribes a Christian to secure a wafer of the host; the Jew then mutilates the host in whatever manner most strikes the fancy of the narrator (he beats it, or stamps upon it, or pierces it with a knife or nails, or cuts it up, or burns it, or grinds it in a mortar), whereupon blood flows from the wafer, some miraculous event occurs (the Jew is struck dumb, or is paralyzed, or the wafer flies out of his grasp, or a celestial voice publicly proclaims his guilt); here the fable ends and stark realism begins— the Jew is apprehended and executed, along with all the other Jews the mob can lay hands on. This theme also became one of the most popular subjects of medieval literature, recurring time and again in every literary form, so that it entered deeply into the consciousness of the masses and of necessity strongly affected their attitude toward the Jew.[5]

*Christian girls desecrate the host at the devil's
instigation*
(Nuremberg, 1567)

*Representation of alleged host desecration by
Jews at Sternberg, 1492*
(contemporary wood-cut)

Preachers and writers loved to expatiate upon the ingenious
tortures to which the Eucharist was subjected—but even more
upon the astounding miracles with which it reacted, for these
were equally essential to the myth. An especially beloved detail
was the physical apparition of the Christ child in the wafer—so
that the alleged mutilation was represented as being practiced
directly upon the Christ. This too was the import of the unfailing
blood miracle. This manifestation was also said to have occurred
once in reverse: in 1338 some Jews were apprehended in Bohemia
reputedly misusing a host and a large number of their coreligionists were promptly put to death for the crime; "and it is extraordinary," the chronicler remarks, as indeed it was, "that from
their wounded, or rather mutilated bodies, no blood flowed." [6]

Another notable feature of many of the accusations is that, like
other such charges, they implicated not individual Jews but
rather the community as a whole. Even when the crime was
directly laid upon individuals, the entire group customarily suffered the consequence. But not unusually the criminals were represented as acting for the group, distributing pieces of a host far
and wide, or inviting the leading Jews of the country to assemble
and participate in the act of desecration. In a good many instances
the proceedings are said to have taken place *in a synagogue,* as
though they were a part of Jewish ritual; in at least two instances
the host desecration supposedly occurred at wedding feasts, ostensibly the culminating ceremonial of the festivities. [7]

Unlikely as it may seem, in view of the all-too-evident hazards
involved, stories of physical attack upon processions bearing the
host in public multiplied, and steps were taken officially to protect the host and its bearers. Already in 1267 the Council of
Vienna decreed that Jews must withdraw to their homes the
instant they heard the bell announcing that a host was being carried through the streets, and must lock their doors and windows. [8]
The "murderers of Christ" must not come near "the body of the
Lord"—a most suggestive ordinance. This prescription was frequently repeated and strictly enforced, perhaps in the end as
much to protect the Jews as the host, for the mob hardly required

the pretext of an actual attack to punish the Jews for their presumptive intent.

The first accusation of host desecration occurred in 1243, at Belitz, near Berlin, when all the Jews of the city were burned on the spot subsequently called the *Judenberg*. It did not become common until the end of the century when a flood of such accusations burst over the Jews and continued in uninterrupted force during the ensuing centuries, resulting in more or less extensive persecution. The last serious case occurred in Berlin in 1510; twenty-six Jews were then burned and two beheaded. The date of the last reported burning of a Jew for stealing a host is 1631. But a charge of host desecration was reported as late as 1836 from Rumania.[9]

Though the primary purpose of this alleged campaign of host mutilation, as Christians saw it, was to reënact the crucifixion—piercing the wafer with knives and nails was the commonest form of torture reported—this was not the sole motive they discerned.

For all their confidence in the objective truth of the dogma of transubstantiation, they could not fail to anticipate a degree of devil-inspired Jewish skepticism—expressed, for example, in the legend of the simple donkey graced with the wisdom to recognize and kneel before the host, while the unbelieving Jewish onlookers persist in their stubborn blindness—and attempt to mock their faith. In one of the early accusations, leveled in Paris, 1290, the Jew who allegedly misused the host was said to have done so to show his coreligionists "how silly the Christians are, who believe in such a thing"—an explanation which, it must be said, makes this the least improbable of all the accusations. From Prague, in 1389, comes the story of an attack upon a monk carrying the host, in which the Jews are alleged to have heaped insult upon injury: to the monk's remonstrances they are said to have mocked him, "You have your Lord God in your hands, let Him protect you." Some 3,000 Jews were exterminated in reprisal for this folly. In 1453 Jews of Breslau are reported to have confessed under torture that they stole the host, as the account naïvely has it, "to see whether God is really present in it."[10]

However, still another motive must have been present in the mind of the accusers. As the masses became acquainted with the doctrine of transubstantiation and tales of the miraculous properties of the Eucharist grew more numerous and marvelous, the host acquired unique importance in the practice of magic; prior to the thirteenth century such use, while not unknown, was quite rare. The wafer rapidly became a favorite ingredient in all sorts of medicinal and magical potions, notably in love philters, and in poisons; in 1303 the Synod of Gubbio in Central Italy ordered the Eucharist and holy oil to be locked up, "so that they cannot be stolen to be used in making poisons." The host was believed to induce greater productivity in field and flock, to counteract the works of Satan, cure disease, even stave off death—Pope Alexander VI is said to have worn a consecrated host in a gold box on his neck, in the expectation that it would protect him against harm and death. It played an especially significant part in the ritual of the witch-cults.[11]

The Jews, as master magicians, could not but have been suspected of desiring to utilize the wafer in their own infamous sorceries. True, there is no direct charge to this effect but it is implicit in the background of the entire host-desecration complex. "It may well be," remarks Schudt,[12] after describing several unorthodox uses to which the host was put by Christians, "that the Jews at times intended to misuse such hosts for their base magic," a suspicion which must have occurred to many more than himself and which occasionally did find a measure of expression. We have already noted the alleged Jewish inclusion of "the body of Jesus Christ" in a poison calculated to spread death over a continent. From Mainz comes another significant piece of evidence. Some time between 1384 and 1387, while Peter of Luxembourg occupied the bishopric, the servants of a rich widow reported that they had heard the sound of a child's crying coming from a box and upon opening the box had discovered there a toad, and a host bleeding profusely from the toad's bites. He immediately ordered an investigation, which produced this story: the widow owned a large stock of grain, and to make sure of getting a good price for it she went to a Jew for help. The Jew instructed her to get him a host, which she did on the pretext that she was ill and required the last sacrament. He it was who placed the host and toad in the box, with the promise that this would bring her the profit she desired. The pattern of this scheme was quite familiar; both culprits were burned at the stake. The significant feature of the story is the toad, which, as everyone knew, represented the devil. To offer a host to the devil was to practice the blackest sort of black magic—of a peculiarly Christian variety too, it may be added.[13]

Moreover, the similarity that we have remarked between the Jew badge and the distinctive sign of the convicted sorcerer was pressed even more sharply by a regulation affecting Christians who had been found guilty of using the Eucharist in magic. They were condemned to wear yellow felt patches in the shape of a host on their garments, "neither more nor less than the primitive Jew badge." [14] A more telling identification of sorcerer and host-desecrating Jew could hardly have been invented. Indeed, Ulysse Robert makes the suggestive observation that the circular Jew badge may have been intended "to represent the host, emblem of the Christian religion which they denied, and which they were condemned to wear on their garments, since they would not accept it in their hearts." The institution of a distinctive Jewish garb was effected by the same Fourth Lateran Council that adopted the dogma of transubstantiation, and the charge of host desecration by sorcerers and Jews developed concurrently with the Jew badge. Whether the two were directly related it is impossible to say with certainty, but we may surmise that in the public mind such an association could easily have been contrived.

Still another feature of the myth would have contributed to such an association. For the therapeutic function of magic also played a part in it. The blood that was believed to spurt from the mutilated wafer was considered of especial utility to the Jews: to counteract the *foetor judaicus* and to cure the secret ailments from which they supposedly suffered. There is something anti-climactic in the final charge made against the Jews in this connection: they used this blood, so it was rumored, as a superior sort of rouge, to redden the pallid cheeks of their young ladies.[15]

Most of these accusations undoubtedly had no material basis and were pure inventions, as the fixed pattern and the miracles indicate; Father Peter Browe, a Jesuit scholar who has specialized in the history of the Eucharist, after examining carefully the extant material, has concluded that the host-desecration charges are uniformly without basis, and that *if* individual Jews were sometimes guilty, *the Jews* never were.[16] Besides, it is known and was known at the time, too, that in a good many instances wafers were deliberately "planted" on or near Jewish premises in order to incite the people. A notorious case of this sort occurred in 1338: a number of Jewish communities in Lower Austria, Steiermark, and Moravia were exterminated when the report spread that a bleeding host had been found in the home of a Jew at Pulkau. Pope Benedict XII, in a frankly skeptical letter, ordered Duke Albert of Austria to investigate—first the attacks, then the investigation. The Duke's report disclosed that a blood-spattered wafer had been criminally placed in some straw outside the Jew's house by a Christian.[17]

It must be said, however, that in some instances there may have been more to the myth than would at first appear. The essential feature of all these stories is the presence of blood on the wafer. It has been shown that a bacterium (dubbed the *Micrococcus Prodigiosus*, by Professor Ferdinand Cohn in 1872, "the microbe of miracles," and known also as the "microbe of bleeding hosts") which grows quite easily on wafers left for a while in dark places generally produces a blood-red coloring matter. It is not unlikely that the actual appearance of red spots on sacred hosts which had become damp and had been exposed to atmospheric dust in which these microbes abound gave rise to the charge that these were blood spots and that the Jews were responsible for the phenomenon. Corpus Christi Day was instituted by Pope Urban IV to commemorate just such a "miracle" when a doubting priest at Bolsena in 1264 reported that "drops of blood" fell from the bread of communion, thus proving the real presence of Christ in the wafer.[18]

Just as Christ resided physically in the host, so he was present in the crucifixes and other representations of him that adorned Christian homes and churches, and so were the other holy personages of Christianity believed to be literally and physically present in their images and paintings. This was not officially sanctioned doctrine, it is true, but it was nonetheless part and parcel of the average Christian's belief. Nothing illustrates this so vividly as the countless legends of Jewish maltreatment of such images and pictures, which parallel the myth of host desecration. These legends, of course, presuppose Jewish acquiescence in the crassest of Christian superstitions, for the ostensible purpose of the Jewish attacks was, as in the case of the host, to insult not alone Christianity but its representative figures. And not to insult them merely but actually to injure them, for the images suffered and bled and retaliated miraculously against their persecutors.[19]

These accusations covered a wide range of offenses: the Jews threw stones and refuse at the images, spat on them, made lewd gestures and insulting remarks, pierced and slashed and shattered them. An early legend relates that the ritual of conversion to Judaism includes the act of stabbing a crucifix.[20] Sometimes in the miracle plays the Jews were represented as re-crucifying the figure of Jesus torn from a crucifix.[21] Tovey repeats the story that in 1268, during a University procession in Oxford on Ascension Day, "a certain Jew of the most consummate impudence" (not to say foolhardiness) violently snatched the cross from the bearer "and trod it under his feet in token of his contempt of Christ." As with the host, if we are to believe the accounts of these incidents, Jews frequently manifested such daring. As late as 1577 a Czech writer charged a Jew with tearing down a crucifix in a church and letting his horse trample on it—in full view of the assembled congregation![22]

Matthew Paris tells a horrendous tale (here recounted in Tovey's inimitable translation) of "a certain rich Jew, having his abode and house at Berkhamstede and Wallingford. . . . This Jew, that he might accumulate more disgrace to Christ, caus'd the image of the Virgin Mary, decently carv'd and painted, as the manner is, to be plac'd in his house of office (*in latrina sua*); and which is a great shame and ignominy to express, blaspheming the image itself, *as if it had been the very Virgin her self* [these are the significant italics of Tovey, who, of course, knew better], threw his most filthy and not to be nam'd excrements upon her, days and nights. . . . Which when his wife saw . . . *wip'd off the filth from the face of the image* [again Tovey's italics] most filthily defil'd. Which when the Jew her husband had fully found out, he therefore privily and impiously strangled the woman her self, though his wife." [23] This story, it must be said, is credible by comparison with the host of similar tales that were current, for it lacks the miraculous and tendentious elements that characterize most of them. Yet, had the tale been true, it is extremely unlikely that Abraham of Berkhamsted, the accused, could have gotten off, as he did, with nothing more than minor damage to his purse.

The medieval chronicles, which were thickly sprinkled with these accounts, were, it must be remembered, *Tendenzschriften*. Written by churchmen, they were intended, as Gregory of Tours expressly admitted, *ad corroborandam fidem Catholicam*, as propaganda for the Christian faith, and therefore they played up prominently the miraculous events that might strengthen the Christian in his faith. They are "narratives in which legend is rationalized and passes for authentic history, in which history is made the pendant of legend, or vice versa. One never knows where the one ends and the other begins." The legends of image mutilation by Jews, and their subsequent miraculous conversion to Christianity were grist for the chronicler's mill, and he did not fail to embroider them artistically into his tapestry version of his times. From the chronicles these tales graduated into the realm of folklore, literature, and drama, so that none could remain ignorant of them.[24] One day a peasant entered a church and found there a picture of Christ, slashed and bleeding. Deeply moved he sank to his knees and uttered a fervent, naïve prayer: "Oh, dear Lord God," he beseeched, "let this be a lesson to you and come not again under the vile, wicked Jews." [25] The author was poking fun at the naïveté of peasants. Yet one could not wish a more vivid demonstration of the impression made by these tales upon simple, pious folk.

Nearly all the medieval chroniclers in the West traced the origin of the Iconoclastic controversy in the time of the Isaurian emperors to the deep-rooted hatred of the Jews for the founders of Christianity and for the Virgin Mary in particular. The Jews were held responsible for the attacks upon images during this episode, and the Iconodules, who defended the use of images, created a series of stories recounting how the Jews were converted by the power of the very images they despised and sought to destroy. "The general line of these stories is usually the same. To insult Christianity a Jew who has by some means or other become possessed of a Christian image or precious object decides to profane it. The object proves its sanctity and power, and the Jew is usually converted." [26]

This type of story remained popular long after the echoes of the Iconoclastic revolt had died away; during the later Middle Ages, indeed, it experienced a notable revival, being endlessly refashioned in its own image, for it flattered the medieval taste. The Reformation sounded its death knell, though it did not perish immediately; with Luther's posting of his ninety-five theses on the church door at Wittenberg the Protestant schismatics took over the role of iconoclasts par excellence and the Catholic Church retired the Jews to the post of understudy.

That these tales, however, represented something more than simple propaganda is indicated, for one thing, by the frequency with which the blood motif appears—the mutilated image usually drips blood. I know of no express allegation that this blood was utilized by Jews, but the parallel runs too close to the salient feature of the host-desecration stories and the ritual murder myth to be wholly without significance. Moreover, a secondary intent behind these stories may well have been to portray the Jewish determination to injure Christendom as well as its foremost figures. We have a story of the near destruction of Rome in 1020 by whirlwind and earthquake as a result of Jewish mockery of a crucifix. Even if we understand this to have been a token of

Christ's wrath, it was nonetheless an effective technique to arouse that wrath and force the Christian world to suffer its consequences. A sixteenth-century writer explains the perplexing failure of Mary to perform miracles in certain places by the presence of Jews there and by their "dreadful abuse" of the Virgin, which curtails her miraculous visitations.[27]

There is considerable evidence, too, that the crucifix was employed in magic and witchcraft by Christians—why not also by Jews? Johann Eck, in his *Ains Judenbüchlin* (1541), after repeating a number of legends about Jewish misuse of holy images, with the resultant miraculous flow of blood, scolds those Christians who despoil wayside crucifixes to use pieces as amulets or for magic, "so that wayside crucifixes are seldom whole." That Eck completely forgot to inquire why these images failed to bleed is no doubt beside the point.[28]

Such direct attack upon the body of Jesus and the saints, however, was apparently too simple and gross a procedure to satisfy the crafty Jews, and, if we are to believe the reports, they had recourse to a more recondite method of wreaking their venom upon the Christians and their Lord. Annually, we are informed, they would fashion from wax an image of the founder of Christianity, and (in the synagogue, some accounts insist) by their magic art transmit through this image to its model and his followers the pangs and tortures they visited upon it. This, too, became a popular theme of medieval literature.[29] One of the earliest poems in the Spanish language, by Gonzalo de Berceo (about 1250), celebrated a miraculous apparition of the Virgin to the Archbishop of Toledo, interrupting the mass with the plaint that the Jews were again crucifying "my son." "The people stirred, with all the clergy, and rushed in haste to the Jewry, Jesus Christ and the Virgin Mary guiding them. Then was their sacrilege discovered! They found in a house of the Chief Rabbi a great figure of wax fashioned like a man—like the Lord Christ was it—set there crucified, fastened with great nails, with a great wound in its side." [30] A number of the first poems to appear in the vernacular were devoted to a similar theme. It is not surprising, then, that the *Siete Partidas* (1263) took formal cognizance of this popular accusation and forbade the Jews to make waxen images of the crucifixion.[31]

What we have here is a version of the famous image magic known and used universally. By sticking pins into, or burning, or otherwise mutilating an image of an enemy it is believed that he will be caused to experience in his own body the effects of such action. Christians did not hesitate to impute to their Jewish neighbors frequent resort to this technique, with which they were themselves quite familiar,[32] with respect not only to the body of Christ but to those of their Christian contemporaries as well. One of the oldest accusations of this sort, preserved in a Hebrew document which has been tentatively dated from the eleventh century or thereabouts, recounts this tale. An apostate from Blois, seeking to take revenge on his former coreligionists, who had presumably persecuted him, conceived a stratagem. One day at Limoges he had a wax image made, which he secretly hid in the cupboard of the synagogue; then he accused the Jews before the Lord of the province of having made a wax figure of him and of piercing it three times annually, at the three Jewish holiday seasons, in order to bring about his death. "Thus did their ancestors to your God, and have they not often done thus to the image of your Lord?" he argued. An investigation ensued, the figure was discovered, and the Jews faced sudden disaster. But in the nick of time (this is a Jewish story, we must remember) the artist who had made the image appeared and disclosed that the apostate himself had ordered it. And so all ended well, except that, as the chronicler sadly comments, the resultant popular agitation against the Jews took a long time to subside.[33]

A famous story tells that when Archbishop Eberhard of Treves in 1066 decreed the expulsion of the Jews unless they accepted baptism, they made a wax figure of him and bribed a monk to baptize it in his name. (According to one account they called in a Rabbi Moses of Worms, "the most renowned magician and necromancer of the time," to make the image.) While the Bishop, on the appointed day, was busy making preparations for the anticipated mass baptism, they set fire to the figure; so soon as it was half burned through the Bishop fell sorely ill and expired that very day while still in the church.[34] The difficulty with this story, if one were otherwise inclined to accept its veracity, is that the operation was supposed to have been performed on a Saturday—the Saturday before Easter, when Eberhard actually died. Its Christian authors bungled one detail: they failed to take into account that Jews would not have kindled and used fire on the Sabbath.

In at least one instance, however, Jews were definitely implicated in a murder plot of this sort, though in an altogether secondary role. The prime movers here were high Church dignitaries. In 1317 Hugues Géraud, bishop of Cahors, with some other clerical conspirators, planned to do away with Pope John XXII; Aymeric de Belvèze, the bishop's treasurer, hired a Jew, Bonmacip, to procure the poison and the wax figurines necessary to carry out the plot. The rite was tested first on Jacques de Via, the Pope's favorite nephew, who did, in fact, die on June 13. Encouraged by this initial success, Aymeric repaired hastily to Toulouse, where he bought some poison from an apothecary and three wax statuettes from the Jew Bernard Jourdain. These statuettes, properly baptized, and the poison (an interesting example of the connection of magic with poisoning) were wrapped in parchment strips on which were inscribed charms directed against the pope and two leading members of the curia, and the whole was baked in loaves of bread and dispatched to Avignon, where the pope was in residence. The plot, however, miscarried; its authors were arrested, tried, and executed that same year.[35]

That churchly sorcerers should have turned to Jews for their material is no doubt a tribute to the Jew's reputation, yet also an ironic commentary on it, for it was the accusers who were actually practicing magic while the defendant was guilty only of catering to an evidently extensive—and Christian—clientele. There must have been good cause for including in the French language a single word, *envoûter*, meaning "to cast one under a spell by transfixing one's image in wax."

CHAPTER NINE

RITUAL MURDER

OF all the bizarre charges against the Jewish people the one that has enjoyed the hardiest tenacity and the utmost notoriety, and has produced the direst consequences, is the so-called ritual-murder accusation. In its popular version it foists upon Jewish ritual the need for Christian blood at the Passover service. The subject of much study and infinitely more polemics,[1] its absurdity has been conclusively established, but the true nature of the accusation has never been made sufficiently clear. The legend as we know it has experienced several redactions. In its early form it was the product of ancient superstition —and of the medieval characterization of the Jew as sorcerer— and stressed primarily, as we shall see, the Jews' need of Christian blood for other than ritual purposes.

It is perhaps difficult for us today to appreciate how deep an impression this blood accusation made upon the medieval imagination. Crowning the diabolic conception of the Jew, it rendered him a figure of such sinister horror even in that blood-stained, terror-haunted period that it is little wonder the common folk came to despise and to fear and to hate him with a deep, fanatical intensity.

The clergy, who were the artificers of public opinion in the Middle Ages, lost few opportunities to play up in the most lurid colors the murderous crimes of this nature attributed to the Jewish people as a group, despite generous efforts by the Papacy to counteract such charges. In fact, nearly all the accusations arose from the clergy, who profited directly from them (not necessarily personally, of course); the martyred "saint" and his shrine brought pilgrims and offerings. It is highly revealing, for instance, that when the alleged murder of William of Norwich in 1144 first aroused interest, the Prior of Lewes, who happened then to be staying in Norwich, tried to get the body for Lewes Priory, even before any proof was forthcoming as to the manner of the boy's death, for he realized that it might become an object "of conspicuous veneration and worship." [2] And of course the chroniclers and other writers and artists of the Middle Ages did their best to render these tales a conspicuous part of medieval folklore. *Kindermörderische Juden* is a common appellation in the medieval German texts; English literature regularly described the Jew as "bloudie." [3] There are even a number of pathetic instances during the fourteenth to sixteenth centuries of impecunious Christian parents offering their children at a price to Jews to be killed, and as late as 1699 a poor woman offered to sell her baby for this purpose to Meyer Goldschmidt, court jeweler to the King of Denmark. [4] One can understand why, in certain parts of Europe down to modern times, parents have frightened their children into obeying them by threatening that the Jewish bogyman will snatch them away. [5]

It is not necessary here to list the accusations of this sort leveled at the Jews during the Middle Ages; suffice it to say that they were always in danger of answering for the death or disappearance of a child and that the danger materialized frequently in large-scale massacres and expulsions. More than 150 charges of ritual murder are listed in the standard works of reference; yet these do not constitute, in all probability, more than a fraction of the whole. [6]

More than one pope felt called upon to deny the truth of this charge, and even the secular authorities, who had no great love for the Jews, were occasionally impelled to extend them their protection in the interest of public order, and perhaps at times of justice too. Many of these cases were deliberately fabricated by their enemies, who would plant the evidence, in the shape of a corpse or a jug of blood, upon Jewish premises, and then raise the alarm. (This plot became a favorite theme of Jewish legend, which naturally had for its happy ending the exposure and punishment of the criminal.) This little game must have assumed

serious proportions to elicit the provision found in several char-
ters—that granted by Bishop Hartmann of Augsburg in 1271, the
charter of 1361 permitting the Jews to return to France after the
expulsion of 1322, the charter issued by Philip the Good of Burgundy in 1374—which specifically exempted Jews from the consequences of dead children being hidden in their homes or gar-
dens.[7]

Probably the oldest report of a ritual-murder charge is from the
pen of a pre-Christian writer, Democritus, who alleged that every
seven years the Jews captured a stranger, brought him to the temple in Jerusalem, and sacrificed him, cutting his flesh into bits.
Apion, who recast this story, reduced the interval between sacrifices to one year, and dramatized his version by introducing an
actual Greek victim to Antiochus Epiphanes during his visit to
the temple, and making this Greek himself recount his tragic fate.
It is assumed that both of these versions are based upon an earlier
pamphlet by one Molon.[8]

The origin of this fable is difficult to track down, but its association with the name of Antiochus Epiphanes offers a clue. It
has been plausibly suggested[9] that it originated as a propaganda
move on the part of the agents of the half-demented King of
Syria to excuse his profanation of the temple in Jerusalem, an act
which aroused the indignation of the entire Hellenistic world, in
whose eyes such sacrilege was an unpardonable crime. Seeking
to vilify the Jewish people and their religion, they concocted out
of various current folklore and ritual motifs the fable that it
was a regular practice of the Jews, in Apion's words, "to catch a
Greek foreigner, and fatten him thus every year, and then lead
him to a certain wood, and kill him, and sacrifice with their accustomed solemnities, and taste of his entrails, and take an oath upon
thus sacrificing a Greek, that they would ever be at enmity with
the Greeks." It should be noticed that even here, in its earliest
appearance, the ritual murder constituted an expression of hostility toward an enemy people, with the purely ritual element of
secondary import; the blood motif is altogether lacking.

Such accusations were far from uncommon in the ancient

world, and others besides Jews were also their victims. It is well known that during the first centuries of the Christian era the Christians themselves were often accused by pagans of killing and sacrificing infants. (Origen charged the Jews with spreading these reports but, as Parkes observes, though individual Jews may have been guilty, it is far from likely that this was part of the Jewish anti-Christian propaganda. No other second-century apologist ascribed these calumnies to Jews, though all mentioned them.) Nor did Christians hesitate, in turn, to accuse their own gnostics and other sectarians of such rites.[10]

So far as the Jews are concerned, this accusation does not make its appearance again until the twelfth century, when it was suddenly revived and given a new and lusty lease on life. However, an incident occurred during the intervening centuries which, while not an instance of the ritual-murder charge, nonetheless closely paralleled it and may have influenced its later resurrection. In the year 415 or thereabouts at Inmestar in Syria, during the Purim celebration a number of Jews, in drunken revelry, hung a Christian boy from a cross and so maltreated him that he died. Later in that century, probably as a result of this and perhaps other excesses, Theodosius II forbade the burning of a Haman effigy and mocking the cross during the Purim festivities. The execrations traditionally heaped upon the head of Haman in jest and the carnival aspect of the Purim celebration could have easily led to imprudent and offensive remarks and gestures, and might just as easily have been misinterpreted by hypersensitive Christians. Possibly an echo of the Theodosian prohibition, and evidence that the observance of Purim still aroused misgivings as to its real intent, is heard in an eleventh-century formula of renunciation of Judaism required of a convert, which anathematizes "those who celebrate the festival of Mordecai . . . and those who nail Haman to a piece of wood, and joining it to the sign of the cross, burn them together while hurling various curses and the anathema against the Christians." An episode similar to that of Inmestar was reported to have occurred during Purim at Bray in Northern France, in 1191, when Jews allegedly made a Christian act the role of Haman and executed him. Cecil Roth suggests that the medieval ritual-murder accusation originated with such acts as this occurring on Purim, which coincided (as occasionally happened) with Easter; but this is making too much of these rare and purely coincidental occurrences. "Authentic" ritual-murder charges are recorded during the twelfth century prior to the Bray event. At most such episodes contributed incidental evidence to substantiate the more serious charge in the popular mind.[11]

In seeking the origins of this charge we must accord some weight also to other, possibly contributory, considerations. Individual Jews were unquestionably guilty of occasional acts that aroused and merited the ire of their neighbors. And the universal tendency to generalize, particularly, it seems, with respect to the Jews, rendered them all suspect because of the guilt of a few. Agobard, for instance, cites several apparently authentic cases of the theft of children in France by Jewish slave traders for sale to the Moors of Spain; and a tenth-century chronicler adds a tale of the castration of boys in Eastern France for sale as eunuchs to the Moorish harems.[12] In 1202 a Jew, Bonefand of Bedford, was accused of "totally cutting off the privy member of one Richard the nephew of Robert de Sutton: to which indictment Bonefand pleaded not guilty, and was very honourably acquitted." [13] Legitimate or not, such reports could not but have exerted a powerful influence upon public opinion.

Jewish "misanthropy" was of course a cardinal item in the hostile propaganda. The ferocity of the American Indian of dime novel fame pales ingloriously before Dio Cassius' blood-curdling description of the Jewish revolt in North Africa at the time of Trajan: "The Jews were destroying both Greeks and Romans. They ate the flesh of their victims, made belts for themselves out of their entrails, and anointed themselves with their blood." [14] If they could display such barbarism when destroying mere heathen, to what lengths would they not go in the war against Christ?

As though impelled by some such rhetorical question, public

authorities in the Byzantine Empire and the Balkan region generally drafted Jews quite often to perform public executions. In 1073
a Jew was forced to pierce the eyes of the ex-emperor Romanos IV
by his successor; and from the thirteenth to the fifteenth centuries
there are a number of instances of Jews being compelled to exe-
cute mutilations and death sentences upon political and criminal
offenders in the Byzantine Empire and later under the Turks, in
Bulgaria, Serbia, Venice, Palermo, and Morocco. In Crete and
other Venetian colonies the Jewish community was forced to
supply the public executioner, and the head of the community
was held responsible for his appearance when required. This
stratagem was not unknown in the West, either; in England too
during the twelfth and thirteenth centuries Jews were obliged
on occasion to act as torturers and executioners.[15] News of such
activities, sifting through to the rest of Europe and edited and
reëdited, certainly did not improve their black repute. So firmly
persuaded was Christendom of their sanguinary habits that almost any mysterious homicide was laid at their door as a matter
of course. It is probably symptomatic that at the very time the
blood accusation was aborning in England and France, Jews
were being charged in Germany with a number of such murders.[16]

All these considerations, however, do not establish the origin
of the medieval blood accusation; some far more pressing and
specific stimulus must have been at work to give the charge the
form and virility it assumed within a short space of time. Even
the "ritual" aspect of the blood accusation, as it first appeared
during the twelfth century, does not provide a wholly satisfying
explanation.

What would seem to be the earliest instance of this charge occurs in a report that in 1096, during the Polovtzian raid on Kiev,
the monk Eustratios was abducted from the Pechera monastery
and sold to Jews in Cherson, who, in about the year 1100 *crucified him in celebration of the Passover.*[17] However, this report
comes from a thirteenth-century account and therefore embodies
the point of view current at the time of its composition, when the

effort to explain such crimes ritualistically had passed into its second stage.

The first "ritual murders" had nothing to do with Passover, or indeed with any Jewish festival. Let us listen to a contemporary chronicler describing the fate of the very first boy martyr, William of Norwich, who disappeared unaccountably in 1144: "The Jews of Norwich bought a Christian child before Easter and tortured him with all the tortures wherewith our Lord was tortured, and on Long Friday hanged him on a rood in hatred of our Lord, and afterwards buried him." Not a very plausible story, but it was based on the statement of a Jewish convert, one Theobald of Canterbury, who obligingly came forward with the explanation that the Jews were required to sacrifice a Christian child annually *at Easter;* the choice of place was made, according to him, by a yearly conference of rabbis, which had met the year before at Narbonne and selected Norwich.[18] His tale evidently did not command much credence at the time, despite the chronicler's tone of assurance, for no Jews were tried or punished for the alleged crime—there was no evidence that a murder had been committed. Yet the mere statement of this convert led to the bringing of identical charges at Gloucester in 1168 and elsewhere. It will not be amiss to repeat here an extract from a contemporary account of the martyrdom of Harold of Gloucester in tribute both to the author and to the logic of the times: "The boy Harold . . . is said to have been carried away secretly by Jews, in the opinion of many, on February 21st, and by them hidden till March 16th. On that night . . . the Jews of all England coming together . . . they tortured the lad placed before them with immense tortures. It is true no Christian was present, or saw or heard the deed, nor have we found that anything was betrayed by any Jew. . . . [But, the boy's wounds having been examined] those tortures were believed or guessed to have been inflicted on him in that manner. It was clear that they had made him a glorious martyr to Christ."[19] Similar charges were made at Blois in 1171, at Bury St. Edmonds in 1181, at Pontoise, Braisne, and Saragossa in 1182, and at Winchester in 1192. There was no trial in any of these cases; rumor was sufficient to establish the martyr-dom of the children.

Theobald's fable of the required Easter sacrifice did not hold up for long, but his story of the annual rabbinical conference en-joyed a much hardier career. It struck a responsive chord in the public fancy, for it spread rapidly through Europe and was often repeated in connection with supposed Jewish crimes of this sort. In time it was expanded to make room for a secret Jewish society whose function it was to kidnap and kill Christian children and distribute the blood to the major Jewish communities, at the bid-ding of the Council, whose permanent meeting place was ulti-mately fixed in Spain. All sorts of traitorous criminal acts were laid at the door of this mythical body.[20]

The earliest explanation of these alleged crimes, therefore, which was widely accepted for a while, held that the Jews *cruci-fied* Christian children, usually *during Passion week*, in order to reënact the crucifixion of Jesus and to mock and insult the Chris-tian faith. Every one of the twelfth-century charges was based upon this motif (except for the case of Robert of Edmondsbury, concerning which we know nothing more than the simple state-ment that "the boy Robert at St. Edmund is martyred by the Jews on the 10th of June" [21]), which carried over into the thir-teenth century. In Norwich in 1235 a number of Jews were prosecuted for circumcising a boy (possibly a convert) "with the intention of crucifying him in celebration of Easter." [22]

The case of Hugh of Lincoln (1255), which achieved tre-mendous notoriety, produced a similar charge. A large number of Jews were in Lincoln at the time to attend the marriage of Belaset, daughter of Magister Benedict fil' Moses. The day after the wedding the body of a boy, who had been missing for over three weeks, was discovered in a cesspool into which he had probably fallen while at play. But a more dramatic explanation of his death immediately suggested itself. Matthew Paris, in describing the alleged murder, related how "the child was first fattened for ten days with white bread and milk, and then how almost all the Jews in England were invited to the crucifixion." [23]

The Jew Copin was forced to confess that the boy was crucified *in injuriam et contumeliam Jesu*. Nearly one hundred Jews were arrested, of whom nineteen, including Copin, were hanged without trial. The rest, after being convicted and sentenced, were ultimately released when, the intervention of the learned Franciscan teacher Adam Marsh having proved fruitless, Richard of Cornwall, who held the Jewry of the Kingdom in mortgage and was naturally anxious to protect his property, interceded in their behalf.

The same accusation was made on the continent, with sufficient frequency to elicit a specific enactment in the *Siete Partidas* (1263) beginning with the assertion: "We have heard it said that in certain places on Good Friday the Jews do steal children and set them on the cross in a mocking manner. . . ." [24] (These early accounts are strongly reminiscent of Apion, as preserved by Josephus, who was highly prized by the Church and widely read among churchmen.)

It was at about this same time that the blood element was introduced in the myth, in conjunction with the crucifixion, as part of a peculiarly Christian conception of a Jewish celebration of Easter. The collecting of the blood was first mentioned in a case at Fulda, in 1235; and in 1247, at Valréas, France, a Jew, after being tortured, confessed that a dead child found with wounds on its forehead, its hands and feet, had been crucified in accordance with a Jewish custom to celebrate communion on Easter Saturday with the blood of Christian children. [25]

The occurrence of a number of such cases during the first half of the thirteenth century, explained in this manner, and the public disturbances that ensued, led the German emperor Frederick II to consult a committee of scholars and distinguished Jewish converts to Christianity from all parts of Europe to ascertain whether the Jews required Christian blood on *Parasceve*—a term frequently used to designate Good Friday (*Judei Christianum sanguinem in parasceve necessarium haberent*). These experts replied (and the reply is worth quoting at some length): "Neither the Old nor the New Testament states that the Jews lust for human blood; on the contrary, it is expressly stated in the Bible, in the laws of Moses, and in the Jewish ordinances designated in Hebrew as the 'Talmud,' that they should not defile themselves with blood. Those to whom even the tasting of animal blood is prohibited surely cannot thirst for that of human beings, (1) because of the horror of the thing; (2) because it is forbidden by nature; (3) because of the human tie that also binds the Jews to Christians; and (4) because they would not wilfully imperil their lives and property." [26] A fair statement indeed, but, it need hardly be said, without much effect on public opinion.

This explanation of the ritual murder, then, stressed the traditional Jewish hostility toward Christendom and the intent of the Jews to burlesque gruesomely the essential fact of the Christian faith, the crucifixion of Jesus, and the sacrament. However, it was too much strain even on the elastic medieval credulity to suppose that Jews celebrated Easter, even in this perverse fashion, and the Easter association was gradually superseded by the Passover motif, which made more sense, of a peculiarly medieval sort. (The alleged *crucifixion* of the monk Eustratios on *Passover*, mentioned above, is thus seen to be a clumsy invention deriving from the transitional phase of the legend.) But the Easter element did not lapse completely and occasionally put in an appearance in the later accusations. We still hear in the sixteenth century that the murder of Christian children and the distribution of their blood among Jews are a "token of their eternal enmity toward Christendom," for "if they had Christ today they would crucify him as their fathers did, but since they do not have Christ, they martyr in his stead an innocent Christian child." [27]

The coupling of the blood accusation with Passover also dates from the first half of the thirteenth century. Richer of Sens, in the *Gesta Senoniensis Ecclesiae* (published between 1239 and 1270), specified that the alleged murder of several children at Fulda occurred on the day before Passover—March 22, 1236. The forced nature of this association is evident from the fact that other contemporaneous accounts definitely establish the correct date as December 25, 1235. The idea caught hold, however—it probably did not originate with Richer, who was no doubt merely repeating what was already common rumor—since it seemed to offer a plausible motive for such crimes, and was so assiduously propagated that Pope Innocent IV in his encyclical *Lachrymabilem Judaeorum Alemannie*, issued on July 5, 1247, to the archbishops and bishops of Germany and France, came to the defense of the Jews and declared that "they are falsely accused that, in that same solemnity [Passover] they make communion with the heart of a slain child. This it is believed their Law enjoins, although it is clearly contrary to the Law. No matter where a dead body is found, their persecutors wickedly throw it up to them." And again, in confirming the *Constitutio pro Judeis* first issued by Calixtus II in 1120, Innocent IV felt impelled to add: "Nor shall anyone accuse them of using human blood in their religious rites. . . ." In 1272, when reissuing this same *Constitutio*, Gregory X added: "The charge is . . . made against the Jews by their enemies that they have stolen and slain these children in secret, and have sacrificed the heart and blood," a charge which he forbade the clergy to countenance. So that it is apparent that during this century the notion was already widespread that Jews required some sort of sacrifice of a Christian child on the Passover.[28]

Yet the early accusations are vague and uncertain about this (as is evident from the papal allusions cited above), and it was only in later centuries that the charge was elaborated. The notion that Jews use Christian blood in baking their Passover unleavened bread, or mix it with their Passover wine, seems to be no older than the fourteenth century, and became a fixed element of the charge only in the fifteenth century. When Martin V reiterated the traditional papal attitude in 1422 his protest was directed against the rumor that Jews "mix human blood in their unleavened bread, which the preachers of various orders spread among the people." One of the important causes adduced for the expulsion of the Jews from Spain was the constantly repeated accusation that they drank Christian blood.[29] A variant that appears to be unique occurs in a purported "confession" under torture of a

Jew in Savoy in 1329 that Jews "compound out of the heads and entrails of murdered Christian children a salve or food called 'aharace' (*Haroseth*), which they eat every Passover in place of a sacrifice; they prepare this food at least every sixth year because they believe they are saved thereby." [30]

Thus, in time the Passover motivation became dominant, and it is in this guise that the legend has retained its popularity until today. But as one inspects the records of the ritual-murder charge during the early centuries of its propagation it becomes impressively evident that other motivations were still more prominently advanced and that these must have exerted a determining influence in fixing the legend in the public mind. It must be remembered that the clergy was usually behind these cases; the official record was created by them and would naturally reflect their theological bias. In these circumstances the popular explanation, if it differed, as it undoubtedly did for a long time, found less and less place in that record. The "ritual" explanation is palpably clerical in origin. But in the early period, before the clerical view was firmly established, and in the occasional later statements that voiced lay opinion without benefit of clergy, the popular view of the matter is quite clearly expressed.

The fact is that most of the early accusations make no mention of either Easter or Passover, or of any ritual purpose whatsoever behind these purported murders; their sole object was alleged to be *the abstraction of the blood, or of other parts of the body*. To cite but a few of these:

1234—Lauda a.d. Tauber: probably at the end of the year (since the attack upon the Jews occurred Jan. 1–3, 1235), Jews accused of murder of Christian child—the first such accusation in Germany.[31]

1235—Fulda: on Christmas day, while their parents are at church five boys killed and their blood collected in bags smeared with wax; connection with Christmas altogether fortuitous;[32]

1267—Pforzheim: on July 1, child killed and its blood collected on folded pieces of linen;[33]

Torture applied to produce a "confession" from
Jews charged with the "ritual murder" of Simon
of Trent

Geschichte des zu Trient ermordeten Christenkindes
(Trent, 1475)

Conjuring the devil from blood secured through
"ritual murder"

Pierre Boaistuau, Histoires prodigieuses (Paris, 1575)

1270—Weissenburg: Jews accused of suspending child by the feet, on June 29, and opening every artery in its body in order to obtain all its blood;

1285—Munich: in October, Jews accused of kidnaping a child;

1286—Oberwesel: "the good Werner" slowly tortured to death by Jews for three days; no mention originally of blood or of a ritual purpose, but later accounts speak of the Jews collecting his blood;

1287—Berne: a boy, Rudolph, tortured, and his head finally cut off;

1293—Krems: Jews kill a boy "in order to get his blood." [34]

Here we have a fair sampling of the recorded cases during the thirteenth century, when the charge really began to flourish (the twelfth-century instances seem all to have been little more than reflexes of the initial accusation made by Theobald of Canterbury). The same lack of ritual motivation pervades the later cases, too. Just a few more citations will indicate this: on July 12, 1462, at Rinn near Innsbruck, a boy was allegedly murdered and his blood then carefully collected in vessels; at the beginning of the seventeenth century this story had been revised to read that the Jews had first drawn off this boy's blood while he was still alive, and that his death had resulted from this operation.[35] Although the fifteenth-century Spanish theologian Alphonso de Spina mentions cases of alleged Jewish child murder he makes no special reference to the use of Christian blood *at the Passover*, and this at a time when the Passover association was quite familiar to everyone.[36] In fact, the fifteenth- and sixteenth-century accusations stress particularly the extraction and collection of the blood, often without bothering to specify its use. In the celebrated case of Simon of Trent, in 1475, the boy was reputedly murdered "to the accompaniment of curses and spells" two days after the beginning of the Passover, when his death could no longer have had any connection with the Passover ceremonial; Jews are alleged to have admitted that they required "fresh Christian blood" because it was a jubilee year (which it was in the *Catholic calendar!* Jews have not counted or celebrated the Jubilee year since early biblical times, if at all).[37]

Right down to modern times such charges reappear without any reference to Passover or ritual. Jews were accused of killing a boy near Neuenhoven (Düsseldorf) and drawing off his blood on the night of July 13, 1834. The notorious Damascus case, involving the murder of the Capuchin Father Thomas and his servant, occurred in February, 1840. The death of a boy, whose corpse was found on June 29, 1891, at Xanten, Rhenish Prussia, was attributed to the Jewish penchant for collecting blood, with no relation to Passover ritual.[38] It is unnecessary to offer additional examples at this point.

As we have noted, it was not the blood alone that was suspected of interesting the Jews but other parts of the body as well. The head and the heart have already appeared in the record; from a Spanish Hebrew source we learn that "some made the accusation that in the house of a Jew they had found a murdered child, whose body was cut open at the heart, and they further said that the Jews had taken out the heart to celebrate with it."[39] There are references to the extraction of the liver also; on November 5, 1447, Pope Nicholas V issued a bull severely castigating the clergy who spread the report that "Jews require the heart and liver of a Christian for the celebration of certain holidays."[40] And it seems to have been a common belief that the Jews made use of the flesh of the victims, too. In Warwick, England, a Jewess was said to have eaten "the mouth and ears" of her victim, while from Spain comes a story of the excision of some flesh from a Christian child, and in Pösing, Hungary, there occurred a trumped-up case in which the Jewish creditors of the accusers were alleged to have cut off the penis and testicles of a boy, besides drawing off his blood.[41] Two accounts of the expulsion of the Jews from France by Philip Augustus in 1182, ten years after the murder accusation of Blois, relate that punishment to Philip's conviction that Jews *eat* Christians. (Though it should be added, however, that other accounts explain this expulsion on the ground of Jewish usury).[42]

From the twelfth to the twentieth century is a long stretch, but other things besides wine and fiddles improve with age: modern anthropologists have uncovered places in Germany and the Balkans where it is still believed that Jews consume human flesh, and not only that—they wash down these anthropophagous repasts with the blood they suck at night from the Christian serving-girls who work for them![43]

CHAPTER TEN

THE BLOOD ACCUSATION

WHY did the Jews require this blood and these organs, then, if not for ritual use? The medieval Christian had no difficulty in supplying the answer. He was too well acquainted with their wide utility not to have imputed a like knowledge to the Jews. Indeed, if anything, the Jews' skill in their application was believed to be far more extensive than any to be found in Christian circles.

One of the most pervasive beliefs of the ancient world, and of the Middle Ages perhaps even more, was in the unexcelled value for medicinal and magical purposes of the elements of the human body. Medieval magic is full of recipes for putting to occult use human fat, human blood, entrails, hands, fingers; medieval medicine utilized as one of its chief medicaments, along with other parts of the human body, blood, preferably blood that had been freshly drawn, or menstrual blood. Thorndike points out that "the story of having sacrificed a pure boy for purposes of magic or divination was a stock charge" made in ancient times among the pagans, and against the early Christians by their pagan enemies, as well as against Jews and heretics in the Middle Ages.[1] Candles made of human fat were particularly prized by thieves on the theory that such candles would render them invisible while lighting up their surroundings. Poisons, as we have seen, often contained human ingredients.

Human blood was notoriously employed in the witches' ritual and sorcery. The use of blood to write the compact with the devil, so characteristic of the later witch-cults, is mentioned as early as the thirteenth century, and significantly, in connection with the Theophilus legend.[2] In fact, the best practice ultimately favored the use of *Jewish* blood for the most successful witchcraft. On July 13, 1784, two women were broken on the wheel in Hamburg for having murdered a Jew in order to get his blood for such a purpose, and until recent times it was still believed in parts of Europe that the pact with the devil must be written in Jewish blood.[3]

The magical utility of the body was entirely familiar to the medieval world. An interesting and especially pertinent illustration of the universal acceptance of this superstition, and incidentally of its usefulness in controversy, was provided during the open strife at Berne in 1507 between the Dominicans and the Franciscans, when the latter unabashedly asserted that their Dominican rivals had used the blood and eyebrows of a *Jewish* child for secret purposes! And when a number of Jews, at about this time, were accused of the murder of a child, a friend unavailingly raised a telling question: "Were there no sorcerers, devil-conjurers or treasure-hunters in the place, who do such things in the course of their sorcery and witchcraft?" [4]

As for the medicinal use of such elements, perhaps the most comprehensive illustration may be taken from a period that would technically be regarded as long past the close of the Middle Ages but which still remained essentially medieval in its point of view, regardless of date; only in synoptic history texts does the medieval period vanish at a given moment. In 1699 there appeared in Frankfort an encyclopedic volume summarizing all the earlier learning on the subject, entitled: *Curieuse, Neue Hauss-Apothec, Wie man durch seine eigne bey sich habende Mittel, als dem Blut, dem Urin, Hinter- und Ohren-Dreck, Speichel und andren natürlichen geringen Mitteln seine Gesundheit erhalten, fast alle selbst vor incurabel gehaltene Kranckheiten . . . heilen . . . möge und könne*, which, besides the blood, urine, excrement, earwax, and sputum mentioned in the title, described the therapeutic use of the bones, marrow, skull, flesh, fat, hair, brain, heart, nails, sweat, afterbirth, semen, menses, and so on.[5] Such medicines have been favored by physicians from earliest times down, apparently, to the present. It was reported late in the nineteenth century that the ignorant country folk in the vicinity of

Graz suspected that the doctors of the local hospital were permitted every year to exploit one human life for curative purposes. "Some young man who repaired thither for toothache or any such slight ailment is seized, hung up by the feet, and tickled to death! Skilled chemists boil the body to a paste and utilize this as well as the fat and the charred bones in their drug store. The people are persuaded that about Easter a youth annually disappears in the hospital for such purposes." [6]

A number of medieval legends directly related the Jews to these activities, as was inevitable in view of their renowned prowess in the allied fields of magic and medicine. Many of these legends originated early in the Christian era and were repeated in countless versions until they became a constant of medieval belief. In one of them a blind Jew, smearing his eyes with the blood of some murdered monks, immediately regains his sight. The story that Constantine the Great, stricken with leprosy for his early persecution of the Christians, was advised by his Jewish physician to bathe in children's blood was popular and widely retold. The earliest version of this tale, by the Armenian Moses of Chorene (who died in 487), attributes this prescription to heathen priests, but the obviously prejudiced distortion was the only one current during the Middle Ages. [7]

Similarly, Richard the Lion-hearted of England, allegedly suffering from leprosy, was given this counsel by a Jewish doctor: "Know that you will recover your health completely, if you can make up your mind to bathe in the blood of a newborn child. . . . But because this remedy is only external, it must be helped out by an additional recipe, which extirpates even the inward root of the malady. Namely, the child's heart must be added, which Your Majesty must eat and consume quite warm and raw, just as it has been taken from the body." Unfortunately for the credibility of this story Richard never suffered from leprosy, and he died of a wound received in battle. There is still another account that Pope Innocent VIII on his deathbed (he was not leprous) called in a Jewish physician who suggested injecting "the lifeblood of boys" into the dying man. [8]

This was the real background of the blood accusation. That such use of human parts, and especially of blood, was inherently abhorrent and inconceivable to the Jew, for magic or medicine or for any other purpose,[9] is of no significance here. What matters is that the medieval world implicitly accepted and tacitly acquiesced in this use, and imputed it to the Jew. Here, in the realm of superstition, we must seek the most compelling motivation behind the medieval blood accusation.

The same Richer of Sens whom we have already encountered reports an interesting case from the town of St. Dié, early in the thirteenth century: One of the Jews of this community, who was renowned among his coreligionists as a great sorcerer and augur, drugged a Gentile serving-girl with a magic potion and cut off a part of her body for some secret purpose. When rumor of this criminal act spread, the girl was called before Philip, the provost of the Duke of Lorraine, and subsequently the Jew was tried and sentenced to death. He was tied to the tail of a horse and dragged to the gallows; but when he sought to offer an explanation of his act the hangman silenced him, for the other Jews had bribed him to do so, lest the culprit reveal something to their disadvantage. He was hung up by the feet, and after two days the Jews cut him down and buried him. So runs Richer's story, and the implication is obvious: not only was this Jew guilty of sorcery, but the other Jews were somehow accessories to the crime, though they escaped his deserved fate through bribery.[10]

Were this story unique one might regard it merely as another example of medieval superstition and dismiss the Jewishness of its villain as incidental to the general conception of the Jew. But not long after, the most notorious of the early blood accusations specifically makes the charge of sorcery, and gives us reason to believe that such crimes were widely held, in the thirteenth century, to be a salient feature of Jewish magical practice.

After describing the crucifixion of Little St. Hugh of Lincoln Matthew Paris continues, "And when the child was dead they took down his body from the cross, and disemboweled the corpse, for what end is unknown; but it was said it was to practice magical arts." Copin, forced to accuse the other Jews of the crime, is reported to have disclosed their purpose in these words: "And when he was dead, and they desired to hide him, being dead, he could not be buried in the earth, nor hid. For the corpse of the innocent was reputed unprofitable for divination, for he was eviscerated for that purpose." [11]

Just as the crucifixion theme left room for "magic arts," so did the introduction of the "ritual" Passover motif fail to oust them. Indeed, for all its popularity the ritual feature of the myth remained somewhat artificial and too "theological" to supplant satisfyingly the more primitive and more "secular" earlier view, which persisted in asserting itself. In 1401 the townspeople of Freiburg, petitioning for the expulsion of the Jews, affirmed that their danger to the community extended far beyond an occasional child murder, for they dry the blood they thus secure, grind it to a powder, and scatter it in the fields early in the morning when there is a heavy dew on the ground (*uff ein towe*); then in three or four weeks a plague descends on men and cattle, within a radius of half a mile, so that Christians suffer severely while the sly Jews remain safely indoors.[12]

Here we have the ultimate combination: murder, blood, magic, poison, in grand alliance aimed at the destruction of Christendom. This fable was repeated often enough, in various guises, to indicate that it was quite generally believed. In fact, its first appearance antedates the birth of the blood accusation proper, and provides a striking instance of the association of well poisoning (the earliest recorded such charge) and the murder of a Christian. We have a report that during the First Crusade, on May 5, 1096, in the city of Worms, "someone . . . dug up a corpse which had been buried a month, and paraded it through the town, crying out that the Jews had killed a Christian, boiled him, and thrown the resulting concoction into various wells in order to poison the water supply." [13] One wonders how a corpse that had been boiled and dispersed could well have been displayed to the mob, but the charge sufficed as a pretext for the Crusaders and

the townspeople to fall upon the Jews. In France, subsequent to
the Black Death, this story took a somewhat different form; this
is the way it went: a Jew prevails upon his impoverished Christian neighbor to sell him the heart of his prettiest child, and a
host; the host is delivered, and the heart too, but in place of the
child's heart a pig's is secretly substituted. The Jew grinds these
up, concocts a mysterious powder, and deposits it in the wells
with the intention of poisoning the Christians of the neighborhood, but instead all the pigs that drink this water perish and
the humans escape unharmed, "since it was not a human but a
swine's heart." [14]

Later centuries added new twists to the worn fable, but it
remained the same despite all the doctoring. A sixteenth-century
account, which purports to relate a recent occurrence, has the
Jew, who has been deceived with a swine's heart instead of the
human heart he ordered (on the pretext, incidentally, of needing
it in his medical practice), bury it "with his sorcery and witchcraft" in a field, whereupon all the pigs in the vicinity rush
wildly to the spot and in mad frenzy destroy each other. "Without doubt his intention was to cause the people to do thus," is the
narrator's redundant comment.[15]

We have still another version of this tale, tricked out this time
with place (Jägersdorf, Silesia) and date (1535), as though to
say, here is a well-authenticated event, who can doubt it? A Jew
offered to purchase her milk from a nursing mother, who sold
him sow milk instead. He then induced a peasant debtor to carry
out his orders, with the promise that his debt would be forgotten
(usury is a useful adjunct to the Jew's diabolic schemes), led
him to a gallows, and had him split open the head of a corpse
hanging there and pour in the milk. "When the peasant had done
this, the Jew instructed him, 'Put your ear to the head. What do
you hear?' The peasant replied, 'The grunting as of many
sows.' The Jew cried out, 'Woe is me! The woman has deceived
me.' The next day all the hogs from a distance of two miles came
together at this spot and killed each other." And again to make
certain its moral is not lost, the account winds up with a

rhetorical question: "Pious Christian, had he procured human milk, how would it have gone?" [16]

Sixteenth-century sources also preserve a quite different plot, based on the blood motif, which is undoubtedly older in origin. "Nowadays," runs the statement, "when the Jews for fear of Christian justice can no longer sacrifice humans, they have nevertheless found another way of offering up human blood, which they secure from barber-surgeons and cuppers; when they have put this in a glass vessel, and set it on burning coals, they conjure up by means of it demons, who do their bidding and answer all questions that are put to them, so long as the blood is kept boiling." [17] A typical bit of witch lore, which helps to explain why so many of the accusations stress the collecting of the blood in glass vessels. And, to prove that this theory is not one man's invention, a woodcut in a work published in Paris in 1575 (Boaistuau's *Histoires prodigieuses*) depicts a Jew "producing the devil from a vessel of blood obtained from a crucified child's body." [18]

But why especially the blood of a child? "They desire innocent Christian blood, not that of an old Christian whose innocence, acquired through baptism, has been forfeited by his subsequent sin," explained Johann Eck after a bit of tortuous exegesis.[19] This *was* a primary requirement of the myth, but not exclusively on the pseudo-theological grounds he advanced. Those familiar with the way of magic understood it well enough. Since time immemorial sorcerers have preferred to work with young children, notably in divinational exercises, and the witch-cults prized the blood and organs of infants above all others. This preference is allied with the importance of *new* things in magic. Children are virginal and uncontaminated; by the special logic of magic "innocent" blood should be most potent. This consideration may not have been present to all minds but it could not have escaped many in the Middle Ages.

However, the Jewish need of blood was so great, and a supply of the highest quality so limited, that in a pinch they lowered their standards, as other sorcerers were known to do in like circumstances. A report from Lublin, in 1636, confirms the popular impression, already called to our attention, that surgeons and barbers offered a secondary source of supply. There a Carmelite monk asserted that Jews had lured him into a house, forced him to submit while a German surgeon bled him, and collected his blood in a vessel while they murmured incantations.[20]

Such an accusation was calculated to strike a receptive note, as indeed it did, for Eastern Europe has proven fertile ground for the proliferation of the myth. Some of the most recent innovations upon this theme come from that region. For example, a book published in Poland in 1716 alleges that Christian blood is used by Jews for every form of magic and witchcraft; these are a few of the specific utilities it possesses: they smear it upon the door of a Christian home to predispose its inhabitants in their favor; they inject it in an egg and give it to a bridal pair to eat during the marriage ceremony, in order to promote fertility; they soak incantation formulas in it and then bury them under the threshold of a house, to bring success to its tenants.[21]

Even the unleavened bread, baked with Christian blood, according to Christian belief, has its peculiar magical virtues— among Christians! The notion is widespread throughout rural sections of Germany and Eastern Europe that a piece of *Judenmatz* has the power to extinguish fires and to immunize a house against fire, to protect houses, men, and beasts against lightning and hail, to protect clothing against moths, prevent the paralysis of various bodily organs which witches know how to produce, etc. It is with good reason, as we can see, that such folk greatly prize a gift of *matzah* and share it with their best friends as a potent token of good will.[22]

If the blood and organs of pretended victims of Jewish blood lust were believed to be destined for magical use, this by no means exhausted their utility in the medieval view. They possessed quite as notable a potency for Jewish magic medicine, and indeed were held to be absolutely essential for the peculiar medical needs of that accursed people. The sources leave no room to doubt that many of the purported murders were thus accounted for by the masses.

The statement that Jews had required the blood of a murdered child "for their own healing" (*ut ex eis sanguinem ad suum remedium elicerent*) occurs early in the thirteenth century— in connection with practically the first case of this sort in Germany, that of Fulda (December, 1235).[23] Just why they should have needed blood for such a purpose we are not told, but it is quite evident that this strange conjecture was related to another fable that gained rapid and convincing currency in that century. Thomas of Cantimpré expounded it at length in his account of the Pforzheim incident of 1267, when he explained that ever since the Jews had called out to Pilate, "His blood be upon us and on our children" (Matt. 27.25) they have been afflicted with hemorrhoids (or hemorrhages). A sage had advised them that they could be cured *solo sanguine Christiano;* they took the advice literally and adopted the custom of annually shedding Christian blood which they applied to their bodies "in order that they might recover from their malady." Thomas comments, as every Christian understood, that it was really the blood of Christ that was meant.[24] This story, allegedly based partly on a sermon by Augustine (which is not to be found in his works) and partly on the statement of a converted Jew, thereafter became a fixed element of medieval folklore and was incessantly repeated. Though the maladies varied the treatment remained constant, and so pressing was the Jews' need of Christian blood believed to be that a sixteenth-century writer expressed the opinion that they were driven to preserve the limited available supply by mixing it with tomatoes, honey, and ginger, "for they cannot dispense with it as a cure for their ailments."[25]

Often as the charge was made, extreme pressure could not fail to produce the anticipated "confessions" to such practices—and with time and free rein to the imagination the scope of these well-controlled admissions expanded considerably. Thus, after several such confessions had been secured, the City Council of Freiburg in Breisgau petitioned Duke Leopold in May, 1401, to expel the Jews from their city since "every seven years all Jews must obtain Christian blood," with which they smear themselves annually, "and also take the blood on their tongues and swallow it for the prolongation of their lives, and particularly from a desire not to stink, for when they lack this blood they stink so foully that no one can remain near them." [26] Similar confessions extracted in Regensburg in 1476 revealed that the Jews drank Christian blood mixed with wine and smeared it on their unleavened bread as a *prophylactic against leprosy*, or else rubbed it on their cheeks to produce a healthy color and to prevent weakness.[27]

The city of Tyrnau produced a set of confessions in 1494 which made possible the following explanations of their need for blood:

"Firstly, they were convinced by the judgment of their ancestors that the blood of a Christian was a good remedy for the alleviation of the wound of circumcision. Secondly, they were of opinion that this blood, put into food, is very efficacious for the awakening of mutual love. Thirdly, they had discovered, as men and women among them suffered equally from menstruation, that the blood of a Christian is a specific medicine for it, when drunk. Fourthly, they had an ancient but secret ordinance by which they are under obligation to shed Christian blood in honor of God in daily sacrifices in some spot or other; they said it had happened in this way that the lot for the present year had fallen on the Tyrnau Jews." [28]

The notion that Jews use Christian blood "to alleviate the wound of circumcision" seems to be a late fifteenth-century invention, for only then do we begin to hear of it. Such a confession was purportedly extracted in 1476, in Baden,[29] and the Endingen incident, which became the theme of the *Endingen Judenspiel*, one of the most popular German dramas of the seventeenth century, demonstrated how the desired confession was elicited. Incidentally, the *Judenspiel* fixes the time of the event as the Feast of Tabernacles, not from any ritual motive but merely because it was an occasion for the assemblage of Jews. In 1462 a Christian family in Endingen was murdered; eight years later the Jews were accused of the deed and forced to admit the crime. Although the confessions mention repeatedly the desire of the Jews for the blood and *heads* of the victims ("Gather the blood diligently, and the heads indefatigably," the rabbi in the play orders his fellow criminals, "for great purposes which we know, for crafty and for profitable uses" [30]), the reason for their interest in the heads is left unexplained. But the use of the blood found a ready explanation: one of the first to be interrogated knew enough to admit that "the Jews require Christian blood at their circumcisions, as an unguent" (*crisam*, the term used, is a peculiarly Christian expression signifying consecrated oil). The next was not so well posted, and it is pathetic to hear him fumbling for the answer his inquisitors obviously expected of him: "His first statement was that the Jews need Christian blood for medical purposes, for it is quite salutary. But this reply did not satisfy us, and we told him he lied . . . whereupon he said they require it for leprosy.[31] Upon this we asked, 'Why then was your son leprous?' and we would not accept this answer. Then the Jew Merckly further testified that the Jews need Christian blood for its fragrance, since they stink fearfully. This answer too we would not accept," and so their inquisition proceeded painfully until finally he hit upon "the truth," that "the Jews require Christian blood for their *crisam* at their circumcisions." Having thus earned his execution in the desired manner, he was offered the usual reprieve: " 'Since you Jews all know so well that Christian blood is so salutary and good, why don't you permit your blood also to be made salutary, and let yourself be baptized?' To which he replied, 'That's for the devil to do.' " [32] His fate sealed, they turned to the others, and in the same way wrenched satisfactory stories from them.

"Leo, the Jew from Pforzheim," obligingly deposed at this same proceeding, "of his own free will, without duress, that once, some eighteen or twenty years ago, he was with his father at a circumcision, and by chance noticed something red in a little dish, and asked what it might be; to which his father replied, if he did not know it, this was Christian blood, which the Jews must have and use at their circumcisions." [33] This statement, a patent effort to please the examiners, provides the clue to this strange conceit. Not long after, the convert Antonius Margaritha, who made no bones about slandering his former coreligionists when it suited him, in a little book describing their ceremonies and customs pointed out that they "use dragon's blood to relieve the infant's pain" after a circumcision. "Dragon's blood" is a dark or blood-red gum of a species of palm (*Calamus Draco, Pterocarpus Draco, Dracaena Draco*), which was commonly applied by Jews to heal the wound of circumcision. [34] Gullible folk, persuaded of the Jewish lust for Christian blood, might easily have mistaken this gum for real blood. That simple people harbored this suspicion is perhaps excusable; but we may question the motives of the responsible churchmen and public figures who concurred in the paradoxical assertion that the operation which distinguished the adherents of the Jewish faith must be brought to a successful conclusion by the application of *Christian* blood.

There are a number of other notions closely related to this one, if not derived from it. We have already remarked on the belief current in the fifteenth and sixteenth centuries that Jewish boys are born with their fingers resting on their foreheads, "as though they were attached to the skin"; several preachers and writers would have us know that only the application of Christian blood makes it possible to free the fingers without seriously endangering the infant's life. "And this blood also has its special uses for girls," is one man's cryptic addendum to the foregoing asseveration. [35] In Hungary the belief has been encountered quite recently that Jews annually strangle a child or a virgin with their phylacteries, draw off the blood and smear the genitalia of their children with it to make them fertile. [36] And finally, the belief that "the Jews are always born blind," which was first voiced in the nineteenth century, is also accompanied by the charge that they smear the eyes of newborn infants with Christian blood to give them vision.[37] These ideas were probably also inspired by the sight of that "something red in a little dish."

The universal popularity of magic charms and potions to relieve the discomforts of childbirth gave rise also to the notion that Christian blood was employed by Jews to ease labor pains, a hypothesis first hesitantly advanced by the convert Samuel Friedrich Brenz in his booklet *Jüdischer abgestreiffter Schlangen-Balg* (Nuremberg, 1614). He wrote: "When a Jewish woman is in childbirth and cannot be delivered, the rabbi takes three strips of parchment made of doe skin, writes something on them and places one upon the head, the other two in the hands of the suffering woman." The composition of the ink used is kept secret by the Jews, but "perhaps" it is Christian blood. Despite the frank dubiety of this insinuation it became a new basis for the blood accusation, and in the same century the Jesuit Raderus carried it further still and charged that every Jewish woman is required to make use of Christian blood when she gives birth. Johann Peter Spaeth of Augsburg, born of Catholic parents, who became a Jew toward the end of the seventeenth century and took the name of Moses Germanus, reported that "even at the present time much of the same sort of thing [false accusations against the Jews] happens in Poland and Germany, where circumstantial tales are told and songs sung in the streets, how the Jews have murdered a child, and sent the blood to one another in quills for the use of their women in childbirth." [38]

It must be added too that, just as with the blood that supposedly flowed from the pierced host, so in connection with these murder charges it was bruited about that Jewish maidens used "pure Christian blood" to rouge their cheeks.[39] Apparently the alleged pallor which was so successfully alleviated by the magic of Christian blood was a consequence of the unremitting hemorrhages with which Jews were afflicted for their crime against Jesus. Or does this supposition weight folk belief with too much consistency?

The credulous medieval imagination thus did not lack for

explanations of the fancied Jewish blood lust. But the strangest explanation of all comes to us from the sixteenth century. Hans Wilhelm Kirchhof in his *Wendunmuth*[40] declares that the Jews smear their dying coreligionists with the blood of innocent Christian children, with the prayer: If the Messiah promised by the prophets has really come, and he be Jesus, may this innocent blood ensure for you eternal life! It has already been pointed out that it was a basic Christian conviction that the Jews were insincere in their rejection of Christ—that only through a devilish contumacy could they persist in what was, to the Christian, not only an illogical but a veritably inhuman attitude. Here we have what purports to be the final and conclusive evidence to this effect. On his deathbed the Jew "plays safe"—perhaps Jesus is the true Messiah, after all! The same story is repeated in a number of sixteenth- and seventeenth-century works, and it may not be amiss to give a fuller version from a later source. This states that when a Jew is dying his face is smeared with fresh Christian blood, or a cloth dipped in this blood is laid on his face, and someone whispers into his ear: "If Jesus, in whom the Christians believe and upon whom they rest their hopes, is the true Messiah, then may this blood of an innocent child who died with faith in his Redeemer help you to eternal life." One source demands that the blood come from a recently baptized child that had been suffocated. If ever there was perverted reasoning, this is it: to argue that Christian salvation was sought through the magic of freshly spilled Christian blood! Yet it must have carried conviction, for it was advanced as a satisfactory explanation of the supposed Jewish habit of child murder.

The older tradition thus underwent an unremitting process of elaboration and improvement. With the field wide open, there could be no limit to the possibilities. The sixteenth century produced a "confession" at Pösing, Hungary, that the Jews had "sucked blood out of a little child with quills and small reeds," because they "must have Christian blood wherewith Jews of the highest rank besmear themselves for their wedding feasts," and another to the effect that the descendants of the ancient priestly caste (*Kohanim*) bathe their hands in this blood before blessing the congregation.[41] In the seventeenth century we encounter such additions, ostensibly based on older sources, as that the use of Christian blood "maintains peace and unity" among the Jews, and renders them "beloved of God." [42] Still more recently it has been charged that on Purim the rabbis send their congregants a dish prepared with Christian blood; that a slaughtered Christian child is a substitute for the paschal lamb, and is sacrificed as an atonement offering for the sins of the Jews; and that on Passover Jews smear Christian blood on their doorposts to ward off the angel of death.[43] This final charge is dated 1816. All these display the ritual element that had come to the fore toward the end of the Middle Ages, but the Passover story has not succeeded in ousting other semi-ritualistic but essentially superstitious features.

This unsavory catalogue must make it apparent that the suspicion of magic, whether per se or as an adjunct of medicine, was behind the accusation of child murder. The many "confessions" that we have drawn upon are tragic testimony to the plight of Jews forced to admit not what was true but what their persecutors believed and insisted upon hearing; testimony, too, to the effectiveness of a propaganda against which the fervid disclaimers of Jews and the protestations of leading Christians were of no avail. Suspicion of the Jew's motives and activities having once fixed the belief in his blood guilt in the medieval mind, it inspired a hunt for plausible explanations to supplement the original, basic charge of satanism and sorcery from which the whole myth sprang. The Easter association, which was among the first widely advanced (at the instance of a converted Jew, be it noted), was patently artificial and improbable: the entire conception was too glaringly Christian and not at all Jewish, and was therefore hardly tenable for long. It was soon superseded by the Passover ritual story, which we must regard as a conscious, though not necessarily a deliberate, effort to improve upon the untenable Easter motivation. It is not difficult to see how a naïve, theology-ridden people could transfer their own belief and practice to another: if the "blood of Christ" could redeem Christians, why should not the Jews seek to profit from its peculiar virtue, and if that blood played so prominent a part in Christian ritual, why not also in Jewish?—allowing, naturally, for the perverse non-Christian course Jews could be expected to follow? [44] But we cannot see in it an essential part of the blood myth in its early form. Indeed, Apion's story seems to have provided the precedent for the ritual phase of the blood accusation, which was little more at the outset than an incidental and supplementary rationalization. The very persistence and expansion of the purely superstitious explanation, whether in conjunction with or independently of the ritualistic, long after the ritual aspect had become a fixed feature of the blood accusation testifies to the basic and ineluctable relation between the two mythical Jews—the sorcerer and the child murderer.

The records of the early accusations are meaningless unless viewed against the background of medieval superstition and seen as another expression of the Christian conviction that the Jews are the spawn of the devil, committed to destroy Christendom, both by direct murder and by indirect magical means. A modern writer who has made a careful study of Christian magic and witchcraft, and who proves himself as credulous and superstition-ridden as the period he examines, expresses exactly the medieval attitude, which is his as well: Jews were persecuted "not so much for the observance of Hebrew ceremonies, as is often suggested and supposed, but for the practice of the dark and hideous traditions of Hebrew magic. Closely connected with these ancient sorceries are those ritual murders. . . . In many cases the evidence is quite conclusive that the body, and especially the blood of the victim, was used for magical purposes." [45] Montague Summers, the writer of these lines believes this "evidence" implicitly. If a present-day Catholic can so readily acquiesce in the charge that Jews used Christian blood for magical purposes, how all-compelling such "evidence" must have been for his medieval predecessors.

PART THREE

THE JEW AS HERETIC

CHAPTER ELEVEN

CHURCH AND JEW

THIS, then, was the Jew as medieval Christendom saw him—sorcerer, murderer, cannibal, poisoner, blasphemer, the devil's disciple in all truth. But how did such a conception arise? What was its origin? And why did it flourish particularly in the thirteenth and fourteenth centuries? What were the factors that suddenly became operative at that time to make the Jew the black beast of Europe? These are inevitable questions. And we can hardly rest content with a portrayal of the medieval conception of the Jew that evades the responsibility of at least attempting to answer them.

It is a striking consideration, in this regard, that despite the virulent anti-Jewish campaign of the early Church, relations between Jews and Christians were not materially embittered. Indeed, the period between the break-up of the Roman Empire and the Crusades—roughly the sixth to the eleventh centuries—was comparatively favorable for the Jews. Their unhappy experience in Visigothic Spain after its conversion from Arianism to Catholicism and the wave of expulsions during the seventh century were the result of *official* antagonism rather than of any strongly felt popular resentment. In general it may be said that social and economic relations remained good. Some Christians continued for a long time to observe their feasts and festivals on the Jewish dates and together with Jews. The constantly reiterated fulminations of Church authorities against close social and religious intercourse between the two groups ("It comes to such a pass that uneducated Christians say that Jews preach better to them than our priests," complained Agobard [1]), against eating and drinking and living with Jews, testify to their unimpaired and cordial intimacy. Even the clergy had to be forbidden from time to time to be friendly with Jews. Reporting his amicable discussions with Rabbi Simeon Hasid of Treves, Gilbert Crispin, Abbot of Westminster in the eleventh century, says: "He often used to come to me as a friend both for business and to see me . . . and as often as we came together we would soon get talking in a friendly spirit about the Scriptures and our faith." [2] In the tenth and eleventh centuries we hear of Jews receiving gifts from Gentile friends on Jewish holidays, of Jews leaving the keys to their homes with Christian neighbors before departing on a journey. In Champagne, where Jews engaged extensively in viticulture and wine making, they freely employed Gentiles in their vineyards, and the rabbis set aside the ancient ritual prohibition against the use of this wine on the ground that Christians are not idolaters. Christians took service in Jewish homes as nurses and domestics, and Jewish traders dealt in ecclesiastical articles. Business relations were markedly free and close, and there are many instances of commercial partnerships between adherents of the two faiths.

Nor did the sporadic dissemination of anti-Jewish propaganda by clerical preachment disturb these generally amicable relations sufficiently to arouse a sense of insecurity and alienness on the part of the Jew. The Jews of France, for instance, called the French language "our language," and some eminent scholars of this period bore French names, e.g., Judah HaKohen, who was known as Léontin, and Joseph, known as Bonfils. The use of French names was even more marked in England, where Norman French was the vernacular of the Jews no less than of the aristocracy; and a similar process of cultural adaptation prevailed throughout Central and Southern Europe. These are assuredly tokens of a cultural and social affinity which could not have flourished in an atmosphere of unrelieved suspicion and hostility.[3]

It will not do to idealize this situation; the distinction between the earlier and the later medieval periods, so far as the popular attitude toward the Jew is concerned, must not be overly formalized. Even in the earlier period, of course, there were signs pointing toward the later attitude, but they multiplied very slowly at first and gathered momentum only in the twelfth and the succeeding centuries, until the slowly changing picture was wholly transformed by that unmitigated hatred of the Jew which we have come to characterize as medieval. Gone were the tolerance and mutual interest expressed in common religious and social observances; gone, too, was the cordiality of personal association and of business dealings. In their place came suspicion and distrust, mutual fear and loathing, to poison the inescapable contact between Jew and Gentile, thrust together as unwilling neighbors by their common physical and psychical environment.

The change in the position of the Jew was effected by a number of factors, notably by the impairment of his legal status under the evolving feudal system, culminating with the abrogation of the right of Jews to bear arms and the introduction of the concept of "chamber serfdom" (*Kammerknechtschaft*—subjection directly to the emperor) in the thirteenth century; by the economic decline he suffered with the development of European society and the emergence of a favored Christian merchant class; by the social upheavals and the deterioration of his social status consequent upon the First Crusade. But these factors all operated against the backdrop of Church policy, which determined public opinion (and therefore juridical and commercial practice as it affected the Jew[4]) and which must in the end bear the major responsibility for the transformation of the popular attitude toward the Jew.

The Christianization of Europe was a slow process and quite superficial at first. England did not become Christian until the seventh century; the Germanic tribes, Saxony, and Bohemia not until the ninth; Scandinavia and Poland not until the tenth; while Prussia and Hungary held out a century longer. It took time for Christian dogma to sink into the popular consciousness and for the new mythology not merely to supplement the older, as it did at the outset, but actually to supplant it. By the tenth or eleventh century this process was nearing completion. (In the eleventh century the papacy was still faced with the task of subjecting its own clergy to the rule of Christian doctrine, as in the important matter of clerical celibacy, for example.) Europe was assimilating the Catholic version of the Christ legend—and its concomitant, the theological Jew.

Perhaps here lies the explanation of the seeming ineffectuality of Church preachment during the period of its establishment in Northern and Western Europe: the Jew of Christian legend bore so little resemblance to the real Jew whom the West knew. He was entirely the creation of theological thinking; an exotic plant that did not speedily take root in the newly converted lands. The European peasant had to learn—and he learned slowly— that he was expected to equate the theological Jew with the neighbor whose friendship he enjoyed and with whom he worked and dealt.

That strange creature had been invented in the eastern half of the Roman Empire during the early struggle of the Church to establish itself. In the effort to prove its superiority to the Judaism it sought to displace, it resorted to the common trick of disputants—mud slinging. It was not content to brand Judaism as a decadent, superseded faith, or the Jews as the murderers of the son of God and the rejected of God Himself—characterizations that in themselves carried serious implications. The early Church established the Christian attitude toward the Jew by ante-dating "the rejection of the Jews and the emergence of the Church to the beginning of revealed history and by emphasizing the position of Abraham as the father of many nations, of whom only one, and that themselves, was chosen," so that the Jews at long last stood revealed as impostors and frauds, contumacious pretenders to an election that was never rightfully theirs. The campaign of slander piled up so many fabulous accounts of Jewish venality and treachery that it became a commonplace to attack Jews for that selfsame *odium generis humani* with which Christian society itself had so recently been tagged by pagan detractors. The attitude fostered by the Church is epitomized in a fifth-century legend of a town in Minorca which, by a miraculous divine privilege, was immune from the presence of snakes, wolves, foxes, and Jews. Any member of these species who happened to enter the town was eliminated by a heaven-sent thunderbolt.[5]

This Jew whom the early Church displayed before its adherents as the authentic article "is not a human being at all," as Parkes has observed.[6] "He is a 'monster,' a theological abstraction, of superhuman malice and cunning, and more than superhuman blindness. He is rarely charged with human crimes, and little evidence against him is drawn from contemporary behavior, or his action in contemporary events." Commenting upon the envenomed diatribes of the fourth-century preacher, Chrysostom of Antioch, Parkes remarks,[7] "It is evident that Chrysostom's Jew was a theological necessity rather than a living person. If he looked different from the actual Jews living in Antioch it was part of the malice of the Jew, one of the snares of the devil, set to catch the unwary Christian."

Once this point had been firmly driven home, one can hardly blame the populace of early Mediterranean Christendom for failing to discern the distinction between the theological Jew and the actual Jew, or for reacting violently upon the clearly implied suggestion of this delineation. The writings and sermons of the militant leaders of the Church inevitably whipped up public opinion and led to wild attacks upon the Jews, which these same leaders often felt bound in all conscience to deprecate. Pope Gregory the Great, toward the end of the sixth century, was frequently fair to the Jews in practice, yet he did not hesitate to attack them in bitter terms as outcasts whom he regarded with horror and loathing. "It is a curious picture," says Parkes, "to think of Gregory turning from the dictation of one of his more flowery denunciations of their diabolical perversity and detestable characteristics to deal with his correspondence, and writing to a bishop who has only been carrying these denunciations into logical action, to remind him that it is by love and charity alone that we can hope to win them, and that even when they do not wish to be converted they must be treated with justice and allowed the undisturbed use of the rights which the Law allows them." [8] Secular legislation naturally followed the Church's cue: "All the

legislation of the Christian Empire, even when designed to protect their lawful rights, is couched in language of abuse and contempt—language singularly unsuited to impressing upon the
recipients of the legislation the sincerity of the legislators."

Herein lies the paradox of Christian policy toward the Jews.
Bitterly condemned and excoriated, they were yet to be tolerated
on humanitarian grounds, and indeed preserved on theological
grounds, as living testimony to the truth of Christian teaching.
Yet the impulse to punish the hated and to convert by all means
the unregenerate constantly warred against the moral and dogmatic scruples which, at best, animated only a small minority of
the more highly placed and responsible clergy.

The center of Christian influence shifted north and westward,
as did that of Jewry, and new populations began to imbibe the
lesson which the Church had so well instilled in its eastern
reaches. For a while the Jew was a human being, wholly disparate
from the figure thus offered as his true representation. But, as has
been suggested, by the beginning of the second millennium of
the Christian era the teaching of the Church was making itself
felt. The unreal Jew of older times still dominated Christian
thought and, as time went on, so well was the lesson learned that
it became increasingly difficult for the people and their clerical
mentors to keep him separate from his real counterpart. The traditional character ascribed to him was transferred to his contemporary activities and being, and whereas in the past the Jew
of legend was the butt of Christian ridicule and hatred, in the
later period the legend expanded to include the contemporary
Jew and all his works.

The paradox persisted and doomed to failure the occasional
efforts of both the state and the Church, conceived as the secular
and the spiritual organs of Christendom, to protect the Jews.
The Jewry-Law of King Venceslas II for Brünn, promulgated
in the year 1268, clearly expresses the contradiction: "Because
of the crime which once their fathers committed against our
Lord Jesus Christ, the Jews are deprived of the protection of their

natural rights and condemned to eternal misery for their sins. Although they resemble us in human form, we differ from them by our holy Christian faith. Therefore Christian goodness teaches us to cast off our harshness, and protect our faith from them; but we must respect their humanity, and not their unbelief." [9]

The logical inconsistency of this was too apparent to escape any but the dullest minds. From the side of the Church we have the repeated and often strongly advanced defense of the Jews by popes and ecclesiastical councils. "Faith must be kept with the Jews," declared the Council of Bourges in 1236, "and no one may use violence toward them; for the Church protects the Jews, since, as it is written, she desires not the death of a sinner." [10] One would have to seek far indeed for a more humane counsel than that of Innocent IV: "If the Christian religion were to give careful heed and rightly analyze by use of reason, how inhuman it is and how discordant with piety for it to afflict with many kinds of molestations, and to smite with all sorts of grave injuries, the remnant of the Jews, to whom, left as witnesses of His saving passion, and of His victorious death, the benignity of the Saviour promised the favor of salvation, it would not only draw back its hands from harming them, but as a show of piety and for the sake of the reverence of Christ, it would, at least, extend the solace of human kindness to those whom it holds, as it were in tribute." But the essential *non sequitur* of the official attitude vitiated all such appeals to Christian virtue; this very statement was elicited by the complacency, if not complicity, of the Archbishop of Vienne in a series of brutal excesses perpetrated against the Jews of his diocese in 1247.[11]

The *Constitutio pro Judeis*, expressly forbidding violence against the Jews, was endorsed by successive popes ten times from its issuance in 1120 until 1250; in the preamble to his reissue of 1199 Innocent III declared: "Although the Jewish perfidy is in every way worthy of condemnation, nevertheless, because through them the truth of our own faith is proved, they are not to be severely oppressed by the faithful." [12] Even the pope hedges; the contradiction sticks in his throat: they are not to be *severely* oppressed. It was this same Innocent III who sponsored acutely oppressive legislation against the Jews.

The secular authorities also sought to protect the Jews, for their own selfish ends: the Jews were a convenient source of funds. The bishops and ecclesiastical rulers, affected by similar secular, as well as ecclesiastical, interests, usually supported the official policy of nonviolent toleration. But popes, kings, nobility, bishops, all had little influence over the populace, which had at long last swallowed the theological conception of the Jew whole, and minus the accompanying theological sophistry. The greatest direct influence upon the people was exerted by the lesser clergy, both secular and monastic, who were, if anything, in advance of their flock in ignorance, fanatical piety, and superstition. Nor was the clergy particularly responsive to the will of the hierarchy, even in more vital matters of doctrine and practice. The first massacres of Jews were directly inspired by clerical preaching, and the murderous bands were sometimes led by priests. William of Newbury, describing the attack upon the Jews of York in 1190, says: "And there were not lacking among the mob many clergymen, among whom a certain hermit seemed more vehement than the rest. . . . The deadly work was urged on before the others by that hermit from the Premonstratensian canonry mentioned above, who . . . was busily occupied with the besiegers, standing in his white garment and frequently repeating with a loud voice that Christ's enemies ought to be crushed. . . ."[13] The later accusations of ritual murder and profanation of the host found their origin and chief support in many of the local clergy, who also readily accepted and propagated the charge of well poisoning. The repeated denials, on the part of popes and church councils, of the truth of such rumors were without effect so long as the overzealous clergy stood between them and the people.[14]

This, then, was the general background of the medieval conception of and attitude toward the Jew: a Church-fostered contempt and hatred which had sunk so deeply into the public consciousness that not even the highest authorities of Church and state were able to meliorate it.

A contributory factor in fixing this background in the public mind also deserves some comment. The Church employed the term Jew as all-inclusive, embracing the entire people, past, present, and future. The principle of corporate responsibility which prevailed during the Middle Ages—taxes were levied on the corporation as a unit, fines or other punishment for the offense of a member were exacted of the entire community or nationality —lent added force to the traditional generalization. This principle was not confined to the Jews or to the Middle Ages. But it affected the Jews with a particular severity. The superstitious crimes that so strongly influenced the medieval conception were considered to be the actions of "the Jews" and not of this or that Jew, and the entire community suffered the penalty for them. The effect of this principle upon the imaginary picture of the Jew, already clearly delineated, may readily be conceived. Indeed, it came to embrace a vast area of official Jewish activity: blood for magical or ritual purposes was procured and distributed at the instance of an official body; bags of poison were dispatched from one community to others; the profanation of wafers and of images was believed to be a solemn communal act.

The decisive turning point in medieval Christian-Jewish relations came with the First Crusade. It was as though the period of indoctrination had reached its peak and the carefully nurtured and stored-up venom had burst its frail restraints and gushed forth in a torrent that overwhelmed Christian and Jew alike. The Crusade launched in 1063 against the Moors of Spain constituted a "curtain-raiser for the main act of 1096." [15] The armies that poured into the Spanish Marches massacred Jews indiscriminately in the name of the Crusade.

What more comprehensible than that the passion generated against "infidels" should seek an outlet wherever unlucky non-Christians chanced to be found? To the masses the Jew was the worst infidel of all—the Christ killer in person; the official distinction was transparently futile. The First Crusade resulted in widespread massacres throughout Western Europe, usually carried out by the bands of *paupères* inspired by religious fanaticism. It is significant that there is no record of ill-treatment of Jews anywhere in Europe by the great nobles of the official army. Three priests, Peter the Hermit, Volkmar, and Gottschalk, were responsible for arousing the masses against the Jews and leading the marauding bands.

In general the civil and ecclesiastical authorities sought to shield the Jews, but their efforts were futile. Even the bishops were powerless against the incitement of these priests; nor did the threat of excommunication deter the mobs. In a number of instances bishops who had invited Jews within the protecting walls of their castles were forced to deliver them up to gangs led by their own clergy. The temper of the times may be discerned in an incident which occurred at Mainz, where the destruction of the Jewish community followed upon the decision of a pet goose to accompany her mistress on the Crusade. The crowd seized upon this as a divine endorsement of the Crusade and forthwith fell upon and slaughtered the Jews! [16]

No marked break followed immediately upon the Crusade, it is true; both groups sought to resume the relationship that had been so savagely interrupted, and except for sporadic outbreaks contacts remained close and cordial for a while longer. But the effects of this experience upon both Jews and Christians never quite wore off. Like a severely debilitating disease which even when cured leaves its telltale scars upon the body of the patient, the First Crusade struck deeply into the spirit of Jewry, leaving irremediable fear and anxiety, a sense of insecurity and desolation, that corroded its inner life and its relations with the now-dreaded Christian world. As for the Christians, the passions then unloosed were not again confined through many centuries. Though the social and economic aspects of Europe might permanently alter and improve, the fanaticism that had been given free rein remained to plague the peace and security of the continent. Minorities were hounded and decimated, not least among them the Jews. And the ancient hostility, generalized and in a measure abstract, underwent a process of elaboration and particularization that produced a host of newfangled superstitions and accusations, and fastened upon the world a conception of the Jew that has not yet been eradicated.

CHAPTER TWELVE

INFIDEL OR HERETIC?

S O much for the attitude of the Church to the Jew, in general. Now to come down to specific cases—what was the immediate origin of the superstitious accusations that emerged in full force during the century or two after the First Crusade? It is in the prevailing attitude toward heresy that we shall find the answer to this question which, however, involves still another: How did the "infidel" Jews come to be popularly identified as heretics, when canon law and the repeated official pronouncements of popes and councils specifically excluded such an identification?

The Crusades are a clue to the unrest that afflicted Christendom. At the height of its catholic power the Church was not unaware of the rise of forces that threatened to destroy its hard-won unity. Even as the See of St. Peter was demonstrating its supremacy in the dramatic scene at Canossa, secular forces were beginning to assert themselves anew and to question the universal hegemony of the Vicar of Christ. Nor was the temporal authority of the Church alone in issue; its internal discipline was, at best, infirm and limited, and worst of all, unorthodox ideologies were once more raising their insolent heads, as they had done in the first centuries of the Church's history, to challenge the doctrinal basis of Catholic belief. The great need of the time was to rally all Christendom once more around its focal city, to draw secular and ecclesiastical forces into an alliance that would accept and realize the Christian ideal of the Church-state. In 1096 began the series of continent-wide expeditions against the Moslems. It is not inconceivable that, just as wise statesmen have done many times before and since, the leaders of the Church hoped to unite Christendom with this onslaught upon an external enemy, in a cause whose idealistic goal must contravene all mundane interests, trusting that the centrifugal forces already manifest would be weakened or destroyed in the process. Though the Crusades need not have been conceived in this Machiavellian fashion, their true historic purpose was indubitably that of a unifying agency.[1]

That the Crusades did not in the end achieve this purpose, and that the rift within Christendom continued to widen, is evidenced by the establishment of the Inquisition, essentially an instrument of unification through propaganda and repression. Whom the Church could not otherwise persuade to conform it was prepared to coerce by force—or else to exterminate. The Inquisition, too, was in the end ineffectual; the Protestant Reformation completed the dread process that had been eating into the vitals of the Church Catholic, and finally divided Christendom permanently, ensuring the prerogative of doctrinal nonconformity.

The Church was, in principle, a totalitarian power, seeking to exercise unlimited dominion in the temporal and spiritual realms, not always unchallenged, but with its confidence in its divine election to this role unshaken. Like all totalitarian powers, it refused to tolerate difference, independence of thought or action, for these imperiled its own position. During its earliest centuries it fought heresy tooth and nail, giving no quarter until each sect in its turn was vanquished; it taught its adherents to shun unorthodox and unlicensed movements within the Church as the devil himself—and not alone to shun them but to extirpate them with the same fury they should display toward its satanic archopponent. For some centuries the Church was little troubled with heretics. But the eleventh and twelfth centuries witnessed a return of organized dissent, part of a broad social movement implying serious revolt against the Church and against the social and intellectual system it embodied, which constituted a real threat to Catholic unity. The Church promptly renewed and intensified its antiheresy propaganda, which was so effective in certain places that it led, during the late eleventh and early twelfth centuries, to several lynchings of heretics by infuriated mobs who regarded the clergy as too lenient. But heresy was not

Heresy

ANTON EISENHUT

so easily checked; when it assumed proportions too vast and too perilous to permit of its being handled effectively by individual action, the Church bestirred itself to arouse the clergy and the people to the danger and created an official organ with express powers to cope with it—the Inquisition.

The state was also a party to this conflict. The Church held that the interests of the state were subordinate to its own in keeping the faith pure; offense to the Divine Majesty was a far greater crime than offense to a secular ruler, and the latter was in duty bound, since his position derived from the former, to destroy the source of the major offense. Moreover the Church advanced the practical consideration that heretics were criminals against the state because they disturbed the public peace, and therefore the state was required to coöperate in rooting them out. The state showed no reluctance in obliging. The early Church had occasionally visited heresy with death, but it remained for secular rulers of the twelfth century and after to adopt officially the death penalty for heresy. Peter II of Aragon, in 1197, was the first to do so; Frederick II made it optional in 1224 and obligatory in 1231, following Pope Innocent III in justifying it on the ground that heresy was equivalent to treason. "Dismissing" or "releasing" the heretic to the "secular arm" was the fiction adopted by the Church to exculpate it from shedding of blood.

This is not the place to examine the origins of this heretical wave; it is enough for our purposes to note the fact of its emergence. Catharists, Albigensians, Luciferans, Neo-Manicheans, Waldensians, Passagii—the opposition to the Church manifested itself under many heads and conquered extensive areas throughout Western and Central Europe. The weak "Episcopal Inquisition" was inaugurated toward the end of the twelfth century to stamp out dissent; when it failed in its purpose the Church embarked upon a more vigorous program. The Albigensian Crusade, a large-scale military operation, launched at the beginning of the thirteenth century—incited, incidentally, by the Cistercian monk Arnold of Citeaux with the sanction of Innocent III—marked the beginning of the "Monastic Inquisition" and of a virile offensive.

The Jews of Provence were victims of this earliest onslaught along with the Albigensian heretics (for all, it should be noted, that Innocent refused to countenance the preaching of the cross against the Jews of that region[2]), and it was evident from the outset that they would have to bear the full brunt of the continuing holy war. This raises our second question, which demands its answer first: by what sophistry could the Jews be included in the category of heretics? Heresy implies a deviation from a prescribed and accepted course but not refusal to pursue that course *ab initio*. By all the rules of logic the Jew was exempt from the brand, and the Church indeed recognized and proclaimed that technical fact. But popular thinking was free of logical restraints. Nor did the practical policy of the Church adhere too slavishly to its logic. In the Christian world the Jew was inevitably looked upon as a heretic—indeed, *the* heretic.

The rationale of this attitude was established quite early. Despite all the evidence to the contrary some of the most influential leaders of the Church in its earliest period were of the opinion that Judaism was not an independent faith but merely a perverse deviation from the one true faith. (We have already noted that the emergence of Christianity was antedated to the beginning of revealed history.) The tendency to treat the Jews as heretics, who knew the truth and rejected it, is very pronounced in the apocryphal gospels which began to appear about the middle of the second century. While the catalogues of heresies compiled by Christian writers included only divagations from orthodox Judaism in the pre-Christian period, for contemporary times they included all Jews. In one of the versions of *The Assumption of the Virgin* the High Priest is made to exclaim: "Do we not believe in Christ, but what shall we do? The enemy of mankind hath blinded our hearts and shame has covered our faces that we should not confess the mighty works of God. . . ." An anonymous fourth-century writer insisted that "the Jews are to be treated as apostates from Christianity, as men who had known the truth and deliberately rejected it." "The opinions of the fourth century [concerning the relation of Judaism to

Christian heresy] were destined to govern the conduct of the Church for more than a millennium," Parkes observes. "It would have greatly simplified the issue had it been possible to equate the two terms, and there are many signs among the theologians and religious writers of the fourth and subsequent centuries indicating their ambition to do so."[3] If this ambition found no *legal* expression, it was nonetheless realized in prevailing opinion. So pronounced and vicious was the Jewish error that public opinion often held it responsible for the rise of other heresies within the Church—the Nestorians were frequently referred to as "Jews" and the Iconoclastic revolt was directly traced to the influence of Jews—and little difference in treatment was meted out to Jews and heretics per se.[4]

So it was that the later Middle Ages inherited a strong tradition placing Jews in the ranks of heretics and subjecting them to the same pitiless persecution. Berthold of Regensburg proclaimed in his sermons that Jews are heretics and their Talmud is full of such damned heresies that it is a crime to let them live; nor was he the only one to apply the adjective "heretical" to the Talmud.[5] A convert to Christianity, invited to return to Judaism, indignantly refused on the ground that his former faith was a *ketzerie* (heresy), a view he could have acquired only from his new coreligionists; and in Spain the crime of subscribing to the *heregía judáica* was imputed to a number of prominent ecclesiastics.[6] This coupling of mutually exclusive terms is to be encountered all through the later Middle Ages. "Arians, Photinians, Nestorians, Jews, and other heretics and fanatics" were indiscriminately lumped together. Luther, who should have been an expert on the subject, rarely missed an opportunity of damning Jews with heretics in one breath; in fact, he referred to the baptism of Jews as a "return to their natural religion."[7]

Moreover, Jews were generally suspected of inspiring the schismatic sects, and the commonest charge against these heresies was that of "judaizing." This popular version of the nature of heresy reached its peak during the Hussite wars (1419–36), when Jews were attacked from the pulpit throughout Central

Europe as sympathizers and abettors of the militant heretics and suffered widespread persecution on this score. In Vienna, where the theological faculty took official cognizance in its minutes of "the alliance of Jews with Hussites and Waldensians," the rabbinic authorities even forbade all discussion of religious matters between Jews and non-Jews in a vain effort to avoid the consequences of this charge.[8] Everywhere the Church and the people discerned the diabolical hand of the Jews turning simple Christians aside from the true faith. Indeed, if Christendom admitted any distinction at all between the two, it was that "the heretics were wrong on some points, whereas the Jews were wrong on all."[9]

Once again we must emphasize the signal division between the official policy of the Church and the realistic policy of its adherents. For all the Church's insistence upon the identity of Jew with heretic in its popular propaganda, the logicians of the Church still could not leap the hurdle of inconsistency involved. After all, the Jews were not and had never been Christians, and could therefore on no logical premise be accused of deviation from a doctrine they had never espoused. In ecclesiastical documents Judaism is categorized as a "perfidy" rather than as a heresy. Indeed, for all its inherent intolerance of difference, the Church officially recognized the right of the Jewish community to persist and to maintain its institutions in the very midst of Christian society. As Baron[10] describes the rationalization of this anomalous lenity evolved by medieval canon jurists: "Mankind as a whole is but the mystic body of Christ. In this *corpus Christi* are included not only Christians, but also infidels. In it, each corporate group, each *universitas*, has a special function, as of a special organ within a human body. The Jewish community, also a member of this universal body, must be maintained as such a *universitas* apart, with as much separation and segregation . . . as possible." Baron justly concludes, "This formula is the more remarkable, the more uncontested the general theory and practice of intolerance became in the Christian world." Highly creditable the formula undoubtedly was, but unfortunately for the

Jews the jurists were very much in the minority. The "general theory and practice of intolerance" far outdistanced all official formulas, however strenuously the Church sought to preserve its position.

The start of the crusade against heresy and the establishment of the Inquisition obliged the Church to delimit the area of operations in accordance with its juridical distinction between infidels and heretics. The former, who wholly denied Christianity, such as Jews, Moslems and pagans, were excluded from the jurisdiction of the Inquisition; only those who "selected" (which is the original meaning of the Greek αἵρεσις) their beliefs, not accepting the full teachings of the Church, were heretics in the special sense that subjected them to the vigilance of that body.

Jews per se were therefore exempt from the solicitous attention of the inquisitorial organs. Only such Jews as had at one time entered the Christian fold and thereafter relapsed came directly within its jurisdiction. The Spanish Inquisition directed its activities not against the Jews of the peninsula and its possessions but against the Jewish pseudo-Christians, the so-called Marranos or Conversos, who secretly persisted in their former faith—or could be charged with doing so—while outwardly professing Christianity. There are instances, though comparatively rare, of Inquisitors compelling Jews, by threats or by force, to accept baptism and forthwith arraigning them as heretics, apostates to Judaism.[11] But it was not really necessary to resort to such crude methods. Every expulsion and persecution produced a large number of converts, many of whom merely feigned conversion, and these, along with those whose conversion had been effected by strong inducements (often of a pecuniary nature) that did not materialize, frequently seized the first opportunity to "return to their vomit," as the medieval euphemism had it, and became actual heretics.

However, it was not unreasonable to apprehend that such reversions were often influenced by Jews, and the Inquisition felt called upon therefore to regard all Jews with suspicion and to try to intervene in Jewish affairs, ostensibly to prevent such activities. The technical limits of its authority having been defined, the Inquisition was speedily granted, or assumed, additional powers that enabled it to circumvent its basic restriction. In at least one instance of very far-reaching assumption of authority the Jews themselves opened wide the breach through which it clambered. This incident bears retelling if only because it demonstrates the avidity with which the heresy hunters pounced upon any pretext to include the Jews among their legitimate prey.

The writings of the famous philosopher and rationalist Moses Maimonides had aroused a heated controversy in Jewish circles early in the thirteenth century, which led to bitter recriminations between his followers and his opponents. In 1232 the orthodox group in the city of Montpellier issued a ban on the Maimonist works, and then rashly invited the Dominicans, who together with the Franciscan Friars were prosecuting the Inquisition, to proceed against the Jewish heretics in the same fashion as against Christian dissenters. The Preaching Orders acceded with alacrity —one is tempted to surmise, even with enthusiasm—and after a search instituted at the command of the Papal Legate in Montpellier all Maimonist books were confiscated, and in December, 1233, the first public burning of Hebrew books was celebrated.

This event provided sufficient precedent for the Inquisition to repeat it elsewhere and to include all classes of Hebrew literature. A month or so after the Montpellier auto-da-fé an estimated 12,000 volumes of Talmudic and other works were publicly destroyed at Paris, and thus having extended its new domain the Inquisition assumed the right to confiscate and burn Jewish writings as it saw fit. In 1239 Pope Gregory IX, instigated by an apostate Jew, Nicholas Donin, now a Dominican friar, who labeled the Talmud an outrageously anti-Christian work, instructed the kings and prelates of France, England, Castile, Aragon, Navarre, León, and Portugal, and the heads of the two Orders to seize all Jewish books and deliver them to the Friars for investigation. The first public disputation of widespread consequence between Jews and Christians ensued, but the defense offered by the Jews did not avail them and in June, 1244, thousands of

Hebrew books were burned at Paris and at Rome. In 1248, after another vain effort of the Jews to protect their remaining literature, the Talmud was again condemned and Jews were forbidden to own copies. Thereafter, during that and the next century, the Inquisition launched one attack after another upon Jewish literature of all sorts and held Jews accountable for the possession of proscribed books. The secular authorities, influenced by the clergy, joined the attack; when Louis X permitted the Jews to return to France in 1315 after their expulsion by Philip the Fair in 1306, the charter he granted them specified that they were not to own copies of the Talmud.[12]

This was the first campaign in the violent war against the Talmud, which continued unabated into modern times, arousing an intense (and uninformed) hatred of that work as the source of Jewish blindness and obstinacy, a book filled with blasphemous attacks upon Christians and Christianity, with curses against Christendom, with foul immoralities and anti-Christian stratagems, with superstition and magic. The sixteenth century saw another attack on the Talmud in particular and Jewish books in general, with the converted Jew Johann Pfefferkorn, backed by the Dominicans, its spearhead in Germany, and the Inquisition playing the same role in Italy. Thanks to the intervention of the humanists and some ecclesiastics the Pfefferkorn agitation produced nothing more than a heated debate, though it aroused much apprehension among German Jews. But in Italy the attack assumed more than literary proportions. In the 1550's all available copies of the "perversely heretical" Talmud were seized and destroyed in a number of Italian cities, and Pope Julius III was asked by the Roman Inquisition to order similar action throughout Christendom. A Venetian commission proclaimed that "every Hebrew work which rests upon the authority of the Talmud [is] entirely condemned by the holy church as heretical, profane, and prohibited."[13]

Thus the Inquisition steadily extended its authority over the Jews, not scrupling to overstep civil and clerical jurisdictional bounds. In 1288, when thirteen Jews were burned at the stake at Troyes as the result of a blood accusation, after a trial of sorts conducted by a Dominican invested with Inquisitorial powers, Philip IV denied the right of the orders to supersede the secular authorities in matters appertaining to Jews.[14] It is evident from the continual conflict between Inquisition and state over this very matter that the friars acted first and debated afterward. Nor was the curia in general more successful in enforcing the official policy of the Church: in 1448 Pope Nicholas V found it necessary to reprimand his Inquisitors publicly and to forbid them to exercise jurisdiction over Jews except in cases of manifest heresy or anti-Catholic activity.[15] Their zeal could not be curbed even by papal intervention. On a number of occasions Jews were directed to defray part of the expenses of the local Inquisitor's office; failure to comply with such demands rendered them punishable by his agents. The extensive powers which the Inquisition gradually accumulated made them liable for a wide variety of proscribed acts, such as inducing a Christian into heresy, sheltering heretics, circumcising Christians, building new synagogues, blaspheming the sacraments, handling the sacred host, etc.[16] If he was not technically a heretic, the Inquisition still managed in devious ways and in many instances to proceed against the Jew as though he were.

Of considerable moment, too, was the fact that the introduction of the Jew badge coincided with the start of the Inquisition and the war against heresy. This chronological correspondence was not accidental by any means. It became the policy of the Church to expose all its enemies to public notice and execration by means of distinctive signs—Jews, Saracens, sorcerers, priests convicted of irregular practices, heretics. These signs were intended to differ for each group, but they varied from place to place, and were often so nearly alike and so clumsily designed (consisting usually of pieces of colored felt sewn on the outer garments) that they could be distinguished from one another only with difficulty, and often not at all. Of all the proscribed groups Jews and heretics were the most commonly encountered in Western Europe. It would have been the most natural thing in the world for the Christian populace to associate the two as members of the same fraternity, a supposition that is amply borne out by the juxtaposition of heretic and Jew, both clearly badged, in medieval illustrations.[17]

In view, therefore, of the unremitting propaganda attack upon the Jew which to all intents and purposes ranked him with the heretic as an implacable enemy of the Church, and of the assumption of authority over him by the Inquisition, whose function it was to stamp out heresy, it must be expected that so far as the popular attitude was concerned any technical distinction that the Church recognized between Jews and heretics was incidental and of no practical import. If dissent was abominable, as the masses had sedulously been instructed, then the Jew was the abomination of abominations, the root and branch of all dissent; no theological distinctions could obscure his true role from the eyes of the common man. The supreme sin of "judaizing" attributed to every least whisper of dissent ensured that. The Jew was the adversary without peer of Christendom, and *ipso facto* he was to be classed with all who sought the destruction of the Church and of Christian society, whether they attacked from within or without, regardless of the finical dialectic of the theologian, of which the common man was wholly innocent, and which was in any event beyond his understanding.

This notion of the Jews' unbounded hatred for all things and persons Christian possesses a peculiar psychological interest. It is curious, though psychologically comprehensible, that just those periods and those men who have made a religion of Jew hatred have most violently damned the Jews for their own dominating passion, hate. "They are full of hate" is the constant refrain of antisemitic literature, medieval as well as modern. Bernard of Clairvaux, who preached the Second Crusade in which so many Jews met a bloody end, could yet inform his congregation in a sermon: "While we pray for the Jews, they persecute and curse us"! The fable was often repeated from the pulpit and the written page that it is a duty incumbent upon every Jew to instruct his children from the cradle to hate Christendom and all its works. Jews were turned out of their ancestral homes and hounded from town to town on the express pious plea that "they are mockers, scorners, and open enemies of Christendom." "Could they but drown all Christians in one spoon," said Johann Eck in the course of one of the most vicious of all anti-Jewish diatribes, "they would eagerly do it." From this background the heresy association derived a peculiar and terrible pertinence, for it expressed not merely a suspicion of doctrinal and ritual divergence, which was bad enough, but a sense of immanent danger. Out of this background arose the picture of the Jew as an *enemy of the people*, never hesitating to betray his closest friend or the city or nation that sheltered him.[18]

A prime feature of this conception, dignified with the authority of such names as Justin Martyr, Jerome, Origen, Agobard, and incessantly reiterated during the Middle Ages, was the accusation that Jews curse Jesus and all Christians daily in their prayers.[19] On the basis of a misunderstanding, possibly innocent at first, when the newborn faith could not fail to be hypersensitive to every breath of implied criticism, the will to hate concocted a miserable libel. One of the so-called "Eighteen Benedictions," composed toward the end of the first century, referred disparagingly to the *minim*, which the early Christians took to mean themselves, though it was actually directed against sectarians within the Synagogue. In order to avoid arousing Christian displeasure, once the Church reached a position where it could make its displeasure felt, or perhaps under direct pressure, the offensive term was later changed to *malshinim*, "slanderers."[20] But the change of a word had no effect upon Christian tradition, which persisted in ascribing slander and execration of Christ to the Jewish service and in time turned up another passage as proof of the contention. This time it was an uncomplimentary reference in the *Alenu* prayer, which bespeaks the unity of all men in the service of one God, to those who "bow down to vanity and emptiness and pray to a God who saveth not." Christians who knew something of Jewish ritual insisted that this meant Christ and his followers, and clinched the argument by demonstrating that the Hebrew term for "and emptiness" has the same numerical value as that for "Jesus"![21] The issue was not academic, for a curse was universally dreaded as an invitation to the spirits, which they might readily accept, to do their worst. Jewish disclaimer of any such intent was of course unavailing, nor did alteration of the text put an end to the accusation and to the physical attacks it inspired. The passage was often blacked out of prayer books by the Inquisitorial censors and was finally deleted altogether from the *Ashkenazic* (North European) ritual after Frederick I of Prussia in 1703 prohibited its recital and posted officers in the synagogues to see that his order was obeyed.[22]

Out of this legend of hate grew a library of tales about murderous attacks upon individual Christians and upon entire communities. Incredible as it may seem, the inhabitants of more than one city professed to believe themselves imperiled by some grandiose plan of the tiny Jewish community to creep up on them unawares and slaughter every last one of them. In Mainz the blowing of the *shofar* (ram's horn) on New Year morning was for a time suspended because the Christians had once taken this to be the signal for a revolt and had ravaged the Jewish quarters.[23]

Thus when we find that in the popular literature the Jew is regarded not merely as one with Christian schismatics but as the ally of the Moorish and later of the Turkish hosts that for a time threatened to engulf Europe, we must recognize this as virtually inevitable. In fact, so basic was this notion of the Jew's hostility that he was almost as a matter of course said to be implicated in every foray against Christian Europe from without, as well as in armed attacks originating with Christian forces—even attacks that never occurred! There was in all probability a substratum of truth in such charges, for the position of the Jews was rarely so secure that they should not have welcomed a change, of whatever sort. But the practically automatic iteration of these accusations and the inherent impossibility of some of them indicate that we are often dealing here with a traditional story pattern rather than with fact.

Tradition has it that when the Catholic Frankish ruler Clovis laid siege to the Arian Visigothic city of Arles in 508 the Jews of the city conspired to betray it to the invader[24] (an act which, in all charity, one should imagine merited at least a miserly word of approbation from the Catholic chroniclers, who nonetheless roundly condemned it as an instance of Jewish perfidy); that Charlemagne succeeded in taking Narbonne only with the aid of Jewish treachery (the city fell to Pepin in 759);[25] and that the Jews betrayed Bordeaux to the Normans in 848. Barcelona was allegedly handed over by them to the Moors in 852, though actually the city was not attacked in that year. They were also accused of betraying Toulouse to the Moors, and in punishment for this deed a Jew was required annually to receive a blow in the face in a public ceremony; yet the Moors never held this city![26]

The consequences of the dissemination of such stories may well be imagined. The penalty exacted in Toulouse was puerile in contrast to the price usually paid. As a result of King Egica's report to the seventeenth Council of Toledo in 694 that the Jews were in communication with the Moors, inviting them to invade the country, all the Jews of the kingdom were reduced to the status of slaves, their property was confiscated, and their children were torn from them and placed in Christian families. Widespread attacks on Jewish communities resulted from the rumor that the Jews had conspired with the Moors of Spain to destroy the Church of the Holy Sepulchre in Jerusalem in 1010. Actually the church was destroyed by Hakim in 1008. Europe experienced in the year 1010 a series of floods, pestilence, and famine, with an eclipse thrown in, which were interpreted as divine punishment for the destruction of the church, so that one may perhaps regard the intense resentment over the alleged Jewish complicity in the event as wholly natural and justified.[27]

The same fable persisted late into the Middle Ages. It was as convenient an excuse as any for despoliation and murder. During the baronial revolt in England the Jewry of London was pillaged by the followers of Simon de Montfort (1263) on the charge that it was plotting to betray the city to the royalists, "having prepared duplicate keys to open the gates and Greek fire to set the houses in flames." The incursion of the Mongols and Tartars under Genghis Khan in the thirteenth century, which reached to the borders of Germany, was said to have been secretly aided by the German Jews, who were alleged to have undertaken to supply the Mongols with poisoned provisions and instead filled the casks with weapons, and who suffered acutely from the rage of the populace.[28] This type of tale was a commonplace of medieval folklore. It is not unusual to encounter the Jew and the villainous Turk, the most powerful external foe and rival of Christendom in the later period, conniving together against their common enemy. When the Turks moved north against the Empire in the sixteenth century, everywhere the cry arose spontaneously that the Jews were in league with them, serving as spies and in general as what we would call today "fifth columnists." They were expelled from Bohemia (1541) and three times from different parts of Austria (1544, 1572, and 1602) because of such alleged activities. "If the Turks should ever come into this country," wrote a citizen of Prague, "which God forbid, it would be because of the Jews, who showed them the way." The Jewish quarter of Candia (Crete) was ransacked in 1538 on the suspicion that Turkish spies were being harbored there; yet, as it happened, the able-bodied Jews were away that day preparing trenches and earthworks in anticipation of the Turkish invasion. In 1684, when the Christian armies attempting to wrest Buda from the hands of the Turks were beaten off, tradition demanded that the Jews be held responsible for the defeat, and accordingly mobs stormed the ghettos of a number of Italian cities and took vengeance on their inhabitants.[29]

The popular literature of course reflected this prejudice. To cite but two out of many instances: Jakob Ayrer's *Comödie von Nikolaus* includes among its dramatis personae the figure of the Jew Moses whose role it is to reveal the secrets of the Christians to the Turkish Sultan; and Barabas, Marlowe's Jew of Malta, is aided and abetted in his villainies by his Turkish slave Ithamore.

Luther often alluded to these tales of collusion as damning evidence against the Jews. So familiar was the association that in many instances it passed into an identification of the two. Thus a Turk, accused of piercing an image of Mary in an early miracle play, was transformed into a Jew in a later version, while in several dramas, such as the Antichrist play of Besançon and the *Mystère de la Sainte Hostie*, the Jew is represented as venerating Mohammed and swearing by his name; the same touch occurs in Robert Wilson's *Three Ladies of London* (1584), by which time it was a conventional element in the portraiture of the Jew, recurring frequently in medieval drama and poetry.[30]

The coupling of the term heretic with Jew and Turk correctly reflects the prevailing view. Politics may make strange bedfellows, but sectarian polemic makes even stranger ones. With the advent of the Protestant Reformation the reprobate partnership gained new adherents. The Church forthwith branded Luther and his fellow sectarians as heretics and "Jews." When four professors of the Sorbonne were tried at Paris in 1534 on a heresy charge, one of the major allegations of the prosecution was that they had secured Greek and Hebrew books from Germany, where they "had been printed by Jews who are Lutherans"! In 1566 the Spanish ambassador to England reported the current rumors concerning the Turkish invasion of Hungary in these words: "Some Catholics think that the heretics are to blame for the enemy's attacks, and some even lay it to the Jews . . . but I can discover nothing particular . . . ."[31] And Luther, who damned vigorously in all directions, saw nothing incongruous in execrating simultaneously as enemies of Christ heretics, Jews, Turks—and papists! Right and left the sectarian disputants of this contentious century hurled the epithet Jew: reformers of one mind against their opponents of another, Catholic against Protestant and Protestant against Catholic. Yet even Luther, not the least adept, came to see that this would not do. There are gradations in mortal sin. At the last, in his *Von den Juden und ihren Lügen* and *Vom Schem Hamphoras und vom Geschlecht Christi*, he repented his haste: it was not fitting that Jews should be included in one category with Turks and papists; they belong in the unique company of only one: the devil—their master, their father, their God.[32]

The effect of this attitude was to place the Jew beyond the pale of human society. The Church enhanced Christian aversion for him by its policy on intermarriage. Not content with prohibiting it "because there can be no fellowship between a believer and an unbeliever," it condemned such a union, with all the weight of threatened penalty at its command, not excluding excommunication and the death sentence, as adultery.[33]

Nothing better illustrates the intensity of this aversion than the medieval attribution of the crime of *bestialitas* to the Christian who married or cohabited with a Jew. In 1222 a deacon, after standing trial before Archbishop Langton, was burned at Oxford on a charge of bestiality: he had embraced Judaism in order to marry a Jewess. E. P. Evans[34] remarks on the irony "that the Christian lawgivers should have adopted the Jewish code against sexual intercourse with beasts, and then enlarged it so as to include the Jews themselves. The question was gravely discussed by jurists whether cohabitation of a Christian with a Jewess, or vice versa, constitutes sodomy. Damhouder is of the opinion that it does, and Nicholas Boer cites the case of a certain Johannes Alardus, or Jean Alard, who kept a Jewess in his house in Paris and had several children by her: he was convicted of sodomy on account of this relation and burned, together with his paramour, 'since coition with a Jewess is precisely the same as if a man should copulate with a dog.' "

CHAPTER THIRTEEN

THE ATTACK UPON USURY

THE usurer was one of the most thoroughly despised and hated members of the medieval community. At best he was a necessary evil, tolerated by the state because the gentry required his services—and exercised sufficient power to scale down their debts by the method of force and expropriation, as well as of repayment. But to the masses he was a wholly unmitigated evil. In an economy of rudimentary capitalism, when trade was insecure and investments often went into unproductive enterprise such as war or castle-building, the high rates which the usurer had to charge were an intolerable burden upon the peasantry and emerging burgher class in the towns, incapable of turning over their capital rapidly enough to meet such rates or of using as a regular technique the *force majeure* available to kings and nobles.

But credit was essential to the expanding economy that was a major product of the First Crusade, and through a combination of circumstances it became the uneasy lot of many Jews to find their economic energies limited to this field. The extinction of the comparatively large-scale Jewish trade with the Orient after the Crusade left them no other economic function, since agriculture and handicrafts were virtually closed to them—though occasional individuals or small communities continued in these pursuits, particularly in certain specialized crafts. The Church, while prohibiting Christian usury and thus restricting effective competition, acknowledged the right of Jews to engage in it, so that for a very short time they enjoyed an advantageous position as moneylenders. An incidental urge in that direction was contributed by the insecurity of Jewish life. Faced with the perennial threat of expulsion and massacre, it was advantageous for them to keep their possessions in a fluid state, easily negotiable and transportable. But perhaps the most telling circumstance lay in the discovery that Jewish moneylending had its fiscal uses: rulers directly fostered it in order to be able to exact a steady flow of tribute, while the constant extortions to which they were subjected obliged Jews to keep a fund of ready cash on hand.[1]

Here was a vicious circle from which there was no escape for the Jew. Society conspired to make him a usurer—and usury exposed him to the cupidity of feudal overlords and to the embittered hatred of the people. So long as he was a source of profit, the state protected him, in a measure. But when Christian competition began to press him hard, as it did in the thirteenth century when Christians realized that easy profits were to be made from moneylending, and when non-Jewish commercial activity increased to such an extent that the Jew no longer counted for much in the field, his importance as a source of governmental revenue vanished. The state's investment in the protection of the Jew no longer paid and was therefore hastily withdrawn. He was mulcted of what little he still possessed and unceremoniously shown the gate. During the thirteenth and fourteenth centuries a number of major expulsions took place in England and on the Continent (the first, in England, in 1290) wholly for reasons affecting the royal exchequer.

"The traditional conception of usury as a Jewish monopoly is a myth." [2] This is the opinion of the leading authorities on the subject. The church's proscription was ineffectual in deterring Christians from entering this lucrative field. The Church actually concentrated its attack even more against Christian usury than against Jewish. Nor was the Jewish moneylender the sole victim of popular resentment, by any means; the Lombards and Cahorsins, and the priests too, when they engaged in usury, as they often did more or less surreptitiously, felt the wrath of their debtors in no uncertain terms. "It is a well-established fact," as Baron points out, "that the Christian Lombards and Cahorsins frequently suffered expulsion with the Jews; indeed in England and France they usually were expelled before the Jews." [3]

Yet, "though medieval testimony is amusingly unanimous in preferring them [Jewish usurers] to their Christian competitors," their brief concentration in this trade permanently fixed its stigma upon them. In the twelfth century the words Jew and usurer had become almost synonymous; Berthold of Regensburg, one of the most representative preachers of the thirteenth century, used the word usurer invariably to identify the Jew.[4] Thus the Jew was obliged to bear the brunt of popular feeling against the money lender from the outset, and long after his short-lived prominence in the field had been preëmpted by others, he still remained *the* usurer in the mass memory and had to suffer for the sins of his successors. Even when Christian usurers were under attack, the Jews could not escape, for they provided the universal standard for odious comparison: the harshest criticism of Christian usurers (and it was made often) was that they were "worse than Jews." Christian usury itself was blamed on them, since "were there but Jews enough, Christians would not have to become usurers"![5] So powerful was, and for that matter still is, the hold of a myth that never had more than a meager basis in fact.

The popular hatred of usurers received the strongest support from the policy of the Church, for Catholicism regarded usury as a grievous sin, more on dogmatic grounds (based on the biblical prohibition[6]) than on social ones: a sin against the Church of Jesus, and therefore against the human race it sought to save. The inevitable increase of Christian moneylending forced the Church to adopt a firm stand.

Usury became a serious matter, the subject of frequent Church and civil legislation, in the twelfth century, and was promptly classed as a crime with sorcery, incendiarism, homicide, sacrilege, and fornication. Pope Alexander III, in 1179, decreed the excommunication of all manifest usurers, and the state soon followed with enactments confiscating the property of usurers who died unrepentant.

But these were feeble measures to counteract the pressing economic need that the moneylender filled, and the Church vainly piled obloquy upon threat until but one final step remained: in 1257 Alexander IV issued a bull officially identifying usury with heresy and placing it under the tender jurisdiction of the Inquisition; and the Council of Vienna in 1311 confirmed this position. The association was not in itself, however, new. In Toulouse as early as 1209 a group had been founded "to drive out heretics and to combat usurers." Matthew Paris spoke of Milan as "a home of all heretics—Paterines, Luciferians, Publicans, Albigenses, and usurers." Pope and council, therefore, merely added formal assent to a verdict already popularly held. The fact that some of the medieval heretical sects were extensively engaged in usury lent added color to the association and made it all the easier to identify the two.[7]

The taint of heresy thus adhered the more strongly to the Jewish people, whose early prominence in the profession singled them out as prime offenders, and at the same time endowed moneylending with a peculiarly heretical odor, especially since the Church expressly and vehemently forbade Christians to engage in it. The relationship between heresy, usury, and the Jewish people was so fundamental to the medieval mind that Bernard of Clairvaux, in appealing to King Louis VII to prevent Jews from exacting what he considered excessive rates of interest from those who took the Cross on the Second Crusade, could make the astounding comment: "I keep silence on the point that we regret to see Christian usurers judaizing worse than Jews, if indeed it is fit to call them Christians and not rather baptized Jews"! Just as heretics were often labeled "Jews" and "Judaizing" was the commonest charge against them, so Christian moneylenders were as frequently condemned for the same crime.[8]

The Jew-heresy-usury equation became a medieval cliché; not even the terminology suffered change. Christian moneylenders were forced to hear themselves slandered as "those other Jews, called Christians," or simply *Kristen-Juden;* in the fifteenth century Christian usury became known in Germany as the *Judenspiess,* the "Jews' spear."[9] At a time when Jews as such had

been unknown in England for several centuries, Sir Francis
Bacon recommended in his essay "Of Usury" (1612) that all
usurers "should have tawny orange bonnets, because they do
Judaize." [10]

It was the Jew's fate that the Church should begin an inten-
sive campaign against usury at the very time when almost no
other economic function was open to him, and during the very
period marked by the successive superstitious accusations. When
the Inquisition took usurers under its wing it expressly included
Jews in this category, branding them not as common miscreants
but as heretics. ("Jews shall desist from usury, blasphemy, and
magic," ran the characteristic trinitarian formula.[11]) And when
the heresy iron branded usurers with the mark of Satan, it was
believed to grace the Jewish usurer more fittingly than all others.

"In almost every city, town and village of France the ingrained
malice of the devil has firmly established synagogues [*sic*] of
usurers and extortioners, commonly called communes; and these
diabolical institutions, forbidden by ecclesiastical constitutions,
are completely wrecking the ecclesiastical system of jurisdiction," wrote the Council of Paris in 1212,[12] by which time the
field had been virtually preëmpted by Christian sinners. Medieval
pulpiteers castigated moneylenders in the most uncompromising
terms. "Unnatural monsters," they were called. "God created
farmers, priests, and soldiers," thundered the preachers and
popular rhymsters in almost identical terms, whether in France,
Germany or England, "but this fourth category [usurers] was
invented by the devil himself." Above the entrance to the church
of Notre Dame at Dijon there was, in 1240, a sculptured figure of
a usurer between the claws of a demon.[13]

The usurer as Satan's creature could be none other than the
Jew, presented over and over in the plays, the legends, the
poetry, the sermons, which were the sole intellectual food of
the masses, as the immortal type of the usurer. That this was an
inevitable conclusion we may well surmise from the vivid portrait of the Jew already familiar to medieval Christians. And the
extant source material offers ample proof that the relation be-

tween Jewish usury and Satan's anti-Christian venom was not overlooked.

In the Passion plays, Judas, often represented as the tool of the devil, plays the typical role of usurer associated in the medieval mind with the Jew. Egged on by demons, he drives a hard bargain, smirking and whining while he cunningly tries to outwit his confederate in crime. After Caiaphas slowly counts out his thirty *pfennigs* hire for betraying Jesus, Judas raises every possible objection to the coins: "this penny is red, this one is sick, this one is broken, this one has a hole in it, this one is improperly stamped, this is too black, look at the long crack in this one, here's one that's dull," etc.[14] And Judas haggles and complains and can hardly be satisfied, while the audience howls with glee and malice at this clever take-off on the devilish Jewish moneylender of its own acquaintance. "The devil's dogs," Hugo von Trimberg, the fourteenth-century minnesinger, calls the Jews, attacking them particularly for their trade in money. A number of medieval tales present the devil as a partner (and not a silent partner, either) in the Jew's usury.[15]

Artists also did not hesitate to portray the devil as an actual participant in Jewish financial operations. The title page of a sixteenth-century diatribe against Jewish usury and wealth depicts three devil-Jews, complete with horns, tails, claws—and Jew badge. A copperplate, dated about 1600, shows the devil sharing in the profits of Jewish moneylending. A seventeenth-century cartoon directed against coin-clipping, portrays a group of Jews engaged in various financial transactions, with the devil prominently represented among them in full Jewish garb, including the Jew badge, like all the rest. The medieval *Arbogastkirche* at Ruffach, in Alsace, has a statue of the devil in company with a Jew tightly grasping a bulging moneybag.[16]

Luther spoke to a responsive and understanding audience when he lashed out, with rabble-rousing accusations and vituperation, against Jewish usury, and concluded with savage irony: "Should the devil not laugh and dance, when he enjoys among us Christians such a fine Paradise, when he, through the Jews, his saints, devours our substance, and in return fills our mouths and nostrils with his effrontery, and mocks and curses God and man, in the bargain?" [17] Devil, Jew, usurer, and heretic have become one and the same creature.

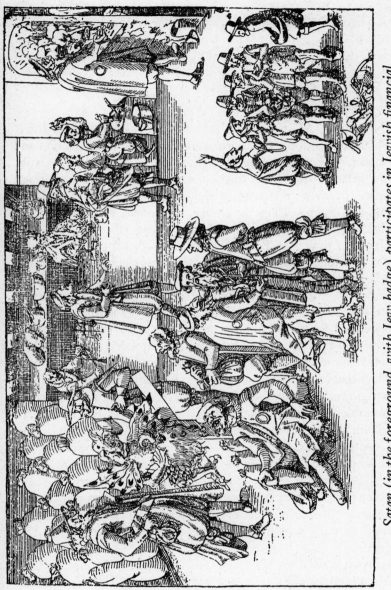

Satan (in the foreground, with Jew badge) participates in Jewish financial transactions

(about 1620)

CHAPTER FOURTEEN

THE CRUSADE AGAINST SORCERY

INDIVIDUAL heresies—and heretics—were short-lived. The Inquisition saw to that. By suasion, persecution, and massacre they were choked off, so that though heresy stubbornly refused to die no one continuing group of individuals remained permanently stigmatized. Only the Jews could not escape the stigma. Even after the Reformation had won the political support that rendered heresy respectable and comparatively safe, they stood out, the sore thumb of "heretical" dissent, in Catholic and Protestant surroundings alike. The popular attitude toward them was already fixed and permanent. But that attitude was not the product of the heretical ascription, simple and unadorned. It was due rather to the sinister connotations evoked by the suspicion of heresy, after centuries of indoctrination had persuaded Europe that the heretic's sin cut far deeper than mere doctrinal or ritual nonconformity.

When magic and heresy were equated, engendering a crusade against sorcery, the syllogism was born which is most directly accountable for the conception of the Jew that has been here described: Jews are "heretics"; heretics are sorcerers; therefore Jews are sorcerers. Here finally we approach the source of the medieval picture of the Jew as supreme sorcerer and agent of the devil. The Church in its campaign against heresy and sorcery created a pattern of occult practice which the masses transferred to the Jew. As we shall see, every one of the major superstitious accusations with which Jewry was plagued derived from this pattern.

Magic was widely accepted and practiced throughout the Christian communities; from the beginning the Church neglected to adopt a consistent policy in dealing with it. The attitude of various Church spokesmen had wavered from a tolerant, half-acquiescent skepticism which took the view that magic was a groundless superstition, with no objective validity, and therefore not to be strongly combated though it should be discountenanced, to bitter condemnation as the manifest work of the devil, altogether real and effective, and meriting the severest measures of repression. More generally, the latter view prevailed; the Church even permitted dissolution of the sacrament of marriage when its consummation was prevented by the arts of the sorcerer, so strong was its faith in his powers. But its efforts at repression were prosecuted with little energy, being limited largely to religious censures, and by the belief that the Christian faith was an effectual countermeasure. William of Auvergne affirmed that magic feats were so seldom performed in Christian lands and in his own time (the thirteenth century) because the power of the evil spirits had been destroyed by Christianity.[1]

Yet his own time witnessed a remarkable efflorescence of the magic arts and an almost universal addiction to them; not alone the common people but the clergy itself, from the lesser priesthood through the highest ranks of the hierarchy, openly subscribed to and practiced them in all their variety. Some churchmen acquired a considerable reputation as magicians, employing their skill even to aid in detecting heretics. Astrology in particular was favored by all ranks, so much so that when sorcery was finally included within the scope of the Inquisition and its manifestions carefully enumerated, astrology was specifically excluded.[2]

A large share of responsibility for this situation must be laid squarely at the door of the Church, though it certainly had not anticipated such an outcome. Its repressive measures were for a long time little better than half-hearted, while its general attitude fostered a belief in the reality of magic and served only to confirm the superstitious masses in their quite comprehensible desire to employ for their benefit whatever forces, natural and supernatural, they believed to be available. How could the denunciation of such practices have had any other effect, when medieval preachers prefaced it with public admissions, amply illustrated, of the ability of witches and sorcerers to perform wonders with the help of the devil and his evil spirits? Even formal theology lent a hand. The belief, for instance, that tempests could be caused by sorcery, which the Church had at first pronounced heretical because it inferred the Manichean dualistic theory which placed the visible world under the control of Satan, was finally accepted as orthodox and permissible; theologians such as Thomas Aquinas proved with much fine-spun dialectic that, "with the permission of God, demons could bring about perturbations of the air."[3]

Moreover, the Church directly stimulated such notions by its own approval of "sacred" magic. It constantly encouraged resort to the "good" spirits, the saints and martyrs of the Church, and to the sacred objects—consecrated water, salt, candles, palms, flowers and herbs, holy fire, relics, etc.—which every diocese proffered for just such purposes. The faithful were taught to carry the Agnus Dei, a figure of a lamb stamped in wax remaining from the paschal candles and consecrated by the Pope; even when Paul II finally forbade their public sale in 1472 he could not resist extolling them as efficacious "in preserving from fire and shipwreck, in averting tempests and lightning and hail, and in assisting women in childbirth."[4]

Even the prominence in medieval belief of the figure of Satan, the source of magic, is in large part attributable to the policy of the Church. "So real and vivid was the Prince of Darkness," to preachers and dramatists, writes Owst, "that their imagination conceived of him in a hundred homely pranks and catastrophes, ceaselessly spying, scheming, fighting against the sons of men with every ingenuity, almost as one of their own flesh and blood, an arch-villain upon the stage of daily life." Equally notable was his role in the stone statuary, the stained glass windows, and especially in the illuminations and miniatures scattered through religious manuscripts. "No corner was too obscure, no capital too scant, to display his claw and his battered nose," says Lenient. There is a fourteenth-century tale of a man so simple—or was he?—that he regularly set a candle before a picture of the devil in his church. From the thirteenth century on, what may be called without exaggeration a veritable cult of the devil obtained in Christian circles.[5] In fact, *disbelief* in the devil and his demons was thereafter unorthodox and actionable. A curious exhibit is the case of that rabbi who was haled before the Inquisition at Rome because he "had denied the existence of demons," and was obliged to recant![6]

It was with its campaign against heresy that the Church firmly fixed the belief in sorcery in the mass psychology. It had argued all along that heresy was the work of the devil, for under no other guidance could honest Christians deviate from the true teaching of the faith—and its contention gained credence from the fact that many of the early heresies embodied Gnostic principles and practices inherited from pre-Christian cultures, and also from the pronounced Manichean dualism evidenced by some of them. Heretics were early castigated as creatures of the devil. But Satan worship constituted sorcery, and thus heresy and sorcery were readily interchangeable concepts. As early as 385 the Spaniard Priscillian and six of his followers were sentenced to death by Emperor Maximus as heretics on a dual charge of Manicheism and magic; the heresy charge was substantiated by the magic charge, on which they were specifically convicted. It is more than probable that in many instances the association was actual, for heretics did practice magic[7]—as did Christians, too—though in the case of Priscillian later opinion tardily reversed the verdict. What is important is that as early as the fourth century heresy and magic were held to be concomitant if not inseparable, a view often expressed thereafter.

The medieval heresies that appeared on the scene in the eleventh and twelfth centuries spread with noteworthy vigor, irritating in the extreme the sensibilities of the Church, which had come to consider its hegemony over the mind and body of the Christian unassailable. On their first appearance the heretics were by no means regarded with animosity by the masses; indeed, they were called *bonhommes,* and Berthold of Regensburg reports the naïve plaint addressed to him after one of his fiery diatribes against the schismatics: "Brother Berthold, how shall we guard ourselves against them, when they are so very similar to good folk?"[8] They were even credited with beneficent supernatural power to avert storms and lightning and other calamities, and the complaint was often heard later that before their extermination lightning had done much less damage.

The Church was faced with the difficult problem of undoing their popularity with the masses. Its attack on heresy simply as a deviation from orthodoxy met at first with no very ardent response (except for isolated instances), especially in those regions most seriously affected by schismatic tendencies. The Church realized that it must have the people with it, that the campaign against heresy must become a popular crusade to be successful, and it turned to a stronger line to arouse the uncertain loyalty of the masses. On the one hand it launched a military campaign against the sects intrenched in Southern France, and established a permanent organ to pursue an unrelenting program of physical extermination; on the other, with a broad sweep of its propaganda brush, it marked all heretics with allegiance to Satan, painted them in dark colors as Satan worshipers, sorcerers, and enemies not only of the Church but of Christian men and women, striving to deliver their souls and bodies to eternal perdition.

No doubt there was some justification for such an attack, for the old Manichean conceptions persisted in a number of these medieval heresies, which worshiped the Power of Evil alongside and on a par with the Power of Good. The Cainites believed the God of the Bible to represent the principle of evil; and there were Luciferan cults which frankly stated the supremacy of Satan. But these notions were by no means predominant in the heresies, most of which were sincere and at the least plausible theosophical or rational critiques of the prevailing theology. Yet the Church indiscriminately branded all with the sins of the few, elaborating even these to fantastic lengths. *Crescit cum magia haeresis et cum haeresi magia,* "heresy grows alongside sorcery, and sorcery alongside heresy," wrote the learned theologian

Thomas Stapleton in 1549, proclaiming as indubitable fact what the Church had been sedulously asserting for some centuries. Indeed, from a condemned superstition the belief in sorcery was elevated by the exigencies of this heresy crusade into a veritable dogma during the thirteenth and fourteenth centuries; in time, refusal to acknowledge its reality could be proclaimed a mark of the "greatest heresy": *Haeresis est maxima, opera maleficarum non credere.*[9]

The new slogan caught on, the people of Europe were off on a wild witch hunt. But so effective and realistic was the propaganda that it produced an unanticipated effect: many of the skeptical were convinced and the ignorant were informed; magic flourished as never before, and witch-cults spread until a large proportion of Europe's population was ultimately caught in them. The more apparent this unwelcome development, the more intense grew the onslaught of the Church, until sorcery and witchcraft had been puffed up into an anti-Church, and for several centuries Europe was embroiled in a fantastic internecine struggle between the embattled forces of Christ and the cohorts of Satan.[10] The excesses to which this struggle led can be visualized from this single incident: the spring of 1586 was delayed in the Rhineland and the cold weather lasted well into June; the Archbishop of Treves burned in the Pfalz a hundred and eighteen women and two men, from whom confessions had been extorted that their incantations had prolonged the winter! It has been reliably estimated that between the years 1450 and 1550 perhaps a hundred thousand witches were put to death, mostly by burning, in Germany alone.[11] Elsewhere, though the figures do not run so high, the attack was pressed with equal vigor.

Prior to the thirteenth century offenses attributed to sorcery were regarded as subject purely to the civil law and were treated as ordinary crimes. With the start of the crusade against heresy a new situation was created, to which secular legislation responded even sooner than ecclesiastical law. The *Treuga Henrici,* an imperial landpeace issued by Henry VII in 1224, contains the earliest reference in secular law to sorcery as equivalent to heresy;

the *Sachsenspiegel,* the oldest German lawbook, compiled at about the same time, curtly includes sorcery with heresy and poisoning as punishable by burning, and the same provision is found in the *Schwabenspiegel,* about a half century later in origin. When the Inquisition was organized it was at first restrained from jurisdiction over offenses of sorcery, but as it perfected its organization it raised this issue and in 1257 Pope Alexander IV, in his bull *Quod super nonnullis,* permitted it to include such offenses when "there is manifest heresy involved." It was in Southern France, scene of the sanguinary attack upon the Albigenses, the first act of the heresy crusade, that heresy and sorcery were first united by the Inquisition, and the first witchcraft trials took place in the last third of the thirteenth century. By 1320 the situation had developed to the point where Pope John XXII could *order* his Inquisitors to hunt down sorcerers and magicians. It is noteworthy that when sorcery thus came under the authority of the Inquisition it came simply as heresy, i.e., not as illicit and harmful acts but as heterodox belief. All heretics were branded as sorcerers and conversely all sorcerers were heretics.[12]

Under this rubric Jews became further accessible to the Inquisition's tender mercies, and so generously were these mercies extended that Philip IV of France, trying to preserve civil authority, was led, as we have seen, to object and instruct his officials in 1302 to withhold all assistance from the Inquisitors in actions against Jews on the score of usury or sorcery unless they were in complete accord with such actions. To cite from among the few recorded cases but a single instance in point, the conviction of Mosse Porpoler of Valencia by the local Inquisitor in 1352 was based on the argument that the magic he had employed to recover some stolen property was abhorrent to the Catholic religion and forbidden by the Jewish as well, and was therefore comprised under the category of *heretical* practice. Such affecting concern for the enforcement of Jewish law was rare indeed. If the full argument is not repeated in other cases of magic involving Jews we may be sure that it was at least by virtue of the

Christian definition of heresy that they entered the purview of the Inquisition. The association between heresy and Satan was made signally manifest to all in the cloak worn by impenitent heretics in Spain, the *sanbenito,* which was decorated with a red cross surrounded by flames, devils, demons, and serpents. A list of practices which the Inquisition published to identify heretics included keeping or invoking familiar demons; pacts tacit or expressed with the devil; insulting or maltreating crucifixes or images of saints; sorcery; divination; etc.[13]

The Inquisition proceeded in its new campaign with vigor and imagination, and it was not long before the people had been completely won over to this conception, which became one of the basic tenets of medieval thought. Sermons, pamphlets, every branch of literature dinned it into their minds until it was a commonplace to encounter all heretics, including Jews, lumped together as creatures of Satan and maleficent sorcerers. Berthold of Regensburg, much of whose preaching was directed against heresy, never tired of reiterating that "Jews, heathen and heretics are lost to the devil." It is interesting that in the Theophilus cycle, for example, the Jewish magician is expressly accused of fostering and practicing heresy in that his prime mission is to dechristianize; in rendering his soul to the devil at the Jew's instance, Theophilus is obliged to renounce Christianity and deny Jesus, to promise never to make the sign of the cross or to worship the image of Jesus. Such demands were characteristic features of the legends about Jewish sorcerers. In the German Antichrist drama the Jews are represented along with other godless heretics as worshipers of the devil. The Protestant heretics were later accorded the same treatment: in the post-Reformation period dramatized disputations between *Catholica* and *Haereticus* were current on the order of the earlier dialogues between *Ecclesia* and *Synagoga,* in which *Haereticus* was aided and spurred on by *Spiritus familiaris,* the devil's advocate.[14]

Witchcraft as such is a notable phenomenon of the end of the medieval period, coming to the fore in the fifteenth century and reaching its height in the sixteenth and seventeenth centuries.

Our picture of medieval witchcraft is derived from none-too-trustworthy sources: the often hysterical descriptions of churchmen and devout Christian laymen, who naturally made witchcraft heresy appear as abominable as they could; the confessions of accused witches, most often half-demented wretches, tortured by their Inquisitors and forced to confess what was expected of them; both sources in turn dressed up for popular consumption by sensational writers who pandered to the taste of their time with excitedly imaginative accounts, lacquered over with pious consternation at the shocking doings they were obliged to relate. One can hardly presume to distinguish here accurate reporting from pure fancy.

No doubt there is a substratum of truth in all these accounts—such witch-cults did exist and their rites must have approximated in some degree the current conception of them. It is, however, difficult to determine to what extent they were remnants of the earlier heretical sects driven under cover by the Inquisition; or a spontaneous outgrowth of the sorcery widely practiced at an earlier time and gradually systematized and organized; or the artificial creation of the Inquisition itself, which by spreading its version of the program of the schismatic groups had actually built up a psychology that brought such cults into being. What seems most probable is that witchcraft was the product of all these elements, the last certainly not the least important, coalescing in a favorable social environment characterized by extreme mass poverty, widespread enervation caused by bad health and conditions of work, epidemic nervous disorders and mass hysteria that overwhelmed from time to time convents and monasteries and entire secular communities. The campaign of the Church, whatever other factors enter into the picture, could not fail to strike deep psychic roots under such circumstances. It is assuredly significant that the rites attributed to these witch-cults were uniformly portrayed as blasphemous burlesques of the Christian ritual and as distinctly and deliberately anti-Christian in character. Witchcraft itself was finally prosecuted as a heresy, and most of the executions of witches were decreed on theological grounds.

Though the earliest detailed accounts of witchcraft date from the first half of the thirteenth century, the features which came to stigmatize it are much older and were long familiar to Christians as distinctive practices of the heretical sects. This fact is of the utmost importance, for it has not generally been recognized that the witchcraft pattern was first fashioned as a weapon in the attack upon schismatic groups. With the development of heresy there grew up "tales of secret conventicles . . . in which the sectarians worshiped the devil in the form of a cat or other beast, and celebrated their impious and impure rites. Stories such as this are told of the Cathari punished at Orléans in 1017, and of their successors in later times. . . . How the investigators came to look for such assemblages as a matter of course, and led the accused to embellish them until they assumed nearly the development of the subsequent witches' Sabbat, is seen in the confessions of Conrad of Marburg's Luciferans, and in some of those of the Templars." Guibert de Nogent, renowned as "the most enlightened and the most impartial man of his time," described in the eleventh century a heretical sect which celebrated its rites with a wild sexual orgy, and then sacrificed an infant by burning and "made of its remains a sort of bread, of which each ate by way of communion." Here we have the express attribution to heretical groups of practices which were later ascribed to the witch-cults. The sacrilegious exercise, first introduced by the clergy of the eleventh and twelfth centuries into their antiheretical propaganda, became the prototype of the later Black Mass.[15]

By the thirteenth century, when the heresy crusade was unloosed, the essential details of the picture were already fixed. The prevailing notion of heretical practice is excellently illustrated in a bull issued by Gregory IX in 1233, instructing the Archbishop of Mainz and Conrad of Marburg to preach a crusade against the heretical sects in Germany: "When a novice is admitted and first enters the school of these reprobates a sort of frog, or as many call it, a toad, appears before him. Some of them kiss it disgracefully on the posterior, others on its mouth, sucking the creature's tongue and spit into their mouths. . . . They sit down to their meal, and when that is over, a statue, which they keep in these schools, strides in, a black tomcat, with its back turned toward them and its tail bent over its back. First the novice kisses this cat on its rear, then the master, and then the others in order. . . . After these ceremonies the lights are extinguished, and they proceed to the most abominable fornication with no regard for shame or relationship. When it happens that more men than women are present, men satisfy their shameful lust together. . . ." [16] This, it must be understood, is a representative picture of *heresy*, graced with the *imprimatur* of the highest authority in Christendom.

The very first victims of the heresy crusade, the Waldensians and Albigensians, were widely attacked in contemporary sermons and literature for just such practices. Indeed, *vaulderie, vauderie*, derived from the Waldensian cult, became the name of the witches' Sabbat, as later *vaudoisie* identified witchcraft in general. The charge of worshiping an animal, in particular a cat or a goat, as the embodiment or representative of Satan, so characteristic of the later accusations against the witch-cults, appears in many early denunciations of heretical sects and is so closely associated with these that folk etymology in Germany traced the word *Ketzer* (heretic) to *Kater* (tomcat); *ketzerie* in Middle High German actually meant "sorcery" as well as "heresy." [17]

CHAPTER FIFTEEN

HERETIC—SORCERER—JEW

WE are not here interested primarily in the history of witchcraft, or in the history of the conflict between the medieval heresies and the Church. If we have had to devote so much attention to these subjects, it was solely with the intention of demonstrating that the Jews were widely regarded as on a par with heretics, if not as heretics themselves, and that the medieval accusations of abominable practices of an anti-Christian and magical nature, such as host desecration, the consumption or other use of Christian blood and flesh, poisoning, etc., were directed against heretics even before they were transferred to the Jews. The ancient antagonism lent itself perfectly to the elaboration of this conception of the Jew which utilized the old charges as a basis upon which to impose the more comprehensive characterization embodied in the concept "heretic" that prevailed in the medieval mind. It is of no point that the Church did not directly charge the Jew, *qua* heretic, with such practices. What matters is that the common people and their clerical mentors made the association,[1] and quite consistently attacked the Jew for activities they believed he *must* pursue in consonance with the generally accepted pattern of heretical-magical practice. If we now bring together the details of this Procrustean pattern we shall see how faithfully the Christian world followed it in its fantastic denunciation of the "demonic" Jew.

It is hardly necessary at this point to do more than recall in passing the attribution of Satan worship to the heretics, to sorcerers, and to witches, which we noticed as the dominant feature of the prevailing conception of the Jew. The fact that Jews had long since been stigmatized in Christian tradition as adherents of Satan made it all the easier to identify them with the typical

heretic as the later Middle Ages conceived him. Indeed, this identification strongly emphasized the satanic element in the popular
notion of the Jew. Heretics and sorcerers were looked upon, all
of them, as tools of the devil and, as we have observed, were
directly accused of doing him homage, while the witch-cults
were notoriously distinguished for their debased and revolting
worship of the devil. All witches were believed to be accompanied and directed by demons or familiar spirits. It is instructive to
compare the graphic representations of the sorcerer and the witch
in medieval art,[2] which consistently emphasize their demonic
characteristics—horns, tails, claws, cloven hoof, and the attendant
demons or devils—with the pictures of the Jew described in the
first part of this book; the latter are at once seen to be nothing but
slavish reproductions of the former.

When the Jew is represented as riding or esteeming highly or
even revering the goat, as he so often is in the Middle Ages, we
must recognize another transference of a distinctive feature of the
heresy-sorcery-witchcraft picture. The devil appeared to his devotees in the shape of an animal; the tomcat of the early heresy
charges became a goat in the later accounts of witchcraft, and
there are numberless tales and pictures of goats receiving the
adulation of witches and sorcerers or serving them as their favorite mount. As is to be expected, the same habits were ascribed to
the Jewish people as a whole, and to complete the transference
cycle, Jews are occasionally specifically represented as sorcerers
and witches, clearly identified by both Jew badge and the accou-
terments of their trade, astride the animal embodiment of their
satanic master.[3]

Nor need we devote much more time to the general charge of
sorcery, which was directly associated with the worship of Satan,
and which was leveled indiscriminately against heretics, and became the prime pursuit of the witches. The catalogue of specific
magical activities charged against the Jews is only a faint copy of
the long list of such crimes attributed to these others. The paucity
of accusations against individuals is really amazing, in view of the
universal conviction that Jews were adepts in this field; one can

Sorcerers paying homage to the devil

Guaccius, *Compendium maleficarum* (Milan, 1626)

A witch's departure for the Sabbat

HANS BALDUNG (1514)

wish for no more conclusive evidence that the conviction was wholly unwarranted. Yet, though the number and variety of the accusations we have recorded fall far short of those chalked up against Christian members of the brotherhood, the reputation of the Jews as sorcerers did not suffer in the least. Rumor saw to it that the general character of the magician should adhere to the Jew even when his specific activity did not warrant such a reputation. Not even the power of transforming themselves into animals, a skill supposedly typical of witchcraft, was lacking in the Jewish repertoire, according to general belief. The theme recurs in a number of medieval legends, and a sixteenth-century mystery play, *La Vie de Saint Martin,* offers in a half-mocking vein an account of a band of Jews celebrating their Sabbath while disguised as bears and wolves, just as the witches were believed to appear during their Sabbat rites. Even the Sabbat itself, with its weird and obscene ceremonial, was traced back to the Talmud by some medieval authorities on witchcraft,[4] while the congregation of witches for the Sabbat rites was commonly designated a "synagogue."

If Jews were accused of desecrating sacred images, abusing the host, and in general burlesquing and blaspheming the ritual and sacraments of the Church, this too was a reflex of the heresy-sorcery crusade. We need not dispute the presumptive guilt of occasional Jewish individuals; but medieval opinion held that the entire people was committed to an official and organized campaign of such reprehensible acts.

Magicians were known to be addicted to the use of consecrated objects in their sorcery: the host was one of the common ingredients of their philters and potions; consecrated oil and water, crucifixes and other such ritual appurtenances were regarded as possessing high magical potency; they favored biblical texts and passages from the liturgy in their conjurations and amulets, mimicked the ceremonial of the Church, and had images baptized to make their charms more potent. Such usages are a common feature of magical practice. The magician is never loath to appropriate for his own purposes purely religious objects and beliefs.

Or perhaps this should be put the other way around: certain religious elements acquire in time an aura of sanctity and power which clothes them, in the eyes of superstitious people, with magical properties, and they thus offer themselves spontaneously to the sorcerer. In practice, the process involves not so much a deliberate act of appropriation on the part of the magician, who is himself a member of the religious group, as it does a utilization of the tools that lie ready at hand. The superstitious belief must exist in the mind of the people before it can be turned to magical use. Christian belief ascribed mystical and supernatural virtues to these objects; why should not the magicians too have prized them highly?

With the attack upon heresy another, far more vicious, motive was disclosed behind these alleged deeds—a deliberate anti-Christian intent. Justifiably or not, heretics had long since been accused of misusing and desecrating consecrated objects—*vide* the Arians, the gnostic sects, Leo the Isaurian and his Iconoclastic followers, the Albigensians, etc. During the Middle Ages this accusation became a regular concomitant of the heresy charge. When the Dominican, Bernard Gui, at the beginning of the fourteenth century, prepared a manual for the guidance of his Inquisitorial colleagues, he took pains to note that a crucial question for the heretic to answer was whether he had stolen a host or consecrated oil from a church. The crime is quite specifically identified in a local ordinance adopted at this time by the town council of Brünn: "Whoever steals God's body is to be burned as a heretic." [5]

As a matter of fact, the heightened emphasis upon host desecration which followed immediately upon the acceptance of the dogma of transubstantiation by the Fourth Lateran Council was directed against heretics, whereas the Jews were not seriously burdened by the charge until the end of the century when it came to be leveled against them too almost as a matter of course. As early as 1233 Gregory IX asserted in the course of his description of the German schismatics whose suppression he demanded: "They also receive each year at Easter the body of the Lord from the hand of the priest, carry it home in their mouths, and throw it into the garbage to the dishonor of the Savior." A significant regulation issued about 1237 by Alexander of Stavenby, Bishop of Coventry, for the government of his diocese, declares that "there are certain persons who, on account of their disdain of Christ, as for example skeptics or others who on account of their contempt, descend into the profound abyss, or others, as for example, wicked Christians and Jews, who on account of their practice of magic, are accustomed to try with outrageous daring various shameful acts against the eucharist and the holy oil." Indeed, heretics who had to answer to the charge of sorcery too, as was very often the case, were obliged to take an oath, on both counts, that they had not committed this crime. The association of "skeptics" and of "wicked" Christians with Jews in the theft of these sacramental objects for magical or other "shameful" misuse is a not infrequent subject of ecclesiastical and secular reproof all through the later years of the Middle Ages.[6]

The spread of the heresies resulted in the alleged elaboration of a regular ritual of such acts of desecration, which in time became a distinctive feature of the witch-cults. At the trial of Lady Alice Kyteler in 1324, the earliest witch trial in the British Isles, it was deposed that "in rifeling the closet of the ladie, they found a Wafer of sacramentall bread, hauing the diuels name stamped thereon in stead of Jesus Christ." Witches were popularly believed to have taken an oath "to trample underfoot and to spit upon all holy images, the Cross and Relics of the Saints; never to use the Sacraments or Sacramentals unless with some magical end in view," and at the Black Mass of the witches' Sabbat a blasphemous burlesque of the mass was enacted, during which the host was variously desecrated by cutting or stabbing, burning, throwing it to the ground, treading upon it, and so on. The famous ointment that gave witches the power to fly was supposedly made of a consecrated wafer, personally secured by the witch at communion, which was fed to a toad that was subsequently burned and its ashes mixed with the blood of a child, unbaptized if possible, and kneaded into a paste.[7]

The dependence of the anti-Jewish charges upon the witchcraft pattern is graphically illustrated in the trial of the Cistercian abbot of Cercanceaux (Department of Sens), in 1323. The abbot, along with other monks and lay persons, was accused of burying a tomcat in a box, with some consecrated wafers for food, intending to flay the cat after nine days and to cut up the skin into strips, for use as powerful magic to secure success in lawsuits, to disclose the whereabouts of lost or stolen articles, and to summon the devil to his service. The defendants were all convicted, but only the laymen were burned—the clerics escaped with life imprisonment.[8] This kind of magic—feeding the body of Christ to the devil—was widely renowned, and evidently highly regarded. When some sixty years later a woman was caught trying her hand at it, as in the parallel incident noted above (p. 115) what simpler way out could there be than to put the blame on a Jew?

Sacrilegious usages were laid at the door of the Jewish sorcerer, as well as of the heretic, at the moment when the medieval heresies made their first open bid for popular support, early in the eleventh century. In his memoirs Guibert de Nogent, who was distinguished for his vehement attacks upon heresy and upon the Jews as its source, tells of a heretical monk who became friendly with a Jewish physician and induced him to reveal the secrets of his sorcery. The Jew conjured up his master, the devil, and when the monk expressed a desire to be initiated into his doctrine Satan told him he would first have to renounce the Christian faith and offer him a sacrifice. And what might that sacrifice be? the monk innocently inquired. "You will make a libation of your sperm," came the reply, "and when you have spilled it before me, you will taste it first as the celebrant should." [9] To one who is familiar with the later accounts of the witches' and sorcerers' ritual the early appearance of the sperm libation and the act of communion with sperm in this context must provide a particularly revealing insight into the development of witchcraft out of purported heretical practice.

Heretics and sorcerers were held guilty of innumerable crimes of poisoning during this period; in fact, it would almost seem that such an accusation was an essential preliminary to the ascription of heretical views, so often did the one lead to the other.[10] The concoction of poisons was a particular skill of magicians. Since heretics were privy to the satanic secrets of sorcery they, too, often had to answer to the charge of poisoning. The witch-cults were believed to have developed this department of magic to a fine art, and many were the hapless wretches burned or torn apart for their reputed addiction to it. It was therefore highly plausible to the medieval mind that the "heretical" Jewish people as a body should conspire to poison all Europe; "once a causal relation had been established between Jews and sorcerers, they [the Jews] were inevitably held accountable for the outbreak of contagious diseases and epidemics, such as the Black Death." [11]

The notion that sorcerers and witches—and therefore heretics, too—required human flesh and blood in their conjurations and rites must be held largely responsible for the belief that Jews also engaged in such practices. According to report, infants, preferably not yet baptized, were sacrificed to Satan. The witches consumed human flesh at their Sabbat feasts—as one writer described the practice in England: "The meate they ordinarily eate is the flesh of young children, which they cooke and make ready in the Synagogue." Human fat was often used in the ointment with which sorcerers and witches smeared themselves before they took to the air. Their love potions required human ingredients. Madame de Montespan was accused of having caused the murder of no less than 1,500 infants in order to ensure the permanence of Louis XIV's affection for her; a vast number of persons, including a crowd of ecclesiastics, were implicated in this case, and as many as 246 men and women of all ranks of society were brought to trial, of whom 36 were sent to the scaffold and 147 were imprisoned.

The utilization of human blood by sorcerers and witches was one of the most widely noted features of their practice, as a host of recorded cases reveals. Besides using it to make poisons, medicines, and love philters, they required it in their blasphemous Sabbat rites to offer as a libation to the devil; to baptize witches at their initiation; to feed to the animals who served as their "familiars"; to write the covenant with the devil; to drink during the mock communion; to mix with foods served at the Sabbat feast or to drink outright as a beverage. In one of the most scandalous cases of this sort during the Middle Ages the Marshal Gilles de Rais, associate of Joan of Arc, was accused in 1440 of having murdered several hundred children in order to procure their blood for such purposes.[12]

Still more evidence of the similarity between the "demonic" Jew and the heretic-sorcerer might be offered; the parallel extends even beyond their purported activities. But some decades ago J. Tuchmann[13] assembled a composite portrait of those attacked by the Church as heretics, sorcerers, and witches, which makes it unnecessary to go into further detail. A bare summary of his study will suffice to demonstrate that in virtually every respect the "demonic" Jew whom we have here described was hardly distinguishable in the medieval mind from these typical enemies of Christendom: They are creatures of the devil, with whom they conclude secret pacts and whom they worship with obscene rites; they offer sacrifices to demons; they conduct secret meetings where they plot foul deeds against Christian society and practice a blasphemous ceremonial; they mock and despise the Christian faith and profane its sacred objects; they stink; their eyes are permanently fixed earthward; they often wear a goat's beard, and at their conventicles disguise themselves with goats' head masks; their heads are adorned with horns, and their wives trail tails behind them; they suffer from secret ailments and deformities; they are cruel and rapacious; they buy or kidnap children and slaughter them in homage to Satan; they consume human flesh and blood; they believe that the sacrifice of an innocent life will prolong their own lives.

Though lacking a single allusion to the Jews this study is as descriptive of the medieval conception of the Jew as of the heretic and sorcerer and witch it actually delineates. One can hardly escape the conclusion that the "demonic" Jew was the product of a transference *in toto* of a prevailing corpus of belief concerning one hated and hunted class in European society to another whose conspicuous independence placed it in a similar category.

The thirteenth century saw the formal beginning of the crusade against heresy and sorcery and the official equation of the two by the spokesmen of the Church, as well as an intensified belief in and addiction to the practices of magic on the part of clergy and laity alike. This same century was distinguished also by a remarkable elaboration of the concept of the Jew as the devil's own sorcerer, by the invention of the host-desecration fable and revival of the myth of image mutilation, and by the emergence of the blood accusation in its medieval form. The chronological correspondence is more than mere coincidence. And when we find this concept subsequently broadened and strengthened, and still further particularized by the poison charges of the fourteenth and fifteenth centuries and by the ascription of specific demonic attributes and functions to the Jew, we cannot fail to discern the influence behind this development in the propaganda and activity of the Inquisition, the growth of the witch-cults, and the universal intensification of superstition.

The mythical Jew, outlined by early Christian theology and ultimately puffed out to impossible proportions, supplanted the real Jew in the medieval mind, until that real Jew to all intents and purposes ceased to exist. The only Jew whom the medieval Christian recognized was a figment of the imagination.

EPILOGUE

STILL THE DEVIL'S OWN

THAT this conception of the Jew permeated every layer of Christian society hardly requires demonstration. There were notable individual exceptions, of course, yet whatever more tolerant attitudes were expressed differed only in degree and barely at all in kind from the one that prevailed generally. Christian civilization was too thoroughly coördinated for it to be otherwise. Even revolutionary modification of the structure and form of that civilization left this attitude unaffected. In time the grip of the Church was loosened and "heresy" came into its own—not only the heresy of denominational independence but equally that of the free intellect and of independent scientific research. The Reformation produced a marked change in the superficial culture pattern of a large part of the West; yet under the surface the Middle Ages still dominated—and dominates—the approach of the masses toward the "Jewish question," which remains as the Middle Ages conceived it: essentially the problem of the good fight against the forces of Satan.

Indeed, the Reformation itself provided still further authoritative channels through which this conception might be propagated. Whatever else in Christendom might change, the Jew remained *in statu quo*. Martin Luther was as intolerant of heresy, though he preferred to call it blasphemy, as his Catholic opponents had ever been. For years he contained himself in the fond hope that the Jews might be won over to his Church. But when he was finally forced to admit that the hope was vain he poured forth his bitterest recriminations upon them. Their iniquity was too great: they were still the arch heretics. Luther, who dared defy the old order, can certainly not be suspected of mere blind plagiarism when he reiterates again and again his complete adherence to the old view of the Jew. His utter sincerity and earnestness are only too evident in his impassioned utterances, that sound as though they had been torn from him almost against his will.[1]

The Gospel is preached in their land to heathen, he wrote, their state destroyed by the Romans. Ever since they wander the earth, driven here and there, with no land, no state, no village, no armed force they can call their own, as has befallen no other people under the sun, always unwelcome guests and beggars. What they, the renowned usurers, extort is in turn wrenched from their grasp when they are robbed or exiled. They are regarded as no better than dogs; whoever harms them or plays a trick on them believes that he has thereby done a good deed. No Jew, since the time of the Apostles, has won esteem in Christendom and before God. Yet their unbelief is still the same as their ancestors'; even the plain sense of Scripture does not convince them. Reason may be won over. Human blindness can be overcome. But Satan is at the right hand of the Jews, and does not permit them to understand.[2]

In a sermon preached September 25, 1539, he recounted several anecdotes justifying the conclusion that even individual Jews experience no permanent change through baptism. One told of a converted Jew in Cologne, who, because of his apparent piety and Christian devotion, was eventually appointed dean of the cathedral; yet after his death when his will was opened it was found that he had ordered the erection of the figures of a cat and a mouse on his grave, to indicate that a Jew can as little become a Christian as the two animals can live together on friendly terms. The same thought is expressed in the Freising cathedral, where there is a picture of the *Judensau* with the inscription: "As surely as the mouse never eats the cat, so surely can the Jew never a true Christian become." It is not required, Luther concluded, nor indeed is it possible to convert the devil and his creatures. The proverb "as lost as a Jewish soul" is altogether justified.[3]

But if reason cannot prevail, there is another more effective method. In his *Von den Juden und ihren Lügen,* one of his last works, he proclaimed it vigorously and forthrightly. No sentimental pity must be permitted to intervene in dealing with the

Jewish problem. Those compassionate saints whose misguided benevolence enabled the Jews to murder and to blaspheme sinned against God, for as Christ is His son and the New Testament His book, so has He through the course of world history rejected the Jews together with their father, the hellish devil. Therefore Christians must undertake energetically, in all earnestness, and not in a spirit of levity, to burn their synagogues, to seize their books, to prohibit their religious exercises and their blasphemies; yes, to settle the matter once for all, the Jews must be driven out of Christian society altogether. An end to this curse upon men![4]

Such was Luther's conclusion. The world moved on, but the Jew must not accompany it. With Luther's blessing now joined to that of the Catholic Church, the old notion of the Jew retained its ancient lustiness into the new times. Luther's fulminations need not be considered a determining influence in the persistence of this conception. Yet we cannot fail to see in them an illustration of how firmly rooted it was in Western culture and a token of its unabated vitality even under the new dispensation. Protestant reform made no difference so far as the Jew was concerned; its attitude toward him remained fixed in medieval tradition. The era of rationalism and liberalism made no difference—it passed the masses by unnoticed. Not until medieval habits of thought—and the social conditions in which they flourish—have been uprooted will there be a difference.

The Christian religion is in disfavor today among certain leading antisemitic circles whose consuming aim it is to destroy all Christian values; among others hatred of the Jew is preached in the name of a hypocritical and false Christianity. Whatever their attitude toward the teaching and the church of Jesus, this one offshoot of medieval Christian fanaticism, antisemitism, makes them kin. The magic of words has transmuted a pernicious medieval superstition into an even more debasing and corrosive modern superstition. Antisemitism today is "scientific"; it would disdain to include in the contemporaneous lexicon of Jewish crime such outmoded items as satanism and sorcery (though these notions, in all their literalness, have by no means disappeared). To the mod-

ern antisemite, of whatever persuasion, the Jew has become the
international communist or the international banker, or better,
both. But his aim still is to destroy Christendom, to conquer the
world and enslave it to his own—and the word is inescapable—
devilish ends.

Still the "demonic" Jew. . . .

NOTES

Sources are cited by author's name;
full titles are listed in the Bibliography.

CHAPTER I. "DEVIL INCARNAL"

1. Cf., e.g., Michelson, pp. 96 f. There had been no Jewish community in England for more than two and a half centuries when Sir Thomas North wrote in his *Diall of Princes* (1568): "Let him take heed also, that he do not call his servants drunkards, thieves, villains, Jews, nor other such names of reproach" (Modder, p. 19).
2. Kynass (p. 7), after a survey of German folk and nursery tales and rhymes, points out that "es gibt keine Lieder die dem Juden freundlich gegenüberstehen." Cf. also M. Bulard, *Le Scorpion* (Paris, 1935); Michelson, p. 70.
3. Cf. Strumpf, p. 18 and p. 39, n. 18; Frankl, pp. 10, 89 ff.; Carrington, p. 8.
4. Strumpf, p. 37, n. 6, quotes the following lines from a French miracle play:
   > . . . chacun homme doit avoir
   > Autant de bien l'un comme l'autre
   > Et nous n'avons riens qui soit nostre.
   > Les grans seigneurs ont tous les biens
   > Et le povre peuple n'a riens
   > Fors que peine et adversité. . . .
5. Browe, *Die eucharistischen Wunder*, p. 1. See also Crane, pp. xix ff., liii ff., and Owst, *Literature and Pulpit*, on the use of *exempla* in medieval preaching.
6. Heise, p. 213.
7. *The Middle Ages* (New York, 1928), p. 25.
8. Justin Martyr expressed the view of the Church and of all good Christians when he said to Trypho: "Your Scriptures, or rather not yours but ours, for you, though you read them, do not catch the spirit that is in them." Cf. Parkes, I, 97, 251 f., 392; also Williams, pp. 33 f., 225, 402.
9. Cf. C. D. Ginsburg, Introduction to Elias Levita's *Massoreth haMassoreth*, pp. 45 f., 47.
10. See, e.g., *Werke* (Weimar, 1920), LIII, 478. Tovey (p. 136) was almost charitable when he wrote: "The Jews are, certainly, bad interpreters of Scripture, and particularly so, with regard to prophecies."
11. M. Paris, *Chron. maj.*, III, 161 ff., V, 340 f.
12. Cf. *JE*, XII, 462 f.; *EJ*, I, 1147 ff.; L. Neubaur, *Die Sage vom ewigen Juden* (Leipzig, 1893).
13. See, e.g., the view of Raymund Martin expressed in his *Pugio Fidei* (1278) —Graetz, *Geschichte*, VII, 150.
14. "The Medieval Conception of the Jew," *Essays and Studies in Memory of Linda R. Miller* (New York, 1938), pp. 171-190; Strumpf, p. 37, n. 5, also

calls attention to the "naive Voraussetzung des Mittelalters . . . die in den Mystères immer und immer wiederkehrt, dass nämlich die Juden von der Wahrheit und Richtigkeit der kirchlichen Anschauung durchdrungen seien, dass sie an die katholischen Dogmen glauben, die hl. Schrift in kirchlichem Sinne interpretierten." Like Roth he accepts the explanation: "Ihre Weigerung zum Christentum überzutreten, sei nur aus ihrem Starrsinn und ihrer Bosheit zu erklären." Cf. also *idem,* pp. 34, 39; Michelson, p. 77.

15. J. H. Greenstone, *JQR,* XXX (1939), 206. How deeply this attitude is inherent in Christian thought was recently illustrated to me when I listened to a prominent liberal Protestant theologian inform a university audience that the man-god Jesus Christ is a "psychological necessity" and that the Jews, in rejecting Jesus, have been "lost" these two thousand years. Beings who do not experience a universal "psychological necessity" must be something other, if not less, than human.

16. Williams, p. 387.

17. Trachtenberg, p. 35, where the subject is treated. A thorough study of the Christian attitude is to be found in Gustav Roskoff's *Geschichte des Teufels* (Leipzig, 1869). 2 vols.

18. "Then was Jesus led up of the Spirit into the wilderness to be tempted of the devil," Matt. 4.1–11; cf. also Mark 1.12, 13; Luke 4.1–13.

19. Cf. Michelson, pp. 15 f., 50. Preachers customarily devoted particular attention to this theme in their Passion Week sermons, cf. Cruel, p. 582.

20. Thus Nicolaus Dinkelspühl, preaching in Vienna in 1420 (Cruel, p. 500); and from a contemporary English preacher, John Myrc, we have this statement: "oure lady was wedded to Joseph, forto deseyve the fende, that he schule wene that he was his fadyr and not conseynet of the Holy Ghost." Owst, *Literature and Pulpit,* p. 512.

21. Luke 23.4, 7–15, 20, cf. also Acts 3.13; Parkes, I, 203, 298; Strumpf, p. 38, n. 11. The twelfth-century mystery, *La Résurrection du sauveur,* presents sympathetically Pilate's plaint that he might have lost his job, and even his life, had he denied the Jews' demand for the death of Jesus:

> Li Jeu, par leur grant envie,
> Enpristrent grant félonie.
> Jo l'consenti par veisdie
> Que ne perdisse ma baillie.
> Encusé m'eussent en Romanie:
> Tost en purraie perdre la vie.

(Michel and Monmerque, *Théâtre français,* p. 12.)

22. Parkes, II, 12, I, 160, 164, 285, 299; Murawski, p. 52.

23. Lifschitz-Golden, p. 14.

24. Strumpf, p. 13.

25. *Idem,* p. 6:

> De mestre aux Juifs encouraige
> Qu'il le tuent par leur oultraige
> Et qu'il le haient com nous faisons;

cf. also the Alsfelder Passion Play (Frankl, p. 11), and the Donaueschinger Passion Play (Roskoff, I, 368 f.), both of which vividly portray the alliance between Judas and the devil.

26. Cf. Strumpf, p. 9; *Cambridge History of English Literature* (Cambridge, 1910), V, 44. In the English Corpus Christi pageant, *The Betraying of Christ,* Judas appeared on the scene in a fiery red wig—a detail of costume

which customarily distinguished the devil in other plays (Modder, p. 15).

27. Lifschitz-Golden, pp. 90, 94 f.; Strumpf, pp. 21, 30.
28. *Dyables d'enfer, ennemys du genre humain; perversorum humani generis inimicorum; demonum humani generis inimicorum;* cf. Lifschitz-Golden, pp. 83, 98, 103.
29. Strumpf, p. 2.
30. Frankl, p. 61, n. 2.
31. Güdemann, III, 207 ff.; Geiger, *Zeitschrift,* III, 298.
32. Cf. Loewe, pp. 43 ff.
33. Lifschitz-Golden, pp. 117 ff.; REJ, LXXXIX (1930), 124.
34. Cf. Goebel, p. 69.
35. Crane, No. 296; Klapper, p. 282; Loewe, pp. 16, 47; see also *idem,* p. 32, for a legend about the devil which was applied to the Jews. Just as the devil does in his realm, so the Jews do on earth, is the obvious moral. One of the most curious descriptions of the Jews is that offered in Spain, probably in the fifteenth century, in which each of their organs is compared to the corresponding organ of *Al Burak,* the fabulous demoniac beast which bore Mohammed to heaven; cf. REJ, XVIII (1889), 238 ff., and XXI (1890), liii.
36. Cf. Michelson, frontispiece; Liebe, pp. 30, 35, 37, 69; Fuchs, pp. 13, 20. On the *Judensau* see Fuchs, pp. 114 ff., 124 ff.; D. Kaufmann, "La Truie de Wittemberg," REJ, XX (1890), 269–273; Stobbe, p. 267, n. 152. Liebe, p. 60, reproduces a seventeenth-century print illustrating these lines, intended more in earnest than in jest:

> Es thut iederman nachfragen,
> Warumb die Juden Ringlin tragen?
> Merkt auff ich will es sagen fein,
> Vielleicht mags die recht ursach sein.
> Erstlich weil sie des Teuffels sindt,
> Drumb man solch zeichen bey ihn findt.
> Denn wen sie denckn ahns ohrt der qual
> Schreyen sie Ô Ô allzumahl.

The same thought appears a century earlier in a Latin rhyme, cf. Bondy-Dworsky, I, 405. For the reference to Crete see Baron, II, 90.

37. Cf. Kynass, pp. 58 ff., 241.
38. Bäch-St., IV, 817.
39. Lewin, pp. 57, 85. One of the most important books in the history of Polish antisemitism, *Jewish Atrocities, Murders, and Superstitions,* by Father Przeslaw Mojecki, contains in the introduction to the second edition (Cracow, 1598) an account of how Satan selected the Jews as his instrument for the destruction of humankind by these methods. See EJ, II, 1002.

CHAPTER II. ANTICHRIST

1. Thorndike, II, 138; cf. also *idem,* pp. 672, 674, 844, 954, 960. The motif is by no means outmoded, it must be noted. Its modern version is to be found in the notorious *Protocols of Zion* which "reveal" in minute detail an alleged Jewish plot to conquer the world. This work is directly rooted

in the Antichrist tradition, and took its earliest form in a Russian volume entitled *The Great in the Little and Antichrist as a New Political Possibility* (1905), whose major theme was the imminent imposition of the reign of Antichrist through his Jewish agents. See on this John S. Curtiss, *An Appraisal of the Protocols of Zion* (New York, 1942).

2. Cf. Baer, II, 515; Parkes, I, 99, 397; Starr, p. 175. The Antichrist theme derives originally from the Jewish notion of the heathen king (Sennacherib-Gog) who will in the end oppose Israel and be defeated by the Messiah. But the satanic pseudo-messianism of the Christian conception is foreign to the Jewish, and probably developed as a direct reaction to the continued Jewish denial of Christ (cf. *EJ*, II, 906 ff.; *JE*, I, 625 ff.; *HERE*, I, 578 ff.; W. Bousset, *The Antichrist Legend* [London, 1896]). Thus the identification of the Antichrist with the anticipated Jewish Messiah is implicit as well as explicit in Christian thought on the subject (though the early Christian literature of the age of persecution singled out the deified Roman emperor as Antichrist, and other enemies of the Church, such as the Gnostics, were also identified as his followers). Bousset, pp. 166 ff., cites the early Church literature. Rabanus Maurus, Archbishop of Mainz (ninth century), wrote: "The Jews dream of the coming of their Christ, whom we know to be the Antichrist: that in the millennium Sodom will once more be raised to its ancient position" (Murawski, p. 36). For a similar apposition by Peter of Blois (end of the twelfth century) see Jacobs, p. 182. The Tortosa Jewry oath toward the end of the thirteenth century required a Jew to swear "per mesías qui es dit Antecrist, lo cual vosaltres esperats" (Amador, I, 572).

3. Starr, p. 104. The motif of the Jewish virgin who would give birth to the Messiah occurs frequently in European literature and lent itself to a (literary?) practical joke, often retold, about the Jewess who, having been seduced by a Christian, persuades her parents that the seed of the Holy Spirit is within her; the news is bruited about and all the Jews in the vicinity gather to welcome the expected Messiah who, alas, turns out to be a girl. One version has it that the Jews, believing that the Messiah would be conceived through "celestial influence," had their most beautiful virgins spend all the eight nights of the Feast of Tabernacles under the stars in their festival huts; of course, the "influence" that discovered them there was quite terrestrial, and Christian, and the consequences were, from the storyteller's point of view, altogether comical. We have here another interesting attribution of Christian ideas to the Jews. See Aronius, No. 418; Schudt, I, 411 ff.; Geiger, *Zeitschrift*, II, 348 and 373.

4. This fable appears in chronicles (cf. e.g., M. Paris, *Chron. maj.*, I, 180), among the *exempla* (Welter, p. 412, n. 5), and in collections of folk tales (Geiger, *Zeitschrift*, II, 356; Strumpf, p. 38, n. 14). See also Graetz, *Geschichte*, IV, 352 f. One tale has a sorcerer assume the role of Messiah (Welter, *loc. cit.*).

5. This account is based upon Preuss, pp. 11 ff. The notion that the Antichrist would be descended from the tribe of Dan, which was very widely held (cf. Bousset, pp. 26, 171, 172; Preuss, p. 16; Williams, p. 280) and substantiated by reference to Gen. 49.17, "Dan shall be a serpent in the way" (a number of writers traced Judas Iscariot to the same tribe, cf. Williams, p. 187, Preuss, p. 16 and p. 34, n. 1), is unquestionably related to the Jewish conception that the Messiah would be derived from this tribe on the

maternal side (cf. *JE*, I, 627; L. Ginzberg, *Legends of the Jews*, V, 368, n. 392, VI, 144, n. 854).

6. One fifteenth-century writer proposes that the harlot mother must be a "Juden wybelin" because "das sol yedoch das böste sin" (Preuss, p. 15). The suggestion that Antichrist is the son of a serpent and a Jewish whore (Bäch-St., IV, 816) contains a double allusion to Satan and to Gen. 49.17. That the relation between Antichrist and Satan is not solely paternal is illustrated by a number of pictures in fifteenth-century works showing the devil hovering behind his son, inspiring his sermons, and in general directing his activities (see Preuss, pp. 35, 36, 38, 40, 41). An anonymous manuscript from the same period, devoted to a discussion of Jewish sins and crimes against Christians, is entitled *Tractatus de Antichristo et discipulus eius* (Scherer, pp. 433 ff.). Another indication of the popular conception of the Jewish Messiah is to be discerned in the notion that "the Jews rejoice when it thunders and lightens because they expect their Messiah to come in such stormy weather" (Margaritha, p. L la-b). Storms were generally believed to shelter demons and sorcerers.

7. *Les Signes d'infamie au moyen âge* (Paris, 1891), p. 104.

8. Strumpf, pp. 16 ff.; Frankl, pp. 27 ff.; Preuss, pp. 28 ff. It should be noted that the German version of the drama, *Das Entkrist Vasnacht*, in contradistinction to the French, follows the Latin original in graciously permitting the Jews to adopt Christianity after the downfall of Antichrist, and thus to enjoy the glories of the millennial era.

9. Preuss, p. 29, n. 1.

10. Lenient, *La Satire . . . au XVIe siècle*, I, 160.

11. *Das Narrenschiff*, p. 213.

12. Preuss, pp. 5 ff., 23 ff., 41.

13. Preuss, p. 17. The conviction that the lost tribes of Israel were still in existence was so ardently held that the famous adventurer David Reubeni, who claimed to be an emissary from an independent Jewish kingdom in the Orient, had no difficulty in securing audiences and support from the Pope and the King of Portugal during the second quarter of the fifteenth century. The widely circulated Prester John correspondence was an important factor in confirming this belief.

14. M. Paris, *Chron. maj.*, IV, 77, 131 ff.; see also H. Bresslau, "Juden und Mongolen," *Zeitschrift für die Geschichte der Juden in Deutschland*, I (1887), 99–102.

15. Geiger, *Zeitschrift*, II, 363 ff.

16. The revival of interest in this figure must be seen as a result of the widespread anxiety about the impending world destruction; see Neubaur, *Die Sage vom ewigen Juden*, and Geiger, *op. cit.*, p. 366.

17. Baring-Gould, pp. 168 f. The legend of Antichrist was known also to the Moslems and they too associated his coming with an uprising of the Jews.

18. Browe, *Die eucharistischen Wunder*, pp. 85 f.; Stern, *Urkundliche Beiträge*, I, 50. When Benedict of York repented his conversion, the chronicler reports, the Archbishop of York burst out "in a spirit of fury," " 'Since he does not wish to be a Christian, let him be the Devil's man.' " So Benedict returned "to the Jewish depravity, like a dog to his vomit" (Jacobs, pp. 105 f.).

19. Such expressions were so frequently employed that there is no point in citing specific references. The statement, however, relating to the invocation of demons is from an "Edict of Faith" issued at Valencia in 1519

(Roth, *Spanish Inquisition*, p. 78). The final quotation is from Grunwald, *Juden in Wien*, p. 5. A legend current among the Kabyle of North Africa probably reflects this European conception: the Kabyle once invaded Spain and slaughtered all the males in a certain city; the women, bewailing their fate, were advised by a wise man to prostrate themselves upon their husbands' graves, whereupon they were impregnated (by the demons that infest cemeteries?) and bore as children the Jews, who then migrated from Spain to Kabyle (Leo Frobenius, *Volksmärchen der Kabylen* [Jena, 1921], I, 103 f.).

The devil-Jew motif is still current. A modern fable has it that a peasant on a Rothschild estate once entered upon a wager with the devil and having outwitted him promptly became a Jew! (Bäch-St., IV, 813). The German educational authorities are today propagating this conception among their children: the first page of a book of nursery rhymes by Elvira Bauer, recently published, displays the statement in bold type, "The father of the Jews is the Devil."

20. Frankl, p. 18: "Die Kinder Gottes, das sind doch wir, die giftigen Würme, das seit ihr, wann hättet ihr uns in eurer Gewalt, als ihr in unserer seit gezahlt, kein Christ erlebte Jahresfrist." Cf. also Lewin, pp. 109, 47; Frankl, pp. 131 f.

21. *Complete Works* of Geoffrey Chaucer, ed. W. W. Skeat (Oxford, 1924), IV, 184, line 1748. In the play *St. Mary Magdalen*, which marks the transition in English literature from mystery or miracle to morality play, "we have a last glimpse of the Jew before he hides himself behind such neutral names as Infidelity or Mammon or Vice or Devil." Here Infidelity, the Vice of the play, proclaims himself a devil, the son of the Devil, announces his name to be "Moysaical Justice" and says that he "sticks so much in Jews' hearts that they will not believe the doctrine and wonders of Jesus" (Michelson, p. 63).

22. Lifschitz-Golden, p. 167.

23. Describing the popular attitude which led to the issuance of the bull *Hebraeorum gens* by Pius V in 1569, expelling the Jews from the Papal States, with the exception of Rome and Ancona, Rodocanachi remarks (p. 186): "On les accusait communément, dans le peuple comme chez les grands et même à la cour pontificale, de commettre les plus noirs forfaits . . . d'être partout, en un mot, les agents de Satan." Cf. also Baer, I, 198.

CHAPTER III. WITH HORNS AND TAIL

1. וְהִנֵּה קָרַן עוֹר פָּנָיו; cf. also Hab. 3.4: קַרְנַיִם מִיָּדוֹ לוֹ, "Rays hath he at his side." See *JE*, VI, 463.

2. Scherer, pp. 341, 547; Singermann, p. 20. The brim of the conical *Judenhut* was often twisted into the form of a pair of horns. In Italy Jews were ordered to wear a black hat with red tassels (or hair) attached, or with striped linen sewn on it (Singermann, p. 28; *EJ*, IX, 546). This costume may at times have approximated the effect of horns and was perhaps intended as a modification of the Vienna decree.

3. "Dieses ist der Juden Teuffel," Liebe, pp. 38, 63; Fuchs, p. 30; *REJ*, VI (1882), 117.

4. *REJ*, *loc. cit.*, and XX (1890), 231; Roth, *Essays and Studies in Memory of Linda R. Miller*, p. 176.

5. I can testify to this from personal experience. It was on a trip through Kansas that I once met a farmer who refused to believe that I was Jewish because there were no horns on my head. And I have since learned that this experience is not uncommon.

6. Cf. Liebe, pp. 35, 92, 105; Kynass, pp. 42, 43, 61, 62, 77, 83 f., 88, 105, 135 f.; Goebel, p. 282.

7. Kynass, pp. 77 f.:

> Der Itzig kam geritten
> Auf einem Ziegenbock
> Da dachten alle Juden
> Es wär der liebe Gott.

8. See the engraving in Schudt, II, 1, between pp. 256–257.

9. Hans Sachs, *Sämtliche Fabeln*, I, No. 172, pp. 489 ff.

10. Robert, p. 23 (cf. also pp. 103 f.).

11. Fuchs, p. 2. The *Gesta Romanorum* has an interesting tale (No. 76) that brings devil, goat, and Jews into suspiciously close juxtaposition.

12. Cf. Reinach, pp. 287, 353; also M. Joel, *Blicke in die Religionsgeschichte zu Anfang des zweiten christlichen Jahrhunderts* (Breslau and Leipzig, 1883), II, 130 ff. Carl Crow recently reported a similar belief among upper-class Chinese that the white man is none too fragrant. Of course there is always the possibility that such an opinion is pure generalization from limited experience with unclean and ill-smelling individuals, or that it is an expression simply of personal prejudice. But when it is widely held despite constant opportunity to check on it, we are justified in seeking some broader psychosociological explanation.

13. Cf. *REJ*, XIX (1889), 249, n. 3, and XX (1890), 101 f., 249; Frankl, p. 133.

14. Güdemann, I, 145:

> ez wart sô grôz nie ein stat
> sie waer von drîzec juden sat
> stankes unde unglouben.

15. Friss, No. 120, p. 161: "dye Juden, dye sneiden, hartneckygen, stinkunden Gotis verreter."

16. *REJ*, VI (1882), 117; Schudt, II, 1, pp. 344 ff.; Chwolson, p. 209. Schudt, IV, 2, p. 165, reports that he discussed this matter with a Jew who seemed to take pride in the peculiar odor of his people, which he attributed to their frequent fasts, and which gives delight to God. This Jew was evidently a student of the classics, for this is the explanation offered by Martial, *Epigr.* IV, 4, 7 (cf. Reinach, p. 287).

17. Cf. Loewe, p. 88, n. 61; Williams, p. 165; Lifschitz-Golden, p. 73; Crane, No. 263. The Moslems have a parallel belief that the grave of Mohammed gives forth a pleasant odor. This conception is altogether foreign to Jewish thought; the only reference to it I have been able to discover is in *Tashbez*, No. 445, where mention is made of the unpleasant odor of the demons in Noah's ark, and this is evidently a reflection of the Christian notion. However, on the foul odor of this earth as it assails the nostrils of a visitor from Paradise, see Trachtenberg, p. 62; on the stench of Hell, see *idem*, p. 67.

18. Berthold of Regensburg, in a sermon, paid the Jews this dubious compliment: "Look," he scolded his congregation, "a stinking goatish Jew honors his holiday better than you do!" (*Siehe, ein stinkender Jude, der die Leute*

anböckset, ehret seinen Feiertag besser als du! Cruel, p. 621). Hans Wilhelm Kirchhof, "to put it delicately," as he said, contented himself with pointing out that Jews "stink like goats" (*Wendunmuth*, III, 366 f.). Cf. also Schudt, II, 1, p. 344: "Alle Juden und Hebräer . . . haben einen gewissen üblen Gestanck dass sie meistens nach Bock Ambra schmäcken."

19. The earliest known reference to this legend is found in a poem by Venantius Fortunatus celebrating the conversion of the Jews of Clermont in 576; cf. Israel Lévi, "L'Odeur des Juifs," *REJ*, XX (1890), 249 ff.; also Schudt, II, 1, pp. 344 ff.

20. Loewe, pp. 28, 31, 32.

21. P. 95.

22. Hans F. K. Gunther, *Rassenkunde des deutschen Volkes*, cited by J. R. Marcus, *Rise and Destiny of the German Jew* (Cincinnati, 1934), p. 41. A street cry current in Austria-Hungary before the first World War (Kynass, p. 109) ran:

> Alle Juden stinken!
> Alle Juden stinken!
> Nur der Laser Jakob nicht.

Could this have been an attack upon poor Laser Jakob for his failure to measure up to the highest Jewish standards? Not long ago a prominent businessman informed his secretary, who was sitting beside him at his desk, that he could smell a Jew twenty feet away. She reported this to me as a rather wry joke: she had been in his employ for several years, but not until that moment, when she told him to hire another secretary, did he discover that she was Jewish!

23. Cf. Schudt, *loc. cit.*; Kynass, pp. 49, 74, 96, 123; Goebel, p. 282, etc.

24. *Historia de los Reyes Católicos Don Fernando y Doña Isabel* (Seville 1870), I, 124 f., cited by Salvador de Madariaga in his *Christopher Columbus* (New York, 1940), p. 130; cf. also Amador, III, 243, n. 1.

25. Cf. *REJ*, XIX (1889), 239 f.; Loewe, p. 31; Güdemann, III, 119, n. 1; *JE*, III, 261; Trachtenberg, pp. 7 f.; Chwolson, pp. 207 f.

26. Cruel, p. 583; Eck, p. J4a; Dubnow, II, 77. One need not look for consistency in these folk beliefs, whose sole purpose is to single out the Jews as *different*: Margaritha (p. K3a) reports that "it is said that the Jews live longer than the Christians, and that they are not subject to such diseases as smallpox, consumption, leprosy, and the like." It is also of interest here to record the opinion of a seventeenth-century anthropologist cited by Schudt (II, 1, pp. 368 f.) as authority for his statement that "God has marked them with certain characteristic signs so that one can recognize them as Jews at the first glance, no matter how hard they try to disguise themselves": one Scriver, "a learned man, has reported concerning the Jews that among several hundred of them he has not encountered one without a blemish or some repulsive feature: for they are either pale and yellow, or swarthy; they have in general big heads and mouths, pouting lips, protruding eyes and eyelashes like bristles, large ears, crooked feet, hands that hang below their knees, and big, shapeless warts, or are otherwise asymmetrical and malproportioned in their limbs."

27. The alleged hemorrhages and male menstruation, e.g., were explained by citing the cry of the Jews before Pilate: "His blood be on us and on our children," Matt. 27.25; cf. *JE, loc. cit.*

28. Chwolson, pp. 207 ff.; cf. also Schudt, II, 1, pp. 345 ff.; *REJ*, VI (1882), 117, and XXI (1890), liii ff.

Notes on Chapter IV   229

29. Notions of specifically Jewish ailments are probably still current. In 1890 a "magician," Wawrzek Marut, convicted by a court in Galicia of disinterring two corpses from a Jewish cemetery, explained that there are two kinds of typhus: the ordinary, which can be banished with the Lord's Prayer, and the "Jewish," which can be conquered only by the application of Jewish bones. Another such case occurred in 1892. See Strack, p. 94.
30. Weller, p. 237; Frankl, pp. 65 f.; Liebe, p. 57. Schudt (II, 2, pp. 11, 13) reports that in 1651 a Jewess at Weisskirchen (Moravia) gave birth to a live elephant; and in 1671 at Glogau (Silesia) another Jewess gave birth to a donkey! It must be said, however, that he does not neglect to mention that similar curious phenomena occur to Christian women too.

CHAPTER IV. "A JEW IS FULL OF SORCERY"

1. Goebel, p. 287.
2. Schudt, II, 2, p. 190; the quotation from Luther is from his essay, "Vom Schem Hamphoras und vom Geschlecht Christi," *Werke* (Weimar, 1920), LIII, 602: "Ein Jüde stickt so vol Abgötterey und zeuberey, als neun Küe har haben, das ist: unzelich und unendlich."
3. Cf. Goebel, p. 282, and Bäch-St., IV, 812 ff. Among the feats still ascribed to Jews the following may be singled out: they charm snakes (St. Gall); make the queen pregnant by means of a magic apple (Greek-Albanian legend); possess magic books (Yugoslavia, East Prussia, Black Forest region); fix a stag's horns on an enemy's head (Posen); bewitch the stable and its occupants (Saarland); tame storms (Oberpfalz); practice bloodletting at a distance by magic (Odenwald); cure sterility, see and exorcise ghosts, do not sink when thrown into the water, etc., etc.
4. For a general discussion of the subject see N. W. Goldstein, "Cultivated Pagans and Ancient Anti-Semitism," *Journal of Religion*, XIX (1939), 355 ff. That there was some justification for this belief is evidenced by Hadrian's alleged statement: "There is no Jewish archisynagogus, no Samaritan, no Christian presbyter in Egypt *non mathematicus, non haruspex, non aliptes*," which, as S. W. Baron (III, 53) remarks, "may not be genuine, but does reflect the actual conditions in many Mediterranean countries." See also L. Blau, *Das altjüdische Zauberwesen* (Strasbourg, 1898); *HERE*, VIII, 278.
5. These citations are to be found in Reinach, pp. 292 (cf. Berliner, I, 114); 253; 165 f., 167, 336; 160; cf. also *idem*, p. 211. On Maria see *HERE*, VIII, 281a, and Pauly-Wissowa, *Real-Encyclopädie der classischen Altertumswissenschaft* (Stuttgart, 1894), I, 1350.
6. *B. Goth.*, I, 9, and I, 12. Cf. Josephus, *The Jewish War*, VI, 5, 4; in *Against Apion*, I, 22, however, Josephus effectively refutes the validity of augury; cf. also Acts 13.6.
7. In his celebrated work, *Against Celsus*, Origen denied the truth of Celsus' charge that Jesus was a magician, and in doing so also felt obliged to defend the Jews against the same accusation. ("They worship angels," Celsus had declared of the Jews, "and are addicted to sorcery, in which Moses was their instructor.") But in his *Commentary upon Matthew* Origen admitted that the Jews are adept in the adjuration of demons and that they

employ charms in the Hebrew language drawn from the books of Solomon. Cf. Thorndike, I, 437; Goebel, p. 68.

8. Williams, p. 132.
9. Parkes, I, 354.
10. See J. Trachtenberg, *Jewish Magic and Superstition* (New York, 1939).
11. In the famous *Mystère de la Passion* the Jews chant as they assemble the ingredients of their brew (Strumpf, p. 5):

> ung peu de selet
> un crapault
> Et avec ce avoir nous fault
> Des cheveux d'un homme pendu
> La langue d'ung serpent volu
> Et la queue d'une couleuvre
> Et encoires pour faire bonne euvre
> Qui aurait l'ueil d'ung blanc corbel. . . .

According to the New Testament, some Jews made the charge that Jesus' miracles were the work of the devil and that he healed by diabolic power (see Matt. 9.34, and 12.24; Mark 3.22). Thus we find the Jews, in the *Mystère de la Passion,* accusing Jesus of practicing magic and of planning

> a faire quelque sorcerie
> ou charmes ou enchanterie
> dont tu es ouvrier moult subtil

(Strumpf, p. 6; cf. also p. 7), and plotting an even more powerful charm to defeat his designs. Medieval preachers (cf. Cruel, p. 500) took occasion to refute this contention. But Jewish sources, while explaining Jesus' miracles as a product of his magic skill (cf. *Sanhedrin* 106b; *Sotah* 47b; *JE,* VII, 171) nowhere ascribe a satanic origin to his alleged magic. It was devil-obsessed Christianity that stressed the relation between Satan and magic. The best-known Jewish tract on Jesus, the famous *Toledot Yeshu* (reprinted in J. D. Eisenstein's *Ozar Vikuhim* [New York, 1928], pp. 228–229), lays his power to perform miracles to his knowledge of the Ineffable Name of God, the most potent force recognized in Jewish magic (cf. Blau, *op. cit.,* pp. 117 ff.; Trachtenberg, pp. 90 ff.), so that he could be worsted only by a subterfuge.

A *midrash* (A. Jellinek, *Bet Hamidrash* [2d ed. Jerusalem, 1938], V, 60 ff.; cf. also *idem,* VI, 11 ff.) credits St. Peter also with knowledge of magic. It relates that Simon Caipha, of his own accord and in order to free the Jews from the annoyance of the trouble-making Nazarene sect, smuggled the Ineffable Name out of the temple, and with its aid performed such wonders as convinced the Nazarenes that he had been sent by Jesus. Thereupon Simon instituted fundamental changes in the Christian ritual which permanently differentiated Christians from Jews. He remained among these Christians until his death, outwardly one of them, but a martyr to his zeal for the inner peace and unity of Judaism.

It is of interest to note also that in the miracle play *Conversion de St. Paul* (cf. Strumpf, p. 20), when Paul preaches his newfound faith in Jesus in the synagogue of Damascus, the Jews recognize him as Saul of Tarsus and charge that his conversion is the result of sorcery.

12. Cf. Trachtenberg, pp. 74 f.; Goldziher, *ZDMG,* XLVIII (1894), 358 ff.; *MGWJ,* LXXVII (1933), 170, n. 1; Bäch-St., IV, 812; W. Ahrens, *Hebräische Amulette mit magischen Zahlenquadraten* (Berlin, 1916).

13. Cf. *REJ*, XLVI (1903), 148; G. Schiavo, *Zeitschrift für romanische Philologie*, XV (1891), 313.
14. See, e.g., W. Baring-Gould, *Curious Myths of the Middle Ages* (Philadelphia, 1869), for the history of several such legends that passed for fact until modern research displayed their absurdity.
15. Stemplinger, p. 11.
16. It is curious to note that the magician Solomon who influenced Christian notions about the Jew is not really Jewish but rather the creation of the Hellenistic and Christian imaginations. Magic was only a minor element in the Jewish legends revolving about the name of Solomon; both in the Talmudic and the later literature his wisdom and his power over nature and over the spirit world are particularly stressed. But the Hellenistic tradition emphasized the magic so strongly (his name itself occurs as a potent constituent in incantations of this period) as to leave its mark permanently upon the legend as it appears in the later Arabic (cf., e.g., the Koran, sura 38.33–37) and European literatures. The early Church held certain conjuring books ascribed to Solomon (which were condemned by the recognized authorities of rabbinic Judaism) in high esteem and preserved considerable fragments of them. See on this fascinating subject G. Salzberger, *Die Salomosage in der semit. Literatur* (Heidelberg, 1907); Goebel, pp. 66 ff.; *JE*, XI, 439 ff.; L. Ginzberg, *Legends of the Jews* (Philadelphia, 1928), VI, 291, 368 f.; Thorndike, II, 279 ff.
17. Peuckert, *Pansophie*, pp. 55 ff.
18. Goebel (pp. 83 f.) suggests that the Zebulon legend is merely another version of the Solomon legend, and is derived from a misreading of that part of the latter which relates to the devil (*diabolos*) stealing the magic books from under Solomon's throne. Cf. also Michelson, p. 93.
19. Lifschitz-Golden, pp. 133 ff.; Güdemann, II, 39 ff., 295 ff.; Williams, pp. 339 ff.; *REJ*, LXXXIX (1930), 123; Vogelstein and Rieger, I, 161 f. Two other figures of magical import deriving from the early history of the Church were the Samaritan, Simon Magus, who, having been held up in early Christian literature as the sorcerer *par excellence,* was often displayed in the later popular literature as the type of the Jewish magician (cf. *HERE*, XI, 514 ff.), and "Longinus the blind Jew," whose name occurs often in medieval charm formulas against bleeding primarily, but also against fever and other ailments, against fire, and to ensure safety and health. This is the name given to the centurion who at the time of the crucifixion recognized and paid homage to Jesus (Matt. 27.54, Mark 15.39, Luke 23.47), or according to another tradition, the soldier who pierced Jesus' side with a spear (John 19.34). In the later Middle Ages Longinus became a Jew, and as such a potent magic influence (cf. Bäch-St., V, 1335).
20. Goebel, p. 287; Schudt, II, 2, p. 210; Bäch-St., IV, 811 and n. 24 on p. 813; Caro, I, 153. Cf. also the story told by the Arab historian Mas'udi (A. Wallis Budge, *Egyptian Magic* [London 1899], pp. 23 f.) of a Jewish magician at Kufa, Mesopotamia, who topped a number of remarkable feats by killing a man, cutting off his head, and then uniting the two again and bringing him back to life.
21. See p. 23 above, and the references there cited.
22. Starr, pp. 95 f.
23. *Idem,* p. 104.
24. Monod, *REJ*, XLVI (1903), 240. The Jews "roamed about the convents

The Devil and the Jews

like troupes of demons, their brothers," Guibert wrote. Luther likewise bitterly attacked his Jewish contemporaries for plunging Christians into sin with their magic, cf. Lewin, p. 84.

25. I am indebted to Professor Guido Kisch for calling this item to my attention; it occurs in the ms. *Regula juris ad decus* (paragraph J 159) from the Breslau Stadtarchiv, which he plans to publish shortly in Part III of his work *The Jewry-Law of the Medieval German Law Books.* He permitted me to examine his photostat copy of the manuscript, and confirmed my opinion that this paragraph is not an interpolation but an integral part of the original document. His comment, in a letter, may be of interest: "You will recall my criticism that there is too much preoccupation with Jews as sorcerers in your book. All the more was I impressed by this paragraph concerning *sorcerers*, with no express reference to Jews, in the midst of all these *Jewry-law* paragraphs."

26. Friss, No. 127, p. 164. On his second offense the culprit was burned.
27. Robert, p. 144.
28. Starr, p. 175.
29. Murawski, p. 35.
30. See Graetz, *Geschichte*, VII, 410, for the text.
31. Liliencron, I, 173:

> Etliche mit grawen har
> lernten erst den talmut
> die heilig schrift ducht sie nit gut. . . .
> Sie heten al gelernet wol,
> ir kunst heist nigromanci
> Satanas was auch darbi,
> wanne sie die rede geteten.

32. *Essendo massimamente la maggior parte di loro Talmudisti negromanti, heretici et vitiosi* (Stern, *Urkundliche Beiträge*, I, 108). This view found judicial expression as late as 1744 when a London court invalidated a bequest left by a Jew for the purpose of maintaining an institution for study of the Talmud on the ground that the legacy was devoted to a "superstitious" purpose—and directed it to be expended instead upon the instruction of foundlings in the rudiments of Christianity! See Roth, *History of the Jews in England*, pp. 203 f.

33. Grayzel, pp. 331, 337; Parkes, II, 140; Thorndike, III, 37.
34. This is a subject that merits more study than it has yet received. The examples here cited are from: Kayserling, *Navarra*, pp. 201 ff.; Amador, I, 572 (Tortosa); Regné, p. 149 (Narbonne); Stern, *Israelitische Bevölkerung*, III, 236 ff. (Nuremberg); *EJ*, IX, 534; see also the articles by Kisch listed in the Bibliography; *REJ*, VII (1883), 253, 255; Scherer, pp. 296 ff.; Baer, I, 1030 and n. 6; Stobbe, pp. 262 f., n. 144; *EJ*, IX, 533-541.

35. Graetz, *Geschichte*, V, 63 f. This canon reflects the displeasure of the clergy over the popular propensity to turn to Jewish rather than Christian ecclesiastics for such services. We have here proof that the people attributed a superior efficacy to the Jewish blessing, no doubt of a magical character. In any event, the evil eye was expressly attributed to Jews during the Middle Ages (cf. Bulard, p. 313) and still is in modern times (cf. Bäch-St., IV, 831 f.); in many places in Germany the evil eye is called *Judenblick* (Wuttke, pp. 149, 163, 444). Belief in the greater efficacy of Jewish prayer is also still to be met with. In the Saarland it was believed that Jews are able by prayer to restore the health of a dying man (Bäch-

St., IV, 813); we find also the notion that if one wishes to encompass the death of an enemy he may do so by giving a Jew a black hen and then praying that his enemy may die (*idem*, p. 815). Wuttke, p. 149, reports that in Hesse, when a very sick man wished to die, he had a rabbi pray for his recovery and long life! But then, it was considered unlucky to meet a priest on the road! Cf. Wuttke, *loc. cit.*; Crane, p. 250; Lecoy de la Marche, *La Chaire française*, p. 426.

36. See the Hebrew accounts in Wiener's edition of *Emek Habacha* (Leipzig, 1858), Hebrew Appendix, p. 9, and A. Neubauer and M. Stern, *Hebräische Berichte über die Judenverfolgungen während der Kreuzzüge* (Berlin, 1892), p. 69; also M. Paris, *Historia anglorum*, II, 9 (where it is stated that women were also excluded because "some women" were suspected of a similar design); Jacobs, p. 100; Prynne, I, 7 f. Parkes, II, 223, 361, points out that the lesser baronage and the young Crusaders, who were heavily indebted to the Jews, took advantage of this opportunity to destroy the records of their indebtedness; but it was the cry of magic that spurred the populace, which was hardly affected by Jewish usury, to initiate these riots.

37. Murawski, pp. 56 f.

38. Regné, p. 193. See Jacobs, p. 264, for an incident relating to a converted Jew who was considered a soothsayer until his predictions went awry. Scherer, p. 433, mentions an anonymous fifteenth-century manuscript which discusses Jewish fortunetelling, with illustrations ostensibly drawn from the Talmud.

39. Cf. Vol. I, pp. 471 ff., II, 1, p. 141, IV, 1, p. 173, and IV, 2, pp. 37 f.

40. Cf. Bäch-St., IV, 816.

41. *JE*, VIII, 256; Solomon ibn Verga, *Shebet Yehudah* (Wiener ed. Hanover, 1855), pp. 109, 122.

42. *Idem*, pp. 115 f. Many dream books attributed to Joseph, Daniel, and other renowned Jewish sages were in circulation in a number of languages: cf. Lea, *Inquisition of the Middle Ages*, III, 447; Thorndike, II, 162, 290 ff.; M. Steinschneider, "Das Traumbuch Daniels und die Oneirokritische Litteratur des Mittelalters," *Serapeum*, XXIV (1863), 193-201, 209-216.

43. *REJ*, VI (1882), 5.

44. Weller, No. 864, p. 360; practically the same story appears in Ludwig Bechstein, *Thüringer Sagenbuch*, I (Leipzig, 1885), pp. 15-16, as a folk tale then still current in Coburg.

45. Lewin, p. 39.

46. Lowenthal, *A World Passed By*, p. 433.

47. Kynass, pp. 51 f.

48. See Thorndike, II, 214 ff., 777 ff., 973, IV, 317; Baer, I, 310, 570, 571, 862; *EJ*, III, 587. Bulard, pp. 236 ff., points out that Jews were often represented as astrologers in medieval Christian art. On the medieval Jewish practice of astrology see *EJ*, III, 585 ff.; Trachtenberg, pp. 249 ff., 311 f.

49. Baer, I, 310 f.; cf. also *idem*, II, 513, 515; G. Scholem, "Alchemie und Kabbalah," *MGWJ*, LXIX (1925), 13-20, 95-110, 371-374, and LXX (1926), 212-219; R. Eisler, "Zur Terminologie und Geschichte der jüd. Alchemie," *MGWJ*, LXIX (1925), 364-371, LXX (1926), 194-201; *EJ*, I, 137-159; *JE*, I, 328-332.

50. Güdemann, III, 156; Dubnow, I, 36 f.

51. Brann, p. 154.

52. Grün, pp. 24 f.; *EJ*, VIII, 1013. It is related that Rabbi Judah Löw also

pursued astrological studies together with Tycho Brahe (*EJ*, III, 587), but Grün (p. 36) shows that it was extremely unlikely that the two even met during the great astronomer's brief and secluded stay outside of Prague from the end of 1599 to his death in October, 1601.

53. Lewin, p. 105; Ackermann, *Münzmeister Lippold*, pp. 11 f.
54. Cf. Thorndike, I, 778 ff., etc., IV, 327; Konrad von Megenberg, *Das Buch der Natur*, ed. F. Pfeiffer (Stuttgart, 1861), pp. 469 ff.; M. Steinschneider, "Lapidarien," *Semitic Studies in Memory of Rev. Dr. Alexander Kohut* (Berlin, 1897), pp. 42–72, and *Die Hebraeischen Uebersetzungen des Mittelalters* (Berlin, 1893), p. 964.
55. Vol. II, 2, p. 393. On amulets in Jewish magic see Trachtenberg, pp. 132 ff.
56. Amador, II, 220, n. 1.
57. Baer, II, 455, 466, 478, 513, 543, 544, etc.
58. *Werke* (Erlangen, 1854), LXII, p. 375. The original of this story is a tale in Kirchhof's *Wendunmuth* (III, 256) about the "sorcery of the Jews."
59. Nathan Hanover, *Yeven Mezulah* (Piotrkov, 1902), p. 15.

Chapter V. Europe Discovers the Kabbalah

1. Gregorovius, p. 27. Benedict XIV, on September 15, 1751, issued a similar ban against Jewish magic; it would seem from the statement of Rodocanachi (p. 266, n. 4), to which my attention was called by Dr. Hermann Vogelstein, that this was merely a reissuance of Pius V's bull. Unfortunately the text is not given so that we cannot be sure, nor is there any indication of the reason for its renewal.
2. Cf. E. Rodocanachi, *La Femme italienne à l'époque de la renaissance* (Paris, 1907), pp. 108, 109 (which Dr. Vogelstein also brought to my notice); Burckhardt, p. 502, n. 4; Gregorovius, p. 30. Schudt (I, 57, IV, 1, p. 24) also remarks on the reputed Jewish skill in love magic and in concocting love philters.
3. Burckhardt, pp. 506 and 503, n. 2 (cf. p. 337, n. 1). Schudt (II, 2, p. 173) has a curious tale of an incident that supposedly occurred in Rome in 1554: 82 women, possessed of evil spirits, were freed of their tormentors by the exorcisms of a Benedictine monk; before he released the demons, however, he forced them to explain why they had taken possession of these women, and learned that the Jews, in revenge for the apostasy of the women, who had formerly been Jewish, had caused them to inhabit their bodies and make (Christian) life miserable for them.
4. The literature both of and on this so-called Kabbalah is very extensive. Christian writers are still generally persuaded that this is the true Kabbalah of the Jews. On the Kabbalah proper see the excellent articles by L. Ginzberg, *JE*, III, 456–479, and G. Scholem, *EJ*, IX, 630–717; on the "practical Kabbalah," see *EJ*, IX, 717–726. *Idem*, pp. 726 ff., contains a brief survey of Christian Kabbalah. Peuckert, *Pansophie*, has a good statement of the influence of Kabbalah upon sixteenth-century Europe; see also Rosenfeld, pp. 35 ff.; Bäch-St., IV, 812.
5. Vol. I, p. 337.
6. S. Dubnow, *Pinkes ha-medinah* (Berlin, 1925), Nos. 307, 440, and p. 285.
7. *Werke*, (Weimar ed.), II, 491, V, 184 ff.

8. One of the most important internationally distributed texts was purportedly translated from a Hebrew work written by one Abraham of Worms in the fifteenth century—see *EJ*, I, 544 f., and G. Scholem, *Bibliographia Kabbalistica* (Berlin 1933), p. 2 (this volume contains a complete listing of authentic and pseudo-Kabbalistic works). The German Jew known as Simon Okes Bogues, mentioned as a magician in Amsterdam in 1610, was no doubt trading on this Kabbalistic reputation (see H. I. Bloom, *The Economic Activity of the Jews of Amsterdam in the Seventeenth and Eighteenth Centuries* [Williamsport, Pa., 1937], p. 24, n. 111).
9. Schudt, I, p. 90, II, 2, p. 212.
10. *EJ*, I, 144; Schudt, II, 2, p. 207.
11. Such exhaustive works as I. Kracauer's *Urkundenbuch zur Geschichte der Juden in Frankfurt am Main von 1150–1400*, A. F. Pribram's *Urkunden und Akten zur Geschichte der Juden in Wien*, M. Stern's *Nuernberg im Mittelalter*, etc., containing thousands of entries from the official local records, do not reveal a single case in point; the brothers Lagumina's *Codice diplomatico dei Giudei di Sicilia* contains just one; F. Baer's voluminous compilation of Spanish records, *Die Juden in christlichen Spanien*, no more than five—and so it goes. Works on witchcraft (e.g., Hansen, Soldan-Heppe, Lea, etc.) and on medieval magic generally (e.g., Thorndike) are no more remunerative.
12. Starr, p. 86.
13. *Jews of Angevin England*, p. 15; cf. *idem*, p. 28. An interesting item in this anthology occurs on p. 153: toward the end of the twelfth century, "Godeliva of Canterbury . . . was passing through the inn of a certain Jew and entered it at the invitation of a Jewish woman. For being skilled in charms and incantations she was accustomed to charm the weak foot of the Jewess"!
14. Baer, I, 343, 608 f. Schudt (IV, 2, p. 333) has a report that some time in the seventeenth century a Jew in the neighborhood of Strasbourg forced a thief, by magic, to return the goods he had stolen, and even to replace that part of it he had already disposed of.
15. Baer, I, 706.
16. Lagumina, I, 508.
17. Baer, II, 379.
18. *Idem*, II, 513.
19. Cf. Schudt, IV, 1, pp. 245 f.
20. Lippold's career and the facts of this case have been thoroughly covered by A. Ackermann, *Münzmeister Lippold*; see also *EJ*, X, 995 f.; K. Burdach, *Vom Mittelalter zur Reformation*, III, Part 1 (Berlin, 1917), pp. 409 f.
21. Printed in full in Ackermann, *op. cit.*, pp. 93 ff.; cf. also *idem*, pp. 55 ff.
22. Philip Augustus was likewise allegedly bewitched by the Jews in order to win his friendship and procure their return in 1198 to the Île de France, whence he had banished them seventeen years before (cf. Güdemann, I, 225).
23. Ackermann, *op. cit.*, pp. 61 ff., 98; see also Heise, pp. 281 f.
24. Vol. II, 2, pp. 210 f.
25. Soldan-Heppe, II, 94.

Chapter VI. Magic and Medicine

1. *Mahzor Vitry,* ed. S. Hurwitz (Berlin, 1889–93), No. 280, p. 247; see also *REJ,* III (1881), 9, n. 1. On Moses ben Yehiel see H. Gross, *Gallia Judaica* (Paris, 1897), p. 513, and Jacobs, pp. 225, 229. The origin and significance of these customs are discussed in Trachtenberg, pp. 178, 179.
2. *Or Zarua* (Zhitomir, 1862), II, No. 423, p. 173; *Mahzor Vitry, loc. cit.;* *Tosafot Moed Katan,* p. 21a; *Kol Bo* (Lemberg, 1860), No. 114; *Yore Deah,* 387.2.
3. *Pesahim,* p. 8b and Rashi ad loc.; *Responsa* of Hayim Or Zarua (Leipzig, 1860), No. 144.
4. *Sefer HaOrah,* ed. S. Buber (Lemberg, 1905), II, No. 127, p. 219.
5. *Sefer Maharil* (Warsaw, 1874), *Hilchot Shabbat;* Güdemann, III, 153; Bäch-St., II, 1417. Some instances of attack upon Jews as arsonists are to be found in Caro, II, 26; Bondy-Dworsky, I, 45, 72, 367, 400, II, 676, 893, 895, 995, 1009, 1015, etc.
6. Liliencron, I, 47, note; cf. Scherer, p. 363. Is it altogether implausible to relate the current vulgar notion that Jews are partial to fires to this superstition?
7. Vol. II, 1, pp. 74 f.
8. Dubnow, I, 204.
9. *Or Zarua,* II, No. 53, p. 12a.
10. Moses b. Eliezer, *Sefer Hasidim Tinyana* (Piotrkov, 1910), p. 7a; Güdemann, I, 136; *Sefer Maharil, Hilchot Mezuzah; Yore Deah,* 291.2. However, the *mezuzah* was regarded among Jews also as a protective device (cf. Trachtenberg, pp. 146 ff.) and is still considered a lucky talisman by a good many Jews and Christians. I have known a nun to carry one in her purse; see also the instance cited by Strack, pp. 75 f.
11.   Des abergloub ist ietz so vil,
               domit man gsuntheit suchen wil;
               wan ich das als zusamen such,
               ich macht wol druss ein Ketzerbuch.
Narrenschiff, p. 71, cf. also *idem,* pp. 98 f., "Von narrichter Arzni," and the description of the typical medieval "Tyriakkremer" cited in Güdemann, III, 198.
12. Crane, p. 248.
13. *Sachsenspiegel,* III, 7, 3. See G. Kisch, "A Talmudic Legend as the Source of the Josephus Passage in the Sachsenspiegel," *Historia Judaica,* I (1939–40), 105–118, and *Jewry-Law,* II, 165 ff.; H. Lewy, "Josephus the Physician," *Journal of the Warburg Institute,* I (1937–38), 221–242. Another medieval legend had it that Titus, being ill and hearing that a Jewish ambassador had been sent from Jerusalem, begged him at once for a remedy without inquiring into his profession (Lewy, *op. cit.,* p. 242).
14. Cf. Stobbe, p. 279; Regné, p. 193; Schudt, II, 2, p. 212; Lewin, p. 102. Several women physicians are also mentioned (Heffner, p. 45; Kracauer, *Geschichte der Juden in Frankfurt,* II, 256 f.); presumably their medicine approximated the sort generally ascribed to all Jewish physicians.
15. Cf. Scherer, pp. 41, 52, 54, 58; Grayzel, pp. 319, 333, 337; *JE,* VIII, 417; Newman, pp. 187 f.

16. Aronius, No. 37; Caro, I, 92 ff.
17. Cf. Güdemann, II, 337; Kracauer, *op. cit.*, II, 258, 263 f.; *MGWJ*, LXXXII (1938), 120. In a complaint dated December 13, 1454, rehearsing the customary pious alarm over the presence in Vienna of a licensed Jewish physician, the medical society of the city gave away its real concern when it pointed out that "jetzt beständig hier zu Wien eilf Doktoren sind," and therefore the city was not in need of additional doctors (Scherer, p. 421).
18. Eck, p. F4b. See also Schudt, II, 1, pp. 389 ff., IV, 2, 184 ff.; Margaritha, p. G4b; Kirchhof, III, 255; Bondy-Dworsky, II, 741; *EJ*, VI, 359. No wonder that Count Nicholas Schlick, recommending a Jewish physician to the "erbaren, namhafften, wolweissenn Burgermaister vnnd Ratt der Staddt Eger" (Bohemia), finds it appropriate to assure them that his patients "nit schad werdet haben" (Bondy-Dworsky, I, 207, No. 327).
19. Frankl, p. 100.
20. Cf. Güdemann, II, 254.
21. Kracauer, *op. cit.*, II, 264. In 1657 the clergy petitioned the Council to rescind the licenses of Jews to practice, its main contention being that Jews are the enemies of God and of Christians and use magical recipes and techniques. Could they do as they please, "hardly one of us would live another hour" (*idem*, p. 267).
22. "Es sei besser mit Christo gestorben, als per Juden-Dr. mit dem Teufel gesund worden" (Krauss, p. 56).
23. Schudt, II, 1, p. 387.
24. *Shebet Yehudah* (Wiener ed.), p. 88; Baer, I, 35, n. 2.
25. Stern, *Urkundliche Beiträge*, p. 29; Grayzel, pp. 155 f., 347; on the employment of Jewish physicians by prelates and kings see *REJ*, XVII (1888), 258 ff., LVII (1909), 268, LXVI (1913), 80, LXI (1911), 37; Saige, p. 23; Newman, pp. 188 ff.
26. Caro, II, 66.
27. See I. *Münz, Die jüdischen Ärzte im Mittelalter* (Frankfort, 1922); S. Krauss, *Geschichte der jüdischen Ärzte* (Vienna, 1930); Carmoly, *Histoire des médecins juifs* (Brussels, 1842); and also Ferorelli, pp. 117 ff.; G. Kisch, *Die Prager Universität*. Lagumina, I, 69–77, records no less than 166 Jewish physicians in Sicily during the years 1362–1492, and many more are mentioned in other documents.

CHAPTER VII. THE POISONERS

1. Vol. II, 50.
2. Bondy-Dworsky, I, No. 14, pp. 7 f.; Güdemann, II, 262; see also Krauss, pp. 54 ff.; Baer, I, 613; and Schudt, II, 1, pp. 391 ff., for a number of such accusations. Johann Pfefferkorn (see p. 82 above) testified that when he was still a Jew, and posing as a doctor, he had attempted to poison Archbishop Albrecht of Magdeburg and Elector Joachim of Brandenburg and members of their courts, but failing in this venture he and his associates had nonetheless managed to kill thirteen Christians by administering poison! (Schudt, IV, 1, p. 245). A curious circumstance warrants special mention of the charge made against a surgeon, David, at St. Quentin, of poisoning a number of persons, including a priest to whom he owed a large sum of money (Caro, II, 104). A Jew indebted to a priest!

3. Baer, II, 47; see also Grayzel, p. 74, n. 147; Stobbe, pp. 180 f.; *Jahrbuch d. Jüdisch-Literar. Gesellschaft*, XIV (1921), 217. A similar view was widely held in Poland at this time; see *EJ*, II, 1004.

4. Lopez was involved in political intrigue, and his enemies seized this means of getting him out of the way; see Michelson, pp. 84 f.; *EJ*, X, 1112 f.; Graetz, *Shylock*, pp. 24 ff.; Friedlander, pp. 17 ff.

5. Aronius, No. 170, item 15; Krauss, pp. 27 ff.; Parkes, II, 216; Amador, II, 497; Newman, *loc. cit.* See also L. Glesinger, "Beiträge zur Geschichte der Pharmazie bei den Juden," *MGWJ*, LXXXII (1938), 111–130, 417–422.

6. Thorndike, III, 525 ff.; cf. also *idem*, II, 860 f., 904 f., and Index, *s.v.* "Poison"; Burckhardt, pp. 440 f. The general esteem in which dispensers of drugs were held may be judged from their associates in this list of wicked people to be found in London in 1192: pimps, actors, eunuchs, effeminates, *apothecaries*, witches, magicians, mendicants, dancers, etc. (Jacobs, p. 148).

7. Dubnow, I, 243; Luther, *Werke* (Weimar, 1914), LI, 195 and *Tischreden* (Weimar, 1916), IV, 338; cf. also Lewin, pp. 39 f. A sixteenth-century Czech diatribe against the Jews (kindly translated for me by Professor Kisch) makes reference to "a Jew who knew how to prepare a poison which would kill a person in four or eight weeks, in a quarter or half a year, or according to one's desire" (Bondy-Dworsky, II, 569). In Brandenburg, in the sixteenth century, apothecaries were forbidden to sell poisonous drugs to "dubious characters, particularly Jews"! (Ackermann, *Münzmeister Lippold*, p. 97, No. 36).

8. Cf. W. Meyer, pp. 38 ff.; Michelson, pp. 79 f. The *cause célèbre* of Dr. Lopez, Queen Elizabeth's physician, may have been the more or less direct stimulus in this instance, but the character of the Jewish poisoner in these plays is so generalized as to represent a recognized type rather than a recognizable individual.

9. Aronius, No. 724–725; Grayzel, pp. 72, 74; *EJ*, II, 982; Scherer, pp. 45, 53, 333; Stobbe, pp. 271 f., n. 162.

10. Cf. Schudt, II, 1, pp. 377 f.; Bäch-St., IV, 827; Grayzel, p. 301, note.

11. Aronius, Nos. 89, 107; Williams, p. 354.

12. Lagumina, I, 389 f., for the translation of which I am indebted to Professor James B. Hopkins of Lafayette College.

13. Scherer, pp. 577 ff.: "Von den Juden. Wan die Juden khauffen wellen auf den Platzen: was sy khauffen wellen, darauf sollen sy zaigen; was sy aber Anruern, das sollen sy khauffen und bezallen nach des verkhauffers gefallen." Cf. also *idem*, pp. 369 ff.; *REJ*, XV (1889), 49; Kayserling, *Navarra*, p. 140; Starr, *Proceedings of the American Academy for Jewish Research*, XII (1942), 70.

14. These were not, however, the very first instances of this sort; twenty-seven Jews were executed at Troppau (Bohemia) in 1163 on a charge of well poisoning (Bondy-Dworsky, II, 886, No. 1110), and similar accusations were apparently made twice in the thirteenth century: Breslau, 1226, and Vienna, 1267 (Bäch-St., IV, 825). Saddling responsibility for an epidemic upon the Jews was not without hoary precedent. Manetho's story that the Jews were expelled from Egypt because they had caused a pestilence was repeated by later Greek and Latin writers as an illustration of Jewish "misanthropy" (Parkes, I, 15 f.).

15. Caro, II, 111 ff.; Parkes, II, 126, 174; Baer, I, 224 f.; Lifschitz-Golden, p. 188; *REJ*, XVII (1888), 219 ff. A current myth that there were many

Jewish lepers in France grew out of the identity in form of the badge worn by Jews and lepers in the Middle Ages (cf. Robert, pp. 146 ff.); legislation relating to the badge covered *Judeis et leprosis* together (*idem*, pp. 11, 148); in Brittany the *cagots* were regarded as a species of leprous Jews (*idem*, p. 174).

16. In the preceding year violent attacks by bands of so-called *Pastoureaux* had destroyed 120 French Jewish communities. There wasn't much left to attack, in any event, in 1321! (cf. Caro, II, 107 ff.; Baron, II, 29).

17. Besides the devastating effect of the plague, from which the Jews suffered at least as much as did the Christians, some 300 Jewish communities in Germany, France, and parts of Spain were totally extinguished by rioting mobs during these two years. This on top of the *Pastoureaux* outbreaks in France, and the Rindfleisch (1298) and Armleder (1337) persecutions in Germany, Bohemia, and Austria (cf. Caro, II, 195 ff., 202 ff.).

18. Geiger, *Zeitschrift*, II, 320; Mauvans, p. 220; Eck, p. F1b.

19. The following account is based upon Caro, II, 206 ff.; Stobbe, pp. 189, 284 ff.; Scherer, pp. 369 ff.; *JE*, III, 233 ff. One will find in these works a discussion, also, of the economic and social background of the riots, which is, of course, important for a complete understanding of what occurred. Our purpose here is to point out the role of the well-poisoning charge in bringing social conflict to a head. See also Ernest Wickersheimer, *Les Accusations d'empoisonnement* (Anvers, 1927). George G. Coulton, in his book, *The Black Death* (New York, 1932), achieves the extraordinary feat of omitting all mention of the Jews!

20. Schudt, I, 457.

21. Heise, pp. 82 f.

22. Lifschitz-Golden, p. 191.

23. Baer, I, 352; Frankl, p. 120. A century later John Trithemius wrote cautiously: "Whether the Jews deserved these persecutions I prefer not to say, but I cannot help wonder who the author of this accusation may have been, for the Jews used the same water as the Christians, and many of them died too during the plague. . . . It must have seemed to many at the time impossible that the small number of Jews, had they really wished to poison all the wells in the world, as they were accused of doing, could have carried out such an enterprise, or could have obtained so great an amount of poison. For this reason many held that the Christians who participated in these attacks were moved thereto more by greed than by love of service of God or by zeal for justice" (Schudt, I, 461 f.).

24. Cf. Graetz, *Shylock*, pp. 10 ff.; Friedlander, pp. 13 ff., 39 ff.

25. IV, 1, p. 299.

26. Stobbe, pp. 287, 288; Bäch-St., IV, 825.

27. "Alle Juden . . . gedenkent cristenheit ze demment mit vergifftende den lufft" (Wiener, p. 236).

28. Stern, *Urkundliche Beiträge*, I, 32; Bondy-Dworsky, I, 95 ff.

29. Kober, p. 133.

30. Bäch-St., *loc. cit.*

31. Schudt, IV, 1, pp. 231, 294.

32. Loewe, p. 78.

33. Schudt, IV, 1, p. 241.

34. Bäch-St., *loc. cit.*

35. Schudt, I, 389.

36. Mauvans, p. 225.

37. Frankl, p. 120. The Jews of Prague were accused in 1705 of attempting to exterminate the Christian populace by distributing fly poison among them! *Historia Judaica,* IV (1942), 113.
38. Vol. II, 1, pp. 323 f. The belief that Jews cause epidemics is by no means extinct yet among the European masses (cf. Bäch-St., *loc. cit.*). Else why have the Nazis so shrewdly exploited it? Almost at the instant of assuming power, in April, 1933, they withdrew the right of Jewish researchers at the Kaiser Wilhelm Institut in Berlin (and presumably elsewhere) to access to typhus, cholera, and other disease germ cultures, lest they deposit these in the reservoirs and other water sources. In September, 1939, the *Völkischer Beobachter* (see *American Hebrew,* September 29, 1939) published a report that during the German invasion of Poland the Jews poisoned the water supplies used by the German troops. And a Berlin dispatch (*New York Times,* November 20, 1939) brought the news that the Jewish community of Warsaw would be strictly confined in a ghetto because "they are dangerous carriers of sickness and pestilence." If the authors of these reports do not themselves believe them, they are evidently confident that their readers will. Here is the account of an eyewitness, Abraham Weiss ("In Nazi Warsaw," *Contemporary Jewish Record,* III [1940], 488), illustrating the technique of exploiting deep-seated folk superstition: "The typhus epidemic swept over all parts of the city and claimed its victims among 'Aryans' and 'non-Aryans' alike. The Nazis, however, decided that the Jewish quarter should be singled out as the 'infection area.' They posted notices to this effect and forced the Jewish community to establish hospitals there for the care of all victims." Doubly shrewd indeed: the Jews suffer all the expense and danger, while their reputation as epidemic makers is confirmed.

CHAPTER VIII. HOST AND IMAGE DESECRATION

1. Wuttke, p. 140. See *HERE,* V, 549 ff., on the early dispute over the Eucharist.
2. "Wer möchte einem kindelîn sîn houbetlîn oder sînin hendelîn oder sînin füezelin abgebîzen?" *Predigten,* ed. F. Pfeiffer (Vienna 1880), II, 270, cited in Strack, p. 34.
3. Grayzel, p. 115; Tovey, p. 104; Rodocanachi, pp. 166 f.; cf. also Browe, *Römische Quartalschrift,* XXXIV (1926), 186.
4. Parkes, II, 32; cf. also Grayzel, pp. 136 ff., and n. 3; Browe, *op. cit.,* 167, 177, and *Die eucharistischen Wunder,* pp. 128 ff.
5. Cf. Browe, *Römische Quartalschrift,* pp. 180 ff.; W. Meyer, pp. 13 f.; Frankl, pp. 125 f.; Loewe, pp. 75 ff.; Strumpf, pp. 29 f.; Lifschitz-Golden, pp. 89 ff., 160 ff.; Fuchs, pp. 180 ff.; Stobbe, p. 292; Liliencron, I, 47; Scherer, p. 363.
6. Bondy-Dworsky, II, 891, No. 1119.
7. Cf. *idem,* I, 134, No. 245; Pauli, No. 556; *MGWJ,* XLIX (1905), 167 ff.; Geiger, *Zeitschrift,* II, 310 f., 313.
8. Caro, II, 190; Browe, *op. cit.,* pp. 187 ff.
9. Cf. *JE,* VI, 481 ff.; Browe, *op. cit.,* pp. 173 ff.; Bäch-St., IV, 819 f.; Scherer, pp. 348 ff., 363 ff., 411 ff., 466 f.; Chwolson, pp. 269 ff.

10. Cf. Güdemann, II, 297; Browe, *op. cit.,* p. 179; Bondy-Dworsky, I, 83; Schudt, I, 220.
11. Cf. Browe, *Archiv f. Kulturgeschichte,* XX (1930), 134 ff., and *Die eucharistischen Wunder,* pp. 89 ff.; Crane, No. 266; Cruel, p. 619; Schudt, II, 1, pp. 316 f., II, 2, pp. 26 f.; Wuttke (1869 ed.), pp. 245, 287, 300.
12. Schudt, II, 2, p. 27.
13. Browe, *Die eucharistischen Wunder,* p. 134 (cf. p. 213 below); and also *Archiv f. Kulturgeschichte,* XX, 142, for the relationship between the toad and the devil. In the Berlin, 1510, case a piece of the host was said to have been baked in a *matzah* (unleavened bread) and hung in the synagogue (*MGWJ,* XLIX [1905], 174; Heise, p. 214). Was there supposed to be a superstitious purpose behind this? Among Christians such a disposition of the host to brink luck or health was not uncommon.
14. Robert, p. 143; cf. also *idem,* p. 113; Browe, *op. cit.,* p. 146.
15. Cf. *JE,* VI, 482; *EJ,* II, 982; Chwolson, p. 275.
16. *Römische Quartalschrift,* XXXIV (1926), 188 ff. Attention should, however, also be called to the opinion of P. Lefèvre (*Revue d'histoire ecclésiastique,* XXVIII [1932], 342) that the accusation made in Brussels, 1370, is "parfaitement authentique. . . . Tout en admettant la prévention courante contre eux à cette époque, il semble difficile, dans l'état actuel de notre documentation, de l'inscrire en faux contre leur culpabilité." The "documentation" includes the usual accusation by an "accomplice," the confessions exacted under torture, etc.
17. Cf. Stobbe, p. 188; Scherer, p. 368; Caro, II, 204; Wiener, p. 50.
18. Cf. *JE,* VIII, 543 f.
19. Jews were probably severe critics of Christian reverence for images, and sometimes openly derided the belief in miracles (cf. Caro, I, 92; Williams, p. 353; Jacobs, pp. 68 f.), a circumstance which must have lent color to such stories.
20. Parkes, I, 292.
21. Lifschitz-Golden, pp. 153 ff.
22. Tovey, pp. 168 f.; Bondy-Dworsky, II, 565 (kindly translated for me by Mr. John Winter of Lafayette College). In 1494 a Jewish cobbler, Isaac Abenul, was imprisoned at Archiaro, in Southern Italy, for having "scratched a cross" in the sole of a lady's shoe, but the royal Camera della Sommaria rejected the evidence as unsatisfactory (cf. Ferorelli, p. 190).
23. Tovey, pp. 128 f., 168 f.; M. Paris, *Chron. maj.,* V, 114; Roth, *History of the Jews in England,* pp. 55 f. Cf. Baer, II, 465, 526, for charges of this sort brought before the Inquisition against Conversos; but see also *idem,* p. xii, on their credibility.
24. Cf. Frankl, pp. 120 ff.; Fuchs, p. 183; Lifschitz-Golden, pp. 95 ff.; H. Loewe, *Die Juden in der katholischen Legende* (Berlin, 1912).
25. "Ach, lieber herrgott, lass dirs ein witzung sein und kum nit mer unter die schnöden, bösen Juden" (Goedeke, *Schwänke,* p. 171, No. 125).
26. Parkes, I, 291 ff. Legend made the Jews responsible for inducing the Caliph Yazid II to carry out a similar program of destruction against Christian images; cf. Starr, p. 91; M. Paris, *Chron. maj.,* I, 330. The exasperation of good Christians at the refusal of the Jews to accept these fables at face value is illustrated in a seventh-century dialogue between a Jew and a Christian, in which the Christian scolds: "How grievous is the obstinacy of these sinful Jews! How many shadow-appearances and

miracles of gushing have taken place, how many times has blood flown
from the icons and the martyrs' relics! Yet these witless fellows, rather
than being converted by such sights, hold them to be imaginary and
foolish!" To which the Jew naïvely retorts that Scripture forbids the
worship of any created thing! (Starr, p. 83).

27. Parkes, II, 33; Vogelstein, p. 137; Geiger, *Zeitschrift*, II, 333.
28. Loewe, p. 53. Cf. also Browe, *Archiv f. Kulturgeschichte*, XX (1930), 140.
A popular *exemplum*, derived from a story of St. Gregory's, told of a Jew
who, finding himself one night in the company of a demon, saved himself by making the sign of the cross (Crane, No. 131; Schudt, II, 1, p. 309).
He might hate and misuse the cross, but he was not averse to profiting
from its "good" magical effect.
29. Cf. Aronius, Nos. 330, 421; Cruel, p. 621; Browe, *Röm. Quartalschrift*,
XXXIV (1926), 170; Loewe, p. 51; Lifschitz-Golden, pp. 79 ff.; Schudt, II,
2, p. 105; Neufeld, I, 69, n. 4. Reports were also current that Jews had
crucified a wooden figure of Jesus (circumstantial detail was never lacking in these tales; this purportedly occurred at Magdeburg in 1301—cf.
Bäch-St., IV, 822), a cat (at Ofen in 1541), and a ram (at Syracuse, Sicily,
in 1113). These last two are mentioned by Schudt, I, 116, 127. On the island
of Crete Jews were accused several times during the fourteenth century
and again in 1449 of crucifying a lamb; see Starr, *Proceedings of the American Academy for Jewish Research*, XII (1942), 65 f.
30. Amador, I, 477; Williams, p. 242.
31. *Siete Partidas*, VII, 24, 2 (Baer, II, p. 45): ". . . oyemos decir, que en
algunos lugares los judios ficieron et facen el dia del viernes santo remem-
branza de la pasion de nuestro sennor Jesu Christo en manera de escarnio
furtando los ninnos et poniendolos en la cruz, o faciendo imagines de cera
et crucificandolas, quando los ninnos non pueden haber. . . ." Thus, according to this version, the wax images were employed only when children were not available.
32. An essential element of such magic among Christians was that the figure
must be baptized, so that it could not be utilized without the coöperation
of the clergy. These were so willing to oblige that special steps had to be
taken against such clerical malefactors, and a distinctive yellow badge, not
unlike the Jew badge, was forced upon them. Cf. Robert, p. 144. Illustrations of the use of image-magic in medieval Europe may be found in
Thorndike, II, 814, 818, 835; Browe, *loc. cit.*, p. 145; *Gesta romanorum*,
No. 102, and pp. 384 ff.
33. I. Lévi, "Le Juif sorcier," *REJ*, XXII (1891), 232 ff.
34. Aronius, No. 160; Schudt, II, 2, pp. 212 f., IV, 2, p. 339. Roskoff, I, 304 f.,
states that the Archbishop's tombstone recorded his death as a result of
Jewish magic.
35. Cf. Guillaume Mollat, *Les Papes d'Avignon* (2d ed. Paris, 1912), p. 44.
I am indebted to Dr. Grayzel for this reference.

CHAPTER IX. RITUAL MURDER

1. See H. L. Strack, *The Jew and Human Sacrifice* (New York, 1909); I.
Scheftelowitz, *Das stellvertretende Huhnopfer* (Giessen, 1914), chap. xii:

"Gibt es im Judentum Ritualmord?"; D. Chwolson, *Die Blutanklage und sonstige mittelalterliche Beschuldigungen der Juden* (Frankfort, 1901); Baron, III, 38, 106; Roth, *The Ritual Murder Libel and the Jews* (London, 1935).

2. Parkes, II, 125. See further, on the profit that accrued to shrines, and the temptation to fake miracles, Cruel, p. 55; Owst, *Literature and Pulpit*, pp. 141, 148; Caro, I, 335; Burckhardt, p. 446.

3. Cf. Frankl, pp. 134 ff.; Fuchs, pp. 183 ff.; Michelson, p. 97.

4. Grunwald, *Vienna*, p. 15; Heffner, p. 28; Cruel, p. 623; Schudt, IV, 2, p. 406.

5. Cf. Kynass, p. 57; Bäch-St., IV, 830; Dubnow, II, 360. In some sections of Germany, into the nineteenth century, a spirit known as the *Jüdel* was believed to make its home in the oven, from which it sallied forth to attack the inmates of the house, the children, in particular. An antidote against it was to smear the mouth of the oven with pork, thus locking it in. The *Jüdel* was evidently a folk representation of the wicked Jew, whose egress could effectively be blocked with the pork! (Güdemann, I, 226, n. 3.)

6. See the lists in *JE*, III, 266 f., and in the works cited in n. 1 above. These accusations still crop up. The most recent important case occurred in Kiev, Russia, in 1911-13. In September, 1928, an instance of the charge was reported from Massena, N. Y., when a child was temporarily missing. The Nazi party has succeeded in revitalizing the myth through its incessant propaganda, the entire May 1, 1934, issue of the notorious *Stürmer* of Nuremberg, an official organ published by Julius Streicher, being devoted to this subject; few issues of the paper omit the illustration of a rabbi sucking blood from an "Aryan" child. The undimmed currency of the myth is sufficient testimony to its deep roots in the popular fancy.

7. Cf. Roth, *op. cit.*; Grayzel, pp. 79 f.; Aronius, No. 751, and Parkes, II, 138, 176, 195.

8. Reinach, Nos. 60, 61, p. 121; Josephus, *Against Apion*, II, 8.

9. E. Bickermann, "Ritualmord und Eselskult," *MGWJ*, LXXI (1927), 171–187, 255–264.

10. Cf. E. Schürer, *Geschichte des jüdischen Volkes im Zeitalter Jesu Christi* (4th ed. Leipzig, 1901-11), II, 552, n. 250; Chwolson, pp. 212 ff.; Parkes, I, 110 f.

11. Cf. Parkes, I, 234; Starr, p. 174; Roth, *Speculum*, pp. 521 f.

12. Caro, I, 138; Parkes, II, 46.

13. Tovey, pp. 65 f.; cf. Jacobs, p. 216.

14. Cf. Bentwich, *JQR*, XXIII (1932-33), 340.

15. Starr, pp. 22 f., 202, No. 149 (not No. 151, as cited in the text); Roth, *History of the Jews in England*, p. 102. Though the Doge declined to relieve the Jews of Crete of this obligation, in 1465 he graciously exempted the Jewish executioner from his duties on the Sabbath and holidays; see Starr, *Proceedings of the American Academy for Jewish Research*, XX (1942), pp. 68, 74 ff.

16. See Aronius, Nos. 311, 322, 323b, 337, 473, 668. Indicative of the general attitude is this incident: in 1343 the grave of a murdered hermit in the Rheinpfalz became the scene of miraculous cures, whereupon large numbers of Jews were burned as his murderers (Caro, II, 205).

17. Starr, pp. 209 f. The Bohemian chronicler Hajek reports the kidnaping of a child by Jews with the intention of killing it, in 1067, but a reference to the yellow Jew badge, which was not worn until the thirteenth cen-

tury, destroys whatever credibility this statement might otherwise claim (Bondy-Dworsky, I, 405, n. 100).

18. Jacobs, p. 19; Roth, *Speculum*, p. 523; Tovey, p. 136; *JE*, III, 260 f.

19. Jacobs, pp. 45 f. The twelfth-century accusations are listed in *JE*, III, 261; Bäch-St., IV, 822.

20. Cf. Aronius, No. 728; Grayzel, p. 265, note; Eck, pp. J4a–b; Loewe, p. 77. Here we have the prototype of the "Elders of Zion."

21. Jacobs, p. 75.

22. M. Paris, *Historia anglorum*, II, 375 (cf. *Chron. maj.*, III, 305).

23. *Chron. maj.*, V, 518; cf. Tovey, p. 136. The long-term effect of such accusations is well illustrated by the legendary fame that speedily surrounded the martyrdom and the miracle-working relics of Little St. Hugh. "The legend entered into the folklore of the English people: it was cited and imitated by Chaucer in his *Canterbury Tales:* it formed the inspiration of many ballads, in English, in French, and in Scots, which were handed down for centuries in the mouth of the peasantry. Thus, in after generations, when no Jew was left in England, it was from the poetical descriptions of this half-legendary event that a large part of the population received its impressions of the despised race" (Roth, *History of the Jews in England*, p. 57). For the extensive medieval literature on this case see Francisque Michel, *Hugues de Lincoln. Recueil de ballades anglo-normandes et écossoises relatives au meurtre de cet enfant, commis par les Juifs en MCCLV* (Paris and London, 1834); Cecil Roth, *Magna Bibliotheca Anglo-Judaica* (London, 1937) A. 8. 157–63; Modder, p. 13.

24. See Chap. VIII, n. 31 above. Other thirteenth-century crucifixion charges were made in Aragon, 1250, London, 1276, and Northampton, 1279 (Bäch-St., IV, 822; Roth, *History of the Jews in England*, p. 78). These lines from the early thirteenth-century Austrian poet, Seifried Helbling (cf. Güdemann, I, 145), indicate how rapidly the notion became a fixed item in medieval thought:

> ez bringet noch alliu jâr
> diu juden kristes marter dar,
> ein kristen sie mordent.

This charge illustrates graphically the time-negating effect of Christian teaching: the crucifixion was a *contemporary* event, always in the forefront of Christian consciousness. The psychology that could countenance such an accusation is revealed in an incident that occurred on May 8, 1147, when the Crusaders from France entered Rameru and in the course of their attack upon the local Jews seized the great rabbinic scholar Jacob Tam. According to a Jewish eyewitness they "inflicted five wounds on his head, saying: 'You are the most distinguished man in Israel; therefore we will avenge on you the crucified one, and wound you in the same manner as you did, inflicting five wounds on our God.'" (Neubauer and Stern, *Hebräische Berichte*, pp. 64, 195, cited by Kisch, *Jewry-Law*, II, 155, n. 99a).

25. *JE*, III, 261; cf. Grayzel, pp. 264 f., n. 2.

26. *JE*, III, 261, 263; Aronius, No. 497; *Historia Judaica*, I (1938-39), 71 f.

27. Loewe, p. 77; Eck, p. K3b. Bäch-St., IV, 822, lists these as additional instances of the crucifixion charge: Prague, 1389; Toledo (La Guardia), 1490; Raus, Poland (Michael), 1547; Siebenbürgen, 1791; Ingrandes, France, 1892.

28. *JE*, III, 263; Roth, *Ritual Murder Libel and the Jews*, pp. 21 f., 97; Grayzel, pp. 271, 275; Bondy-Dworsky, I, 33; Stern, *Urkundliche Beiträge*, I, 6. It is

a curious circumstance that so much of our information concerning this charge comes from papal pronouncements denying its truth and forbidding its dissemination (cf. Roth, *op. cit.*, and M. Stern, *Päpstliche Bullen über die Blutbeschuldigung* [Munich, 1900]). Gregory X went so far as to "ordain that Christian witnesses shall not be heard against Jews in such cases . . . and that Jews shall not be imprisoned for such frivolous causes, except, which we do not believe, when they are caught in the act" (Bondy-Dworsky, *loc. cit.;* cf. Vogelstein, *Rome*, pp. 175 f.; Grayzel, p. 274, n. 4).

29. Cf. Bondy-Dworsky, I, 95 ff. (also *idem*, pp. 328 f.); Stern, *Urkundliche Beiträge*, I, 32; Amador, III, 429.

30. Stern, *op. cit.*, I, 9; Strack, p. 190. The influence of this changed emphasis is to be noted in a fifteenth-century account of the case of William of Norwich, which transferred his martyrdom from Easter to "a feast of Passover" (Jacobs, p. 19). Although red wine is preferred for the Passover ritual, Rabbi David b. Samuel Halevi of Ostrau (seventeenth century) pointed out that "nowadays we are prevented from using red wine because of false accusations" (*Magen David Orah Hayim*, 472.9). Eight times in sixty years (1623–84) we find the Lithuanian *Vaad* adopting legislation to deal with the effects of the ritual murder charge (Dubnow, *Pinkes Hamedinah* [Berlin, 1925], Nos. 9, 110, 307, 440, 684, 725, 768, 781).

31. Aronius, No. 469.

32. *Idem*, No. 474; Strack, p. 178.

33. Aronius, No. 728; Strack, p. 182.

34. Strack, pp. 183 ff.; Scherer, p. 348.

35. *JE*, III, 262; Scherer, p. 593.

36. Williams, p. 278, n. 4.

37. Jews were also subsequently forced to confess that they had mixed the blood in their unleavened bread and wine. An indication of how such cases were created is provided by the fact that the alleged crime followed a series of vitriolic attacks upon the Jews during Lent in sermons by the notorious Franciscan Jew baiter Bernadin da Feltre, who, indeed, *predicted* that the Jews would attempt some such act against Christendom. This case aroused a tremendous stir, became a favorite literary topic, and the type after which many later accusations were modeled. Cf. Scherer, pp. 597 ff.; *JE*, III, 263; Geiger, *Zeitschrift*, II, 308; Liliencron, II, 13 ff.

38. Strack, pp. 206, 207, 215.

39. *Shebet Yehudah*, No. 62.

40. Bondy-Dworsky, I, 116 ff.; Stern, *op. cit.*, I, 46; Baer, II, 315.

41. Roth, *History of the Jews in England*, p. 121, n. 6; Eck, p. M2b; Friss, pp. 404 ff.

42. Parkes, II, 379; Scherer, p. 435, prints this extract from an anonymous fifteenth-century lampoon, which quotes the Jew as proudly proclaiming:

> Es wer vil mer zu schreiben not,
> Wie wir den christen tuen den tod
> Mit mancher wunderlicher pein
> An iren clein kindelein.
> Wir fressen dann ir fleisch vnd pluet
> Vnd glauben, es kumb uns wol zu guet.

43. Bäch-St., IV, 825. It is probably in order to point out also that Catholic missionaries in China and Frenchmen in Madagascar have been accused by the natives of killing children and using their hearts in some mystic

rites, and that in Egypt, too, Christian physicians have had to answer to the charge of eating the hearts and drinking the blood of Moslem patients (cf. Stern, *op. cit.*, II, 64, n. 4).

CHAPTER X. THE BLOOD ACCUSATION

1. Cf. Strack, pp. 50 ff.; Thorndike, I, 62, 249, 418 f., 629, II, Index, *s.v.* "Blood," and "Human body, use of parts of."
2. Roskoff, I, 347.
3. Bäch-St.; I, 1438, IV, 815.
4. *JE*, III, 264; Eck, p. a1a.
5. Strack, p. 19; cf. also Thorndike, II, *loc. cit.*
6. V. Fossel, *Volksmedicin und medicinischer Aberglaube in Steiermark* (Graz, 1886), cited in Summers, p. 161. See Bäch-St., I, 1436 f., 1443 f., on the extensive medicinal uses of blood in particular.
7. Parkes, I, 293, 296.
8. Strack, pp. 62 ff., 138 f.; Frankl, p. 17.
9. Cf. the works cited in chap. ix, n. 1, above, and also Trachtenberg, pp. 129, 203.
10. Aronius, No. 749; Aug. Digot, *Histoire de Lorraine* (Nancy, 1856), II, p. 144.
11. *Chron. maj.*, V, 517: "Et cum exspirasset puer, deposuerunt corpus de cruce, et nescitur qua ratione, euiscerarunt corpusculum; dicitur autem, quod ad magicas artes exercendas"; and *idem*, p. 518: "inutile enim reputabatur corpus insontis augurio, ad hoc enim euiscerabatur."
12. Cf. Stobbe, p. 288. The statement closes with what may be construed as a disarming effort to tell the whole truth, in justice to the Jews: "Aber an grossen töden, die das land durchgant, habent sie nit schuld." This is really a generous admission, coming only half a century after the Black Death.
13. Parkes, II, 69.
14. Schudt, I, 461, citing Basnage, *Histoire et religion des Juifs*, VII, chap. xviii, Par. 19, p. 1824.
15. Eck, p. F3a.
16. *Idem;* Schudt, IV, 1, p. 298, recounts the same tale as having occurred in Coburg, Franconia.
17. Quoted by Schudt, IV, 1, p. 61.
18. Friedlander, p. 7.
19. P. K3a.
20. Dubnow, I, 100.
21. *Idem*, p. 173. See *EJ*, II, 1004, for a number of cases in Poland during the sixteenth and seventeenth centuries.
22. Bäch-St., IV, 815.
23. Aronius, No. 474; *JE*, III, 261.
24. Aronius, No. 728; *JE*, *loc. cit.;* Cruel, p. 622.
25. Eck, p. K1a ("And even those Jews who do not need Christian blood for their health still murder Christians out of hate," he insists); cf. also Kirchhof, III, 366: "die Jüden vermögen ohne Christen blut nicht sein oder leben."
26. Stobbe, pp. 288 f.; Wiener, p. 236. Abraham a Santa Clara also alleges

that Christian blood is required to counteract the Jews' "hateful, nasty and abominable stink" (Frankl, p. 133).

27. Stobbe, p. 289, note.

28. Strack, p. 202; see also *idem*, pp. 174 ff., and I. Loeb, *REJ*, XX (1890), 25 f., on the reputed use of Christian blood by Jews as a medicament. The story told by Johann Eck (p. B2b) of the murder of a child in the vicinity of Genoa in 1452 by a number of Jews, who dipped various fruits into the blood and then ate them, is evidently intended to convey a similar moral.

29. Stobbe, *loc. cit.;* cf. also Frankl, p. 133.

30. *Endinger Judenspiel*, pp. 39 f., ll. 595 ff.:
> Dass blut derselben bhaltet flissig,
> die häupter auch gantz unverdrissig,
> zue grossen sachen, die mir wissen,
> zue brauchen künstlich und zue gniessen.

The effect successfully achieved throughout the play is that Jews require the blood and heads for secret, mysterious purposes. Cf. also p. 26, ll. 211 ff.:
> Zue dem so ist der christen bluet
> zue vil sachen gar nutz und guet,
> wie dass soll wissen gschwinde meister,
> die haben sonderliche geister.

31. *Malenzye*, cf. Lexer, *Mittelhochdeutsches Handwörterbuch, s.v.* "malenzie," "malâterie."

32. See the text of the confessions printed at the end of the *Endinger Judenspiel*, pp. 95, 97.

33. *REJ*, XVI (1888), 242.

34. Margaritha, p. H3b; *JE*, III, 264.

35. Cf. Eck, p. J4a; Cruel, p. 583.

36. Bäch-St., I, 1439.

37. Dubnow, II, 77.

38. Chwolson, pp. 205 ff.; Graetz, *Geschichte*, X, 264. According to a popular rumor Moses Germanus was finally, for some unspecified reason, finished off by a Jewish poisoner, cf. Schudt, I, 274.

39. Cf. Frankl, p. 134.

40. Vol. III, p. 367; cf. also Frankl, p. 133; Chwolson, pp. 193 ff.

41. Friss, p. 410; Strack, p. 204; Chwolson, p. 183.

42. Frankl, p. 133.

43. Chwolson, pp. 183 ff.; Dubnow, II, 73. In Oldenburg it is believed that Jews bathe in Christian blood (Bäch-St., I, 1439).

44. Of course, the psychology of the blood accusation cuts far deeper. Medieval Christianity was possessed of a blood obsession that is artlessly exposed in all the religious and folkloristic literature. Preachers and writers dwelt at inordinate length (sermons lasting an entire day were by no means uncommon) and with fond minuteness upon the sufferings of Jesus, inventing new refinements of torture for the delectation of their audience, and almost sensibly reveling in the blood that dripped with every sentence. One of the characteristic touches, for instance, was to the effect that Jesus sweated real blood while he prayed, before Judas betrayed him (not merely "*as it were* great drops of blood" as Luke 22.44 has it). In the same way the gruesome details of the alleged child murders were

multiplied and embellished with barbaric delight, different sources vying
with one another to excel in the description of the mutilation and bleeding
of the victims. Somehow blood—the blood of Christ, of martyrs and saints,
of slashed images and mutilated hosts, of murdered children—seems to have
been one of the foremost themes of popular Christianity. One cannot
escape the impression that an abysmal guilt feeling drove Christendom
to re-murder Jesus, the personification of its uneasy conscience, time without end, and to seek release by projecting its guilt upon the Jews, washing
clean the stain on its conscience with the blood of Jesus' people. This
takes us into another realm, with which we have no business here. But it
is a matter worth considering.

45. Summers, p. 195.

Chapter XI. Church and Jew

1. Williams, p. 355.
2. Jacobs, pp. 7 ff.; cf. also *idem*, p. 78.
3. See Parkes, I, 119, 222, II, 16 ff., 40 ff., 49 ff.; S. Zeitlin, *JQR*, XXXI (1940),
   30 f.; Rabinowitz, pp. 130 ff.; Baron, II, 40 ff., III, 108 f.; Roth, *History of
   the Jews in England*, p. 93; Adler, pp. 21, 122; *Germania Judaica*, Introd.,
   pp. xxxiv ff.; A. Berliner, *Persönliche Beziehungen zwischen Christen und
   Juden im Mittelalter* (Halberstadt, 1881). It is worth noting that the Hebrew commentaries of Rashi on Bible and Talmud have turned out to be
   the most important repository of Old French, and that Isaac ben Moses
   performed the same service for Old Czech in his *Or Zarua*, where he also
   speaks of Czech as "our language" and of Bohemia as "our country."
4. For a discussion of the influence of Church policy upon secular legislation
   see Scherer, pp. 50 ff.; Kisch, *Jewry-Law*, II, 151 ff.
5. Parkes, I, 97 ff., 204
6. Vol. I, p. 158; see also *idem*, pp. 297 ff.
7. *Idem*, p. 166.
8. *Idem*, pp. 220 f.; see also pp. 210 ff. The following quotation is from *Historia Judaica*, I (1938–39), 33.
9. Kisch, *Proceedings of the American Academy for Jewish Research*, VI
   (1935), 259 f.; cf. Bondy-Dworsky, I, 41 f.
10. *REJ*, XVII (1889), p. 215, n. 2.
11. Grayzel, pp. 264 f. A century earlier we have this forthright injunction
    from the pen of St. Bernard, addressed to the clergy and people of Eng-
    land, France, and Germany: "You should not persecute the Jews, you
    should not slay them, you should not even put them to flight" (Jacobs,
    p. 22).
12. Parkes, II, 211 f.; Grayzel, pp. 76 f., 93 f.
13. Jacobs, pp. 122, 123.
14. Parkes, II, 85 f., 125 ff.; Grayzel, pp. 79 ff.; Caro, I, 288 ff.; Rabinowitz,
    pp. 126 f.; F. Murawski, *Die Juden bei den Kirchevätern und Scholas-
    tikern* (Berlin, 1925).
15. Parkes, II, 58; Regné, pp. 63, 92 f.
16. Parkes, II, 72; cf. also *idem*, pp. 62 ff.

Chapter XII. Infidel or Heretic?

1. Cf., e.g., James Bryce, *The Holy Roman Empire* (New York, 1887), p. 159: "It was indeed in these wars, more particularly in the first three of them, that the ideal of a Christian commonwealth . . . was once for all and never again realized. . . . The religious feeling which the Crusades evoked . . . turned wholly against the opponent of ecclesiastical claims, and was made to work the will of the Holy See, which had blessed and organized the project." See also *idem*, pp. 200 f., and *HERE*, IV, 350: the most notable result of the Crusades was the "increased importance of the Papacy, as the embodiment of the unity of Christendom, and the leader in the call to war."
2. Caro, I, 299; Newman, p. 310.
3. *Historia Judaica*, I (1938–39), 32; cf. also his I, 102 f., 203, 239 ff., 255 f., 300 ff., II, 12; Murawski, p. 50; Williams, p. 319.
4. Starr, pp. 90 f., cf. also *idem*, p. 76; Newman, pp. 304, 613 ff.
5. Cf. Cruel, p. 62. The poet Helbling (Frankl, p. 46) wrote in the thirteenth century: "ez war wol der in verbut ir ketzerlichez talmut, ein buch valsch und ungenaem."
6. Maharil, *Responsa,* No. 233 (quoted in Güdemann, III, 145, n. 5); and Amador, III, 270, n. 1.
7. Frankl, p. 58; Lewin, pp. 4, 6, 7, 12, 31, 45, 65, 106, 107, etc. The juxtaposition of "Jew" and "heretic" is extremely common in the late medieval sources.
8. Cf. Bondy-Dworsky, I, 101, II, 910; Scherer, p. 410; Kracauer, *Geschichte der Juden in Frankfurt*, pp. 159 ff.; Güdemann, III, 155. A century later Kirchhof (*Wendunmuth*, II, 189) dared his readers to make this wager:

   In Böhmer wald wandern ohn gfahrig,
   Ein kätzer, ohn irrthumb verharrig
   Und ein Jud, der nicht ist halssztarrig,
   So leicht man ietzund finden kann,
   Also weisze raben, schwartze schwaan,
   Wett, oder must verloren han.

9. Newman, pp. 131 ff., and Index, *s.v.* "Judaizing"; Parkes, II, 30; Güdemann, I, 223 f., II, 92. It was reported of a heretical sect that appeared in the town of Monforte, Lombardy, during the eleventh century, that "they adored idols after the fashion of pagans, and sought to celebrate their foolish sacrifices with the Jews" (Coulton, *Inquisition and Liberty*, p. 9); the Jews had ceased offering sacrifices with the destruction of the temple by the Romans in the year 70.
10. Vol. II, pp. 46 f.
11. Parkes, II, 139.
12. Cf. Newman, pp. 317 ff.; Parkes, II, 172; Scherer, pp. 46 ff., 51, 55; Grayzel, pp. 336 f., 341 f. There is some uncertainty concerning the date of the burning of the Talmud in France, cf. Graetz, *Geschichte*, VII, 405 ff.; Grayzel, pp. 240, 252; Vogelstein, p. 396, n. 22.
13. Stern, *Urkundliche Beiträge*, I, 107: "Ogni opera Hebraica che si serve dell' autorità del Talmuth tutto dannato dalla santa chiesa come heretico, prophano et prohibito"; cf. *idem*, pp. 73 f., 99 ff., on this movement. On the Pfefferkorn agitation and the ensuing controversy between Reuchlin

and the Dominicans see Graetz, *Geschichte*, IX, 477–506, and Index, *s.v.* "Pfefferkorn."

14. Caro, II, 80.
15. Stern, *op. cit.*, I, 47.
16. These offenses are cited from an order of Philip the Fair in 1299 instructing his officials to hand over the offending Jews to the Inquisition; cf. Saige, pp. 235 f.; Parkes, II, 140. A discussion of the relations between the Inquisition and the Jews may be found in Parkes, II, 136 ff., and Newman, pp. 303 ff.
17. Cf. Robert, pp. 107 ff., 116 ff. "Ce qui montre bien que les miniaturistes ont attaché à la roue un caractère d'infamie, c'est qu'ils ne donnent pas ce signe aux Juifs dont le rôle sera honnête ou indifférent" (*idem*, p. 112).
18. Cf. Cruel, pp. 499, 622; Haenle, p. 23; Eck, p. E2a; Schudt, II, 1, pp. 355 ff., has a long dissertation on this subject. See also Bäch-St., IV, 818, 824, 826.
19. Cf. Murawski, pp. 21, 49; Williams, pp. 34, 260, 353; Aronius, No. 89; Güdemann, II, 260; Scherer, p. 435; Graetz, *Geschichte*, VIII, 70 f.; Schudt, II, 2, pp. 244 ff.
20. Cf. Graetz, *op. cit.*, IV, 400 ff.; I. Elbogen, *Der jüdische Gottesdienst in seiner geschichtlichen Entwicklung* (Leipzig, 1913), pp. 51 f.; A. Z. Idelsohn, *Jewish Liturgy and Its Development* (New York, 1932), pp. 102 f.
21. The letters of the Hebrew alphabet also serve as numerals.
22. Cf. L. Zunz, *Die Ritus des synagogalen Gottesdienstes* (Berlin 1919), p. 147; Elbogen, *op. cit.*, pp. 80 f.; Idelsohn, *op. cit.*, pp. 116, 316; Schudt, II, 2, pp. 244 ff., and III, 198 ff. Of course, it is true that Jews and Christians traded cuss words and insulting epithets, though it must be said that most of the honors went to the Christians, who need not fear uttering them aloud and could take violent exception to Jewish indulgence in this game. Christians objected that Jews greeted them abusively, used insulting expressions in place of "Christ" or "church," etc., which was undoubtedly so. What other means did Jews have to express their resentment? The term *sheketz* ("abomination"), to denote a Christian, which came into use in the fifteenth century or thereabouts, was feeble and even dignified reprisal for the vile abuse they had to bear. Jews were being called "stinking dogs," fit only to have "pigs defecate in their mouths"; "each one ought to be placed under an outhouse." "Such expressions are made for polite society," remarks Güdemann (III, 206, n. 4), "compared to other, untranslatable indecencies" that crowded the pages of "serious" works on the Jewish question.
23. Cf. Parkes, I, 133 ff.; Scherer, pp. 467 f.; Schudt, I, p. 390, IV, 1, pp. 274 f., 298 f., 304; Güdemann, III, 153.
24. I. Lévi, *REJ*, XXX (1895), 295 ff.
25. I. Lévi, *REJ*, XLVIII (1904), 199 ff.; Regné, pp. 13 ff.
26. Parkes, II, 33 f., 43; J. Mann, *Texts and Studies in Jewish History and Literature* (Cincinnati, 1931), I, 16 ff.
27. Parkes, I, 368, II, 37 ff.
28. Roth, *History of the Jews in England*, p. 61; M. Paris, *Chron. maj.*, IV, 77, 131 ff.; H. Bresslau, *Juden und Mongolen*.
29. Cf. Bondy-Dworsky, I, 336 f., 447, note, II, 567; Pribram, I, 8, 32, 45; Schudt, I, 89, 344; *JE*, III, 416; Starr, *Proceedings of the American Academy for Jewish Research*, XII (1942), p. 69. Schudt (II, 1, p. 298) alleges that Jews tried to betray the city of Frankfort when it was besieged by the Swedes in 1635.

30. Lewin, p. 74; Frankl, p. 107; Michelson, pp. 77, 79; Lifschitz-Golden, p. 97; Strumpf, pp. 29, 39, n. 17.
31. *Historia Judaica*, II (1940), 98; J. R. Marcus, *Hebrew Union College Jubilee Volume* (Cincinnati, 1925), p. 380.
32. Frankl, p. 58; Lewin, *passim* (see the references in note 7 above) and p. 91; Newman, pp. 617 f.; Geiger, *Zeitschrift*, II, 330, 370 ff.
33. Cf. Parkes, I, 174, 182, 351, and Appendix I, Part 2, *s.v.* "Intermarriage"; and Starr, p. 144, for the early clerical and secular legislation on this subject, which was preserved in the medieval law codes. On punishments meted out to Jews who had relations with Christians, see Stobbe, pp. 266 f., n. 151; and Scherer, p. 585, who cites this account of the savage treatment accorded a Jew apprehended *in flagrante delicto:* "Anno Christi 1536. Ist ein Jüde in Praga in Behemen gewesen, so mit einer Christin gebulet vnnd drüber ergriffen; da hat er müssen sein Mennlich Glied zu einem Spunde eines gepichten brennenden Fasses hinein stecken und wurde jm darzu auffs Fass ein schartig stumpff messer geleget. als jm nu die hitze so grimmig wehe gethan, hat er jhm mit dem Messer sein Gliedt vor schmertz abgeschnitten. Vnnd da er nun also blutig hat darvon lauffen wöllen, hat man böse hunde an jhn gehetzet, die ihn zurissen haben" (from Hondorff, *Promptuarium exemplorum* [Frankfort 1572], p. 350 a). As Scherer points out, this seems to have been an act of "lynch justice" and not based on law, though, according to an ordinance of 1422 in Mainz, a Jewish "adulterer" was to have his *Ding* cut off and an eye gouged out. Still, this penalty could be compounded for a fine.
34. *The Criminal Prosecution and Capital Punishment of Animals* (London 1906), p. 152.

CHAPTER XIII. THE ATTACK UPON USURY

1. In Angevin England, for example, in the latter half of the twelfth century, when there were about two thousand Jews among the total population of some one and a half million, the Jews were obliged to account annually for one twelfth of the total royal income (about £3,000 out of £35,000); in 1187, through fines, fees, tallages, special imposts, etc., the royal exchequer derived £60,000 from the Jews, as against another £70,000 from all the rest of England! Jacobs (from whom these figures are derived—see pp. xviii f., and p. 382) puts the matter quite justly: "They acted the part of a sponge for the Royal Treasury," he says; "they gathered up all the floating money of the country, to be squeezed from time to time into the king's treasure-chest. . . . The king was thus . . . the sleeping-partner in all the Jewish usury, and may be regarded as the archusurer of the country." Moreover, the king's right to confiscate the estates of Jewish usurers, prescribed by canon law, immeasurably strengthened his political power over the barons and clergy whose debts would thus ultimately fall into his hands. See also the very interesting defense of Jewish usury by King Ladislaus of Bohemia, in Bondy-Dworsky, I, 173 ff.
2. Parkes, *Historia Judaica*, I (1938-39), 37; cf. also his Vol. II, chaps. viii and ix.
3. Vol. III, p. 107; see also Cecil Roth, "The Most Persecuted People?" *Menorah Journal*, XX (New York, 1932), 136-147.

4. Cf. Aronius, p. 319.

5. Güdemann, III, 182 ff.; Geiger, *Zeitschrift*, II, 348, III, 297; Pauli, No. 192.

6. Ex. 22.25, Deut. 23.19, enforced by the supposed direct prohibition of the Gospel, Luke 6.35: *Mutuum date, nihil sperantes* (Vulgate), "Lend, hoping for nothing again" (A. V.), but now translated (R. V.): "Lend, never despairing." "Usury," of course, meant lending on interest in general, no matter what the rate.

7. Parkes, II, 283 ff., 288 f.; Newman, pp. 194 f., 197 ff. On the general subject see F. Schaub, *Der Kampf gegen den Zinswucher, ungerechten Preis und unlauteren Handel* (Freiburg, 1905).

8. Caro, I, 223; Newman, p. 197.

9. Brant, pp. 148, 188; Kirchhof, V, 131; Güdemann, III, 192, 276 ff.

10. Modder, p. 33.

11. Cf. the decree of Louis IX, the saint, 1254 (Graetz, *Geschichte*, VII, 410), and of the Council of Beziers the following year (Grayzel, pp. 336 f.).

12. Parkes, II, 284.

13. Owst, *Literature and Pulpit*, p. 554, and n. 1; Güdemann, III, 189; Lecoy de la Marche, *La Chaire française*, pp. 116 ff., 416 ff.; Crane, Nos. 168 ff.

14. Frankl, pp. 88 f.: "Der pennigk ist roit, disser ist krank, disser ist doch zurissen, disser hot ein hole, disser hot ein falsch zeichen, disser ist doch swarcz, disser ricz ist zu maile langk, der ist blien," etc.

15. Güdemann, III, 188, 191; Lenient, *La Satire en France au moyen âge*, pp. 182, 185. Schudt (I, 258) ascribes to Edwin Sandys the statement that in Italy, on being baptized, Jews were required to forswear the devil and all his works, including usury.

16. Fuchs, p. 13; Liebe, pp. 18, 37, 69.

17. *Werke* (Weimar, 1920), LIII, 521.

Chapter XIV. The Crusade against Sorcery

1. Cf. Lea, *History of the Inquisition of the Middle Ages*, III, 416 ff., and *Materials*, pp. 105–198; Thorndike, II, 343.

2. Thorndike, III, 18 ff.; during the thirteenth and fourteenth centuries there are many instances of ecclesiastics being charged with poisoning, sorcery, murder, image-magic, etc.; see also Lea, *loc. cit.*

3. Cruel, pp. 617 ff.; Owst, *Literature and Pulpit*, p. 112; Lea, III, 414 f.

4. Lea, *Inquisition of the Middle Ages*, III, 410. Geiler von Kaisersberg, a fifteenth-century preacher, after recounting many miraculous cures as proof of the effectiveness of such items, proceeded as follows: "You see then that when something is consecrated to the honor of a saint, or is brought into contact with his relics, it becomes similarly useful. Thus, one can use St. Anthony water, that is, water in which his relic has been dipped, against fire in a bodily organ; St. Humbrecht's water against the bite of a mad dog; St. Peter's water may be drunk to counteract a cold fever; St. Agatha's bread is used against fire; for a sore throat one may tie around the neck a candle consecrated in honor of St. Blaise; St. Valentine's water is good for epilepsy." Catholic spokesmen actually urged upon their flocks such applications of consecrated objects. Cf. Cruel, *loc. cit.*

5. Owst, *op. cit.*, pp. 93 ff., 112 f., 146, n. 7, 512; Lenient, *La Satire en France au moyen âge*, pp. 173 ff., 402 ff.; Cruel, p. 267; Roskoff, I, 350 ff. The last-

named writes (I, 317): "Alle Schriftsteller, welche den Teufelsglauben des Mittelalters besprechen, stimmen in der Wahrnehmung überein: dass die Vorstellung vom Teufel und die Furcht vor seiner Macht innerhalb des 13. Jahrhunderts den Gipfelpunkt erreicht und von da ab die Gemüther beherrscht."

6. Stern, *Urkundliche Beiträge*, I, 176, No. 38: "Die 31 Januarii 1608. Rabbi, qui negaverat existentiam daemonis, revocavit et fuit dictum, ut detestaretur propositionem."

7. For a discussion of the Gnostic heresies and magic see Thorndike, I, 360–384.

8. Güdemann, I, 220: "Bruder bertholt, wie sülle wir uns vor in behüten, so lange daz sie güten lüten so gar gliche sint?"

9. M. Summers, *Geography of Witchcraft* (London, 1927), p. 469; Jakob Sprenger, *Malleus maleficarum* (Lyons, 1669), III, 25; cf. also *idem*, I, 1. Sprenger was an Inquisitor in the Rhine provinces.

10. See on this subject: H. C. Lea, *A History of the Inquisition of the Middle Ages* (New York, 1911), III, 432 ff.; and *Materials Toward a History of Witchcraft*, ed. by A. C. Howland (Philadelphia, 1939), 3 vols.; M. Summers, *The History of Witchcraft and Demonology* (London, 1926); *The Geography of Witchcraft* (London, 1927); Margaret A. Murray, *The Witch-Cult in Western Europe* (Oxford, 1921) (though the approach of these last two writers is open to serious criticism, they have assembled much valuable information); J. Français, *L'Eglise et la sorcellerie* (Paris, 1910); J. Hansen, *Quellen und Untersuchungen zur Geschichte des Hexenwahns und der Hexenverfolgung im Mittelalter* (Bonn, 1901); W. G. Soldan and H. Heppe, *Geschichte der Hexenprozesse* (3d ed., revised and edited by Max Bauer, 2 vols. Munich, 1911). J. Hansen, "Inquisition und Hexenverfolgung im Mittelalter," *Historische Zeitschrift*, LXXXI (1898) 385–432, and *Zauberwahn, Inquisition und Hexenprozess im Mittelalter* (Munich, 1900), pp. 292 ff., devotes special attention to the relation between the Inquisition's campaign against heresy and the spread of the belief in magic. See also *HERE*, VIII, 308.

11. Lea, *A History of the Inquisition of the Middle Ages*, III, 549; Bertrand Russell, *Religion and Science* (New York, 1935), pp. 97 f.

12. Cf. Lea, *op. cit.*, III, 432 ff.; Français, pp. 63 ff., 272 ff. In his treatise of 1325 on astrology Geoffrey of Meaux declared that one born under a certain conjunction will incline to incredulity and adhere to sorcery and heresy (Thorndike, III, 289). The coupling of sorcery, heresy, and incredulity (i.e., heterodoxy) as naturally associated is a noteworthy token of the popular view.

13. Caro, II, 80; Baer, I, 343; Lea, *loc. cit.*, and *A History of the Inquisition of Spain* (New York, 1906), II, 93 f. A medieval copper engraving portrays "Heresy" as a nude woman, with horns, tail, and cloven hoof, just as Jews and sorcerers were commonly pictured (Soldan-Heppe, I, facing p. 130).

14. Lifschitz-Golden, p. 123; Strumpf, p. 39, n. 20 and n. 23; Loewe, p. 56.

15. Lea, *A History of the Inquisition of the Middle Ages*, III, 495 f., 534; *REJ*, XLVI (1903), 243 f. Cf. also Roskoff, I, 326 ff., II, 124 ff.; Soldan-Heppe, I, 137.

16. Cf. Soldan-Heppe, I, 142 ff., and the engraving portraying heretics celebrating their orgiastic rites, *idem*, facing p. 138.

17. Lecoy de la Marche, *La Chaire française*, p. 427; Güdemann, I, 221; M.

Lexer, *Mittelhochdeutsches Handwörterbuch, s.v.* "ketzerie." *Ketzer* was often spelled *kätzer* (see, e.g., Brant, *Narrenschiff*, p. 197, and Chapter XII, n. 8, above).

Chapter XV. Heretic-Sorcerer-Jew

1. The fourteenth-century Breslau code mentioned above (p. 67), which Professor Kisch intends to publish shortly, includes under the rubric *Juden* not only the significant passage relating to sorcerers, but immediately preceding it a paragraph (J 158) concerning *heretics*, again with no express reference to Jews. The combination in this context provides a strikingly pat illustration of the Jew-heretic-sorcerer pattern.

2. An excellent collection is to be found in Grillot de Givry's *Le Musée des sorciers, mages et alchimistes* (Paris, 1929); also in the Munich, 1911, ed. of Soldan-Heppe.

3. Cf. de Givry, *op. cit.*, pp. 36, 62, 63, 68, 70, 71, 74, etc.; Soldan-Heppe, Index, *s.v.* "Teufel, als Bock"; Johann Scheible, *Das Schaltjahr* (Stuttgart, 1846–47), III, 212.

4. Bulard, p. 48; Güdemann, I, 225; cf. also J. Scheible, *Das Kloster*, II (Stuttgart, 1846), 223 f.; *REJ*, XX (1890), 231.

5. Browe, *Archiv für Kulturgeschichte*, XX (1930), 146, and *Die eucharistischen Wunder*, p. 133. The same document from which the Brünn enactment is derived also recounts an incident in which two Christian students who had stolen some hosts and offered them for sale to the Jews of the city, who reported this to the authorities, were arrested and executed as heretics.

6. Soldan-Heppe, I, 144; Grayzel, p. 329; cf. the decree issued by Henry IV of Castile in 1465 (Baer, II, 331) ordering that Jews, Moors, and "wicked Christians" who desecrate the host are to be prosecuted as heretics: "Somos informados que algunos judios e moros han procurado algunas veces de aver la hostia consangrada e de quebrantar la ara consangrada e de tomar la crisma e olio e las otras cosas consangradas para hacer algunos maleficios en injuria de nuestro sennor e de su santa eglesia e de nuestra fe, en lo qual algunas veces han seido participantes algunos malos christianos."

7. Cf. Thorndike, II, 27; Loewe, p. 53; Murray, p. 148; Summers, pp. 89, 145 ff.; Lea, *History of the Inquisition of the Middle Ages*, III, 500; *Materials*, pp. 237, 240, etc.; Peuckert, *Pansophie*, pp. 358 f.; Bäch-St., IV, 414 ff.; Browe, *Die Eucharistie als Zaubermittel im Mittelalter*. The cross, the crucifix, and images of Jesus, Mary, and the saints, were also believed to be misused by the witch-cults; see, e.g., Bäch-St., V, 478 ff.

8. Browe, *op. cit.*, p. 147; cf. Lea, *Materials*, p. 780.

9. *REJ*, XLVI (1903), p. 240.

10. See Thorndike, II, Index, *s.v.* "Poison," for a number of such cases in the thirteenth and fourteenth centuries.

11. Joesten, pp. 10 f. "Der Juden ketzerliches gift legten si all in di prunnen," wrote a medieval rhymster (Liliencron, I, 47). Cf. Lea, *Materials, passim;* Burckhardt, p. 502, Murray, pp. 124, 125, 258, 279 f., etc., and Soldan-Heppe, Index, *s.v.* "Gift," for instances of the use of poisons by the devotees of witchcraft.

12. Examples of infant murder and of the uses to which the bodies and blood

were put abound in the records of the trials of sorcerers and witches; see in particular Lea, *History of the Inquisition of the Middle Ages*, III, 407, 468 ff., 502, 504 f.; *Materials*, pp. 233, 237, 239, 240, 780, 915 f., etc.; Murray, pp. 49, 80, 81, 84, 100, 150, 153, 156 ff., 209 ff., 213 ff., 225; Summers, pp. 144 f., 160 f.; Soldan-Heppe, Index, *s.v.* "Kindesmord."

13. "Les Fascinateurs," *Mélusine*, IV (1888–89), *passim*.

EPILOGUE. STILL THE DEVIL'S OWN

1. "Ach mein Gott, mein lieber Schöpfer und Vater," he wrote in his *Vom Schem Hamphoras*, "du wirst mir gnädlich zu gut halten, dass ich (gar ungern) von deiner göttlichen, ewigen Majestät so schändlich muss reden wider deine verfluchten Feinde, Teufel und Juden. Du weisst, dass ichs tu aus Brunst meines Glaubens und zu Ehren deiner göttlichen Majestät: denn es gehet mir durch Leib und Leben" (*Werke* [Weimar, 1920], LIII, 605).

And again he writes: "Wohlan, es möcht vielleicht der barmherzigen Heiligen einer unter uns Christen denken ich machte es ja zu grob und unesse wider die armen, elenden Juden, dass ich so spöttisch und höhnisch mit ihnen handele. Ah Herr Gott, ich bin zu geringe dazu, solcher Teufel zu spotten; ich wollts wohl gern tun, aber sie sind mir zu weit überlegen mit Spotten, haben auch einen Gott, der ist Meister mit Spotten, und heisst der leidige Teufel und böser Geist. Was ich demselben zu Verdriess spotten künnt, das sollt ich billig tun, er hätte es auch wohl verdient" (*op. cit.*, pp. 590 f.).

It is not incomprehensible, then, that a character in a miracle play (*Miracle de S. Hildefonse* by Gautier de Coincy), a saint, no less, should thus conjugate the verb *haïr* with respect to the Jews (Lifschitz-Golden, p. 135):

> Moult les hai, et je les haiz,
> Et Dieu les het, et je si faiz
> Et touz li mons les doit haïr. . . .

2. *Werke* (Weimar, 1897), XIX, 599, 600 ff.
3. Lewin, pp. 76, 82, 90. Luther's story, which occurs also in the *Tischreden* (*Werke* [Erlangen 1854], LXII, 371), is derived from a tale in Kirchhof's *Wendunmuth*, III, 255. The Freising inscription reads: "So wahr die Maus die Katz nit frisst, wird der Jud ein wahrer Christ," evidently a current saying of the period (Frankl, p. 56, n. 1). This popular medieval theme (cf. Frankl, pp. 54 ff.; Güdemann, III, 146 f.; Geiger, *Zeitschrift*, II, 335, n. 1, 345, III, p. 297) was by no means of recent origin. A seventh-century legend records a saying then current among Christians: "When a Jew is baptized, it is as though one baptized an ass" (Parkes, I, 290). Baptism might temporarily efface the Jew's demonic odor, but in the long run it didn't take! Even after centuries of devout Catholicism the stigma of Jewishness, with all it implies in the popular imagination, can remain a barrier between the descendants of the converts and their Christian neighbors. The Chuetas of Majorca are an outstanding instance in point (see Baruch Braunstein, *The Chuetas of Majorca* [Scottdale, Pa.], 1936). The Nazi insistence that blood is thicker than baptismal water is therefore not without substantial precedent.
4. *Werke* (Weimar, 1920), LIII, 535 ff.

BIBLIOGRAPHY

ABRAHAMS, ISRAEL. Jewish Life in the Middle Ages. Philadelphia, 1896.

ACKERMANN, A. Der märkische Hostienschändungsprozess vom Jahre 1510. *MGWJ*, XLIX (1905), 167–182.

————— Geschichte der Juden in Brandenburg a. H. Berlin, 1906.

————— Münzmeister Lippold. Ein Beitrag zur Kultur- und Sittengeschichte des Mittelalters. Frankfort, 1910.

ADLER, ELKAN NATHAN. London (Jewish Communities Series). Philadelphia, 1930.

ADLER, MICHAEL. Jews of Medieval England. London, 1939.

AHRENS, W. Hebräische Amulette mit magischen Zahlenquadraten. Berlin, 1916.

AMADOR DE LOS RIOS, JOSÉ. Historia social, política y religiosa de los Judíos de España y Portugal. Madrid, 1875–76. 3 vols.

ARONIUS, J. Regesten zur Geschichte der Juden in fränkischen und deutschen Reiche bis zum Jahre 1273. Berlin, 1902.

BÄCH-ST.—BÄCHTOLD-STÄUBLI, HANS, ed. Handwörterbuch des deutschen Aberglaubens. Berlin-Leipzig, 1927–39. 9 vols.

BAER, FRITZ. Die Juden in christlichen Spanien. Berlin, 1929–36. 2 vols.

BARING-GOULD, S. Curious Myths of the Middle Ages. Philadelphia, 1869.

BARON, SALO W. A Social and Religious History of the Jews. New York, 1937. 3 vols.

BAUER, J. Les Juifs de Bédarrides. *REJ*, XXIX (1894), 254–265.

————— Les Juifs de la principauté d'Orange. *REJ*, XXXII (1896), 236–250.

BENTWICH, NORMAN. Of Jews and Hebraism in the Greek Anthology. *JQR*, XXIII (1932–33), 181–185.

————— The Graeco-Roman View of Jews and Judaism in the Second Century. *idem.*, 337–348.

BERGL, JOSEPH. Geschichte der ungarischen Juden. Leipzig, 1879.

BERLINER, ABRAHAM. Persönliche Beziehungen zwischen Christen und Juden im Mittelalter. Halberstadt, 1881.

————— Geschichte der Juden in Rom. Frankfort, 1893. 2 vols.

————— Aus dem inneren Leben der deutschen Juden im Mittelalter. 2d ed. Berlin, 1900.

BICKERMANN, E. Ritualmord und Eselskult. *MGWJ*, LXXI (1927), 171–187, 255–264.

BOAISTUAU, PIERRE. Histoires prodigieuses. Paris, 1575.

BÖCKEL, OTTO. Die deutsche Volkssage. Leipzig, 1914.

BONDY, GOTTLIEB and DWORSKY, FRANZ. Zur Geschichte der Juden in Böhmen, Mähren, und Schlesien. Prague, 1906. 2 vols.

BOUSSET, W. The Antichrist Legend, a Chapter in Christian and Jewish Folklore. Trans. by A. H. Keane. London, 1896.

BRANN, M. Geschichte der Juden in Schlesien. Breslau, 1896–1917.

BRANT, SEBASTIAN. Das Narrenschiff. Ed. by Karl Goedeke. Leipzig, 1872.

BRESSLAU, HARRY. Juden und Mongolen, 1241. *Zeitschrift für die Geschichte der Juden in Deutschland*, I (1887), 99–102.

BROWE, PETER. Die Hostienschändungen der Juden im Mittelalter. *Römische Quartalschrift für christliche Altertumskunde und für Kirchengeschichte*, XXXIV (1926), 167–197.

———— Die Eucharistie als Zaubermittel im Mittelalter. *Archiv für Kulturgeschichte*, XX (1930), 134–154.

———— Die eucharistischen Wunder des Mittelalters. Breslau, 1938.

BULARD, MARCEL. Le scorpion, symbole du peuple juif dans l'art religieux des XIVe, XVe, XVIe siècles. Paris, 1935.

BURCKHARDT, JACOB. The Civilization of the Renaissance in Italy. Trans. from the 15th ed., by S. G. C. Middlemore. New York, 1935.

CALISCH, EDWARD N. The Jew in English Literature. Richmond, Va., 1909.

CARDOZO, J. L. The Contemporary Jew in the Elizabethan Drama. Amsterdam, 1925.

CARLEBACH, EPHRAIM. Die rechtlichen und sozialen Verhältnisse der jüdischen Gemeinden: Speyer, Worms und Mainz. Leipzig, 1901.

CARO, GEORG. Sozial- und Wirtschaftsgeschichte der Juden im Mittelalter und in der Neuzeit. Frankfort, 1908—Leipzig, 1920. 2 vols.

CARRINGTON, HERBERT. Die Figur des Juden in der dramatischen Litteratur des XVIII. Jahrhunderts. Heidelberg, 1897.

CHWOLSON, D. Die Blutanklage und sonstige mittelalterliche Beschuldigungen der Juden. Frankfort, 1901.

COULTON, GEORGE GORDON. The Inquisition. New York, 1929.

———— The Black Death. New York, 1932.

———— Inquisition and Liberty. London, 1938.

CRANE, THOMAS F. The Exempla or Illustrative Stories from the Sermones Vulgares of Jacques de Vitry. London, 1890.

CRÉMIEUX, A. Les Juifs de Marseille au moyen âge. *REJ*, XLVI (1903), 1–47, 246–268.

CRUEL, R. Geschichte der deutschen Predigt im Mittelalter. Detmold, 1879.

CURTISS, JOHN S. An Appraisal of the Protocols of Zion, New York, 1942.

DEBRÉ, MOSES. Der Jude in der französischen Literatur von 1800 bis zur Gegenwart. Ansbach, 1909.

DUBNOW, S. M. History of the Jews in Russia and Poland. Trans. by I. Friedlaender. Philadelphia, 1916–20. 3 vols.

ECK, JOHANN. Ains Judenbüechlins verlegung. Ingolstadt, 1541.

EJ—Encyclopaedia Judaica. Berlin 1928–35. 10 vols.

Endinger Judenspiel. Ed. by Karl von Amira. Halle, 1883.

FALB, ALFRED. Luther und die Juden, Munich, 1921. A strongly anti-semitic presentation.

FEHR, HANS. Massenkunst im 16. Jahrhundert. Berlin, 1924.

FERORELLI, NICOLA. Gli Ebrei nell'Italia meridionale dall'età romana al secolo XVIII. Turin, 1915.

FRANKL, OSKAR. Der Jude in den deutschen Dichtungen des 15., 16. und 17. Jahrhundertes. Mährisch-Ostrau, 1905.

FREIMANN, A. and KRACAUER, F. Frankfort (Jewish Communities Series). Philadelphia, 1929.

FRIEDENWALD, HENRY. Apologetic Works of Jewish Physicians. *JQR*, XXXII (1941–42), 227–255, 407–426.

FRIEDLANDER, GERALD. Shakespeare and the Jews. London, 1921.

FRIEDMAN, LEE M. Robert Grosseteste and the Jews. Cambridge, 1934.

FRISS, ARMIN. Monumenta Hungariae Judaica. Budapest, 1903.

FUCHS, EDUARD. Die Juden in der Karikatur. Munich, 1921.

GEIGER, LUDWIG. Geschichte der Juden in Berlin. Berlin, 1871. 2 vols.

———— Die Juden und die deutsche Literatur des 16. Jahrhunderts. *Zeitschrift für die Geschichte der Juden in Deutschland*, II (1888), 308–374, III (1889), 295–298.

———— Die deutsche Literatur und die Juden. Berlin, 1910.

Germania Judaica, von den ältesten Zeiten bis 1238. Ed. by I. Elbogen, A. Freimann, and H. Tykocinski. Breslau, 1934.

Gesta Romanorum. Trans. by Charles Swan and revised by Wynnard Hooper. London, 1904.

GEYER, RUDOLF and SAILER, LEOPOLD. Urkunden aus Wiener Grundbüchern zur Geschichte der Wiener Juden im Mittelalter. Vienna, 1931.

GIVRY, GRILLOT DE. Le Musée des sorciers, mages et alchimistes. Paris, 1929.

GLESINGER, LAVOSLAV. Beiträge zur Geschichte der Pharmazie bei den Juden. *MGWJ*, LXXXII (1938), 111–130, 417–422.

GOEBEL, FRANZ M. Jüdische Motive im märchenhaften Erzählungs- gut. Gleiwitz, 1932.

GOEDEKE, KARL. Schwänke des sechzehnten Jahrhunderts. Leipzig, 1879.

———— and TITTMAN, JULIUS. Liederbuch aus dem sechzehnten Jahrhundert. Leipzig, 1867.

GOLDSTEIN, N. W. Cultivated Pagans and Ancient Anti-Semitism. *Journal of Religion*, XIX (1939), 346–364.

GOLDZIHER, IGNAZ. Hebräische Elemente in muhammedanischen Zaubersprüchen. *ZDMG*, XLVIII (1894), 358–360.

GRAETZ, HEINRICH. Geschichte der Juden. 3d and 4th eds. Leipzig. 11 vols.

———— History of the Jews. New York, 1927. 6 vols.

———— Shylock in der Sage, im Drama, und in der Geschichte. 2d ed. Krotoschin, 1899.

GRAU, WILHELM. Antisemitismus im späten Mittelalter: Das Ende der Regensburger Judengemeinde 1450–1519. Munich and Leip- zig, 1934. An antisemitic presentation.

GRAYZEL, SOLOMON. The Church and the Jews in the XIIIth Cen- tury. Philadelphia, 1933.

———— The Avignon Popes and the Jews. *Historia Judaica*, II (1940), 1–12.

GREGOROVIUS, FERDINAND. Der Ghetto und die Juden in Rom. Berlin, 1935. Reprinted from Wanderjahre in Italien, I, Stuttgart, 1853.

GRIMM, JAKOB. Deutsche Mythologie. 4th ed. Berlin, 1875–78. 3 vols.

GROSS, HEINRICH. Gallia Judaica. Paris, 1897.

GRÜN, NATHAN. Der hohe Rabbi Löw und sein Sagenkreis. Prague, 1885.

GRUNWALD, MAX. Geschichte der Juden in Wien, 1625–1740. Vienna, 1913. Reprinted from Vol. V of Geschichte der Stadt Wien, pub. by the Altertumsvereine zu Wien.

———— Vienna (Jewish Communities Series). Philadelphia, 1936.

GÜDEMANN, MORITZ. Geschichte des Erziehungswesens und der Cul- tur der abendländischen Juden während des Mittelalters und der neueren Zeit. Vienna, 1880–88. 3 vols.

GUTTMANN, J. Das Verhältniss des Thomas von Aquino zum Juden- thum und zur jüdischen Litteratur. Göttingen, 1891.

HAENLE, S. Geschichte der Juden im ehemaligen Fürstenthum Ansbach. Ansbach, 1867.

HANSEN, JOSEPH. Inquisition und Hexenverfolgung im Mittelalter. *Historische Zeitschrift*, LXXXI (1898), 385–432.

———— Zauberwahn, Inquisition und Hexenprozess im Mittelalter. Munich and Leipzig, 1900.

———— Quellen und Untersuchungen zur Geschichte des Hexenwahns und der Hexenverfolgung im Mittelalter. Bonn. 1901.

HECHT, EMANUEL. Die Geschichte der Juden im Trier'schen. *MGWJ*, VII (1857), 179–191.

HEFELE, KARL. Die franziskanische Wanderpredigt in Italien während des 15. Jhr. Tübingen, 1912.

HEFFNER, L. Die Juden in Franken. Nuremberg, 1855.

HEINEMANN, ISAK. Article "Antisemitismus," in Pauly-Wissowa, Real-Encyclopädie der classischen Altertumswissenschaft, Supplementary Vol. V, Stuttgart 1931, 5–43.

———— The Attitude of the Ancient World toward Judaism. *Review of Religion*, IV (1939–40), 385–400.

HEISE, WERNER. Die Juden in der Mark Brandenburg bis zum Jahre 1571. Berlin, 1932. (Historische Studien, Heft 220.)

HERE—Hastings, James, ed. Encyclopaedia of Religion and Ethics. New York, 1928. 13 vols.

HILDENFINGER, P. Documents relatifs aux Juifs d'Arles. *REJ*, XLI (1900), 62–97.

HOENIGER, R. Zur Geschichte der Juden Deutschlands im frühern Mittelalter. *Zeitschrift für die Geschichte der Juden in Deutschland*, I (1887), 65–97, 136–151.

JACOBS, JOSEPH. The Jews of Angevin England. London, 1893.

JE—The Jewish Encyclopedia. New York, 1901–1906. 12 vols.

JOESTEN, DR. Zur Geschichte der Hexen und Juden in Bonn. Bonn, 1900.

JQR—*Jewish Quarterly Review.*

JUSTER, JEAN. La Condition légale des Juifs sous les rois visigoths. Paris, 1912.

———— Les Juifs dans l'empire romain. Paris, 1914. 2 vols.

KATZ, SOLOMON. The Jews in the Visigothic and Frankish Kingdoms of Spain and Gaul. Cambridge, 1937.

KAYSERLING, M. Die Juden in Navarra. Berlin, 1861.

———— Geschichte der Juden in Portugal. Leipzig, 1867.

KIRCHHOF, HANS WILHELM. Wendunmuth. Ed. by Hermann Oesterley, Tübingen, 1869. 5 vols.

KISCH, GUIDO. Research in Medieval Legal History of the Jews.

Proceedings of the American Academy for Jewish Research, VI (1934–35), 229–276.

———— Die Prager Universität und die Juden, 1348–1848. Mährisch-Ostrau, 1935.

———— The Jewry-Law of the Medieval German Law Books, Part I. *Proceedings of the American Academy for Jewish Research*, VII (1935–36), 61–145; Part II, *idem*, X (1940), 99–184.

———— Studien zur Geschichte des Judeneides im Mittelalter, *Hebrew Union College Annual*, XIV (1939), 431–456.

———— Nuremberg Jewry Oaths. *Historia Judaica*, II (1940), 23–38.

———— A Fourteenth-Century Jewry Oath of South Germany. *Speculum*, XV (1940), 331–337.

———— The Yellow Badge in History. *Historia Judaica*, IV (1942), 95–144.

KLAPPER, JOSEPH. Erzählungen des Mittelalters. Breslau, 1916.

KOBER, ADOLF. Cologne (Jewish Communities Series). Philadelphia, 1940.

KRACAUER, I. Aus der inneren Geschichte der Juden Frankfurts im XIV. Jahrhundert. Frankfort, 1914.

———— Urkundenbuch zur Geschichte der Juden in Frankfurt am Main von 1150–1400. Frankfort, 1914.

———— Geschichte der Juden in Frankfurt am Main. Frankfort, 1925–27. 2 vols.

KRACAUER, J. L'Affaire des Juifs d'Endingen de 1470. *REJ*, XVI (1888), 236–245.

KRAUSS, SAMUEL. Geschichte der jüdischen Ärzte. Vienna, 1930.

KYNASS, FRITZ. Der Jude im deutschen Volkslied. Greifswald, 1934.

LAGUMINA, BARTOLOMEO and GIUSEPPE. Codice diplomatico dei Giudei di Sicilia. Palermo, 1884–1909. 3 vols.

LAMM, LOUIS. Zur Geschichte der Juden in Lauingen und in anderen pfalzneuburgischen Orten. Berlin, 1915.

LANDA, M. J. The Jew in Drama. London, 1926.

LAZARD, L. Les Juifs de Touraine. *REJ*, XVII (1888), 210–234.

LEA, HENRY CHARLES. A History of the Inquisition of the Middle Ages. New York, 1911. 3 vols.

———— Materials Toward a History of Witchcraft. Ed. by Arthur C. Howland. Philadelphia, 1939. 3 vols.

LECOY DE LA MARCHE, ALBERT. Anecdotes historiques, légendes et apologues tirés du recueil inédit d'Étienne de Bourbon. Paris, 1877.

———— La Chaire française au moyen âge. Paris, 1886.

LEFÈVRE, P. La Valeur historique d'une enquête épiscopale sur le miracle eucharistique de Bruxelles en 1370. *Revue d'histoire ecclésiastique*, XXVIII (1932), 329–346.

LENIENT, CHARLES. La Satire en France ou la littérature militante au XVIe siècle. Paris, 1877. 2 vols.

———— La Satire en France au moyen âge. 3d ed. Paris, 1883.

LÉVI, ISRAEL. Le Juif de la légende. *REJ*, XX (1890), 249–252.

———— Le Juif sorcier. *REJ*, XXII (1891), 232 ff.

———— Saint Césaire et les Juifs d'Arles. *REJ*, XXX (1895), 295–298.

LEWIN, REINHOLD. Luthers Stellung zu den Juden. Berlin, 1911.

LEWY, HANS. Josephus the Physician: A Mediaeval Legend of the Destruction of Jerusalem. *Journal of the Warburg Institute*, I (London, 1937–38), 221–242.

LIEBE, GEORG. Das Judentum in der deutschen Vergangenheit. Leipzig, 1903.

LIFSCHITZ-GOLDEN, MANYA. Les Juifs dans la littérature française du moyen âge. New York, 1935.

LILIENCRON, R. VON. Die historischen Volkslieder der Deutschen vom 13. bis 16. Jahrhundert. Leipzig, 1865–66. 2 vols.

LINSENMEYER, ANTON. Geschichte der Predigt in Deutschland von Karl dem Grossen bis zum Ausgange des vierzehnten Jahrhunderts. Munich, 1886.

LOEB, ISIDORE. La Controverse religieuse entre les chrétiens et les juifs au moyen âge. *Revue de l'histoire des religions*, XVII (1888), 311–337; XVIII (1888), 133–156.

———— Le Juif de l'histoire et le Juif de la légende, *REJ*, XXI (1890), pp. xxxiii–lxi.

LOEWE, HEINRICH. Die Juden in der katholischen Legende. Berlin, 1912.

LOWENTHAL, MARVIN. A World Passed By. New York, 1933.

———— The Jews of Germany. New York, 1936.

LUTHER, MARTIN. Eine vermanung wider die Juden. In: Werke (Weimar, 1914). LI, 195 f.

———— Von den Juden und ihren Lügen. In: Werke (Weimar, 1920). LIII, 412–552.

———— Vom Schem Hamphoras und vom Geschlecht Christi. In: Werke (Weimar, 1920). LIII, 573–648.

MARGARITHA, ANTONIUS. Der gantz Jüdisch glaub. Augsburg, 1530.

MAURY, L. F. La Magie et l'astrologie dans l'antiquité et au moyen âge. 4th ed. Paris, 1877.

MAUVANS, BARSILON DE. Les Juifs de Provence. *Annales des Alpes* (1897–98), pp. 214–226.

MENCZEL, J. S. Beiträge zur Geschichte der Juden in Mainz im XV. Jahrhundert. Berlin, 1933.

MEYER, CARL. Der Aberglaube des Mittelalters und der nächstfolgenden Jahrhunderte. Basel, 1884.

MEYER, WILHELM. Der Wandel des jüdischen Typus in der englischen Literatur. Marburg a. L., 1912.

MGWJ—Monatsschrift für die Geschichte und Wissenschaft des Judenthums.

MICHEL, FRANCISQUE. Histoire des races maudites de la France et de l'Espagne. Paris, 1847. 2 vols.

———— and MONMERQUE, L. J. N., eds. Théâtre français au moyen âge. Paris, 1885.

MICHELSON, H. The Jew in Early English Literature. Amsterdam, 1926.

MILANO, ATTILIO. Gli ebrei in Italia nei secoli XIo e XIIo. Città di Castello, 1938.

MODDER, MONTAGU F. The Jew in the Literature of England to the End of the Nineteenth Century. Philadelphia, 1939.

MONOD, BERNARD. Juifs, sorciers et hérétiques au moyen âge. *REJ*, XLVI (1903), 237–245.

MÜNZ, I. Die jüdischen Ärzte im Mittelalter. Frankfort, 1922.

MURAWSKI, FRIEDRICH. Die Juden bei den Kirchenvätern und Scholastikern. Berlin, 1925.

MURRAY, MARGARET A. The Witch-Cult in Western Europe. Oxford, 1921.

NEUBAUR, L. Die Sage vom ewigen Juden. 2d ed., Leipzig, 1893.

NEUFELD, SIEGBERT. Die Juden im thüringisch-sächsischen Gebiet während des Mittelalters. 2 parts. Berlin, 1917-Halle, 1927.

NEUMAN, ABRAHAM S. The Jews in Spain. Philadelphia, 1942. 2 vols.

NEWMAN, LOUIS I. Jewish Influences on Christian Reform Movements. New York, 1925.

OSBORN, E. B. The Middle Ages. New York, 1928.

OUVERLEAUX, E. Notes et documents sur les Juifs de Belgique sous l'ancien régime. *REJ*, VII (1883), 117–138, 252–271.

OWST, G. R. Preaching in Medieval England. Cambridge, 1926.

———— Literature and Pulpit in Medieval England. Cambridge, 1933.

PARIS, MATTHEW. Historia anglorum. Ed. by Frederic Madden. London, 1866–69. 3 vols.

———— Chronica majora. Ed. by H. R. Luard. London, 1872–83. 7 vols.

✓ Parkes, James. The Conflict of the Church and the Synagogue. London, 1934. Cited in the Notes as Parkes, I.

—————— The Jew in the Medieval Community. London, 1938. Cited in the Notes as Parkes, II.

—————— Christian Influence on the Status of the Jews in Europe, *Historia Judaica*, I (1938–39), 31–38.

Pauli, Johannes, Schimpf und Ernst. Ed. by Johannes Bolte. Berlin, 1924. 2 vols.

Perreau, Pietro. Educazione e coltura degl'israeliti in Italia nel medio evo. Corfu, 1885.

Peuckert, Will-Erich. Article "Jude" in Bäch-St., IV (1931), 808–833.

—————— Pansophie. Ein Versuch zur Geschichte der weissen und schwarzen Magie. Stuttgart, 1936.

Pflaum, H. Les Scènes des Juifs dans la littérature dramatique du moyen âge. *REJ*, LXXXIX (1930), 111–134.

—————— Der allegorische Streit zwischen Synagoge und Kirche in der europäischen Dichtung des Mittelalters. *Archivum Romanicum,* XVIII (Florence, 1934), 243–340.

Philipson, David. The Jew in English Fiction. Cincinnati, 1911.

Preuss, Hans. Die Vorstellungen vom Antichrist im späteren Mittelalter. Leipzig, 1906.

Pribram, A. F. Urkunden und Akten zur Geschichte der Juden in Wien. Vienna and Leipzig, 1918. 2 vols.

Prynne, William. A Short Demurrer to the Jewes. London, 1656.

Rabinowitz, L. The Social Life of the Jews of Northern France in the XII–XIV Centuries. London, 1938.

Regné, Jean. Étude sur la condition des Juifs de Narbonne du Ve au XIVe siècle. Narbonne, 1912.

Reider, Joseph. "Jews in Medieval Art" in Essays on Antisemitism. Ed. by Koppel S. Pinson. New York, 1942, 45–58.

Reinach, Theodore. Textes d'auteurs grecs et romains relatifs au Judaisme. Paris, 1895.

REJ—Revue des Études Juives.

Robert, Ulysse. Les Signes d'infamie au moyen âge. Paris, 1891.

Rodocanachi, Emmanuel. Le Saint-Siège et les Juifs: Le Ghetto à Rome. Paris, 1891.

Rosenfeld, Beate. Die Golemsage und ihre Verwertung in der deutschen Literatur. Breslau, 1934.

Roskoff, Gustav. Geschichte des Teufels. Leipzig, 1869. 2 vols.

Roth, Cecil. Venice (Jewish Communities Series). Philadelphia, 1930.

—————— Feast of Purim and the Origins of the Blood Accusation. *Speculum,* VIII (1933), 520–526.

———— The Ritual Murder Libel and the Jew. London, 1935.

———— The Spanish Inquisition. London, 1937.

———— The Medieval Conception of the Jew. *Essays and Studies in Memory of Linda R. Miller.* New York, 1938, 171–190.

———— A History of the Jews in England. Oxford, 1941.

RYDBERG, VIKTOR. The Magic of the Middle Ages. New York, 1879.

SACHS, HANS. Dichtungen. Ed. by Karl Goedeke. Leipzig, 1870–71. 3 vols.

———— Sämtliche Fabeln und Schwänke. Ed. by Edmund Goetze. Halle, 1893–1913. 6 vols.

SAIGE, GUSTAVE. Les Juifs du Languedoc antérieurement au XIVe siècle. Paris, 1881.

SALZBERGER, GEORG. Die Salomosage in der semitischen Literatur. Berlin, 1907.

SARTORI, PAUL. Sitte und Brauch. Leipzig, 1910–14. 3 vols.

SCHEID, ELIE. Histoire des Juifs de Hagenau. Paris, 1885.

———— Histoire des Juifs d'Alsace. Paris, 1887.

SCHERER, J. E. Die Rechtsverhältnisse der Juden in den deutsch-österreichischen Ländern. Leipzig, 1901.

SCHIAVO, G. Fede e superstizione nell'antica poesia francese. *Zeitschrift für romanische Philologie,* XIV (1890), 89–127, 275–297; XV (1891), 289–317.

SCHLAUCH, MARGARET. The Allegory of Church and Synagogue. *Speculum,* XIV (1939), 448–464.

SCHUDT, JOHANN JAKOB. Jüdische Merckwürdigkeiten. 4 parts. Frankfort and Leipzig, 1714–18.

SCHWARZ, IGNAZ. Geschichte der Juden in Wien bis zum Jahre 1625. Vienna, 1913. Reprinted from Vol. V of Geschichte der Stadt Wien, pub. by the Altertumsvereine zu Wien.

SINGERMANN, FELIX. Die Kennzeichnung der Juden im Mittelalter. Berlin, 1915.

SMITH, LUCY T. and MEYER, PAUL, eds. Les Contes moralisés de Nicole Bozon. Paris, 1889.

SOLDAN, WILHELM G. and HEPPE, HENRIETTE. Geschichte der Hexenprozesse. 3d ed., revised and edited by Max Bauer. Munich, 1911. 2 vols.

SPRENGER, JAKOB. Malleus maleficarum. Trans. by Montague Summers. London, 1928.

STARR, JOSHUA. The Jews in the Byzantine Empire. Athens, 1939.

———— Jewish Life in Crete under the Rule of Venice. *Proceedings of the American Academy for Jewish Research,* XII (1942), 59–114.

STEMPLINGER, EDUARD. Antiker Aberglaube in modernen Ausstrah
lungen. Leipzig, 1922.

STERN, MORITZ. Urkundliche Beiträge über die Stellung der Päpste
zu den Juden. 2 parts. Kiel, 1893–95.

———— Die israelitische Bevölkerung der deutschen Städte: III,
Nuernberg im Mittelalter. Kiel, 1896.

STOBBE, OTTO. Die Juden in Deutschland während des Mittelalters.
Berlin, 1923.

Y STRACK, HERMANN L. The Jews and Human Sacrifice. New York,
1909.

STRAUS, RAPHAEL. Regensburg and Augsburg (Jewish Communities
Series). Philadelphia, 1939.

STRAUSS, R. Die Juden im Königreich Sizilien unter Normannen und
Staufern. Heidelberg, 1910.

STRUMPF, DAVID. Die Juden in der mittelalterlichen Mysterien-,
Mirakel- und Moralitäten-Dichtung Frankreichs. Ladenburg a. N.,
1920.

SUMMERS, MONTAGUE. The History of Witchcraft and Demonology.
London, 1926.

TAYLOR, HENRY O. The Medieval Mind. 4th ed. London, 1927. 2
vols.

THORNDIKE, LYNN. A History of Magic and Experimental Science.
New York, 1923–34. 4 vols.

TOVEY, D'BLOSSIERS. Anglia Judaica. Oxford, 1738.

TRACHTENBERG, JOSHUA. Jewish Magic and Superstition. New York,
1939.

TUCHMANN, J. Les Fascinateurs. *Mélusine*, IV (1888–89), *passim*.

ULRICH, JAKOB. Französische Volkslieder. Leipzig, 1899.

———— Proben der lateinischen Novellistik des Mittelalters. Leipzig, 1906.

VIDAL, PIERRE. Les Juifs de Rousillon et de Cardagne. *REJ*, XV
(1887), 19–55; XVI (1888), 1–23, 170–203.

VOGELSTEIN, HERMANN. Rome (Jewish Communities Series). Philadelphia, 1940.

———— and RIEGER, PAUL. Geschichte der Juden in Rom. Berlin,
1895–96. 2 vols.

WELLER, EMIL. Die ersten deutschen Zeitungen. Stuttgart, 1872.

WELTER, J.-TH. L'Exemplum dans la littérature religieuse et didac-
tique du moyen âge. Paris, 1927.

WICKERSHEIMER, ERNEST. Les Accusations d'empoisonnement
portées pendant la première moitié du XIVe siècle contre les
lépreux et les Juifs; leurs relations avec les épidémies de peste

(Communication faite au Quatrième Congrès International d'Histoire de la Médecine [Bruxelles, avril 1923]). Anvers, 1927.

WIENER, M. Regesten zur Geschichte der Juden in Deutschland während des Mittelalters. Hanover, 1862.

WILLIAMS, A. LUKYN. Adversus Judaeos, A Bird's-Eye View of Christian *Apologiae* until the Renaissance. Cambridge, 1935.

WISSELSKI, ALBERT. Märchen des Mittelalters. Berlin, 1925.

WUTTKE, ADOLF. Der deutsche Volksaberglaube der Gegenwart. 3d ed. Berlin, 1900.

ZDMG—Zeitschrift der deutschen morgenländischen Gesellschaft.

ZIMMELS, H. J. Beiträge zur Geschichte der Juden in Deutschland im 13. Jahrhundert. Vienna, 1926.

INDEX

Abraham, 64, 73, 162
Abraham of Berkhamsted, 119
Abraham of Worms, 235, n. 8
Adam, 64, 73
Adonay, 69
Africa, 108, 128, 226, n. 19
Against Celsus, 229, n. 7
Agobard, 68, 100, 128, 159, 182
Agnus Dei, 198
Ahasuerus, 40; *see also* Jew, Wandering
Ailments, Jewish, 50 ff., 116, 229, n. 29
Alard, Jean, 187
Albert, Duke of Austria, 117
Albigensians, 173 f., 202, 206, 211
Albrecht, Archbishop of Magdeburg, 237, n. 2
Albrecht, Count of Saxony, 75
Alchemy, 72 ff., 79, 82, 83
Alenu, 182 f.
Alexander, 40, 44, 63
Alexander of Stavenby, 212
Alexander III, Pope, 190
Alexander IV, Pope, 191, 202
Alexander V, Pope, 69
Alexander VI, Pope, 115
Algiers, 80
Alphonse of Poitiers, 95
Alsace, 103, 193
Alsfelder Passion Play, 222, n. 25
Ammianus Marcellinus, 47
Ammon, 44
Amsterdam, 235, n. 8
Amulets, 58, 61, 63, 67, 74 f., 82
Amulo, 100
Antichrist, 32 ff., 223 ff.
Antiochus Epiphanes, 126
Antiqua Judaeorum, 110
Antisemitism, modern, 1 ff., 49
Apion, 126, 132, 155
Apple, magic, 229, n. 3
Aquila, 44
Aquinas, Thomas, 34, 193

Arabs, 72; *see also* Moors; Saracens
Aragon, 101, 106, 178, 244, n. 24
Aretino, Pietro, 77
Arians, 111
Ariosto, Ludovico, 77
Aristotle, 63
Arles, 184
Armenians, 17
Armleder, 239, n. 17
Arnold of Citeaux, 173
Arson, 89 f.; *see also* Fire
Asher, tribe of, 51
Astrologer, devil as, 48
Astrology, 72, 79, 103, 197
Assumption of the Virgin, 174
Attack, upon Jews, 71, 75, 79 f., 86, 114, 166, 183 ff., 239, n. 17; *see also* Black Death
Augsburg, 52, 105
Austria, 117, 185, 228, n. 22, 239, n. 17
Aventin, Johannes, 102
Avignon, 69, 72, 97, 103, 107, 123
Ayrer, Jakob, 185

Babylon, 34, 35, 40, 41
Bacon, Francis, 192
Baden, 149
Balkans, 38, 129, 139
Baptism, of Jews, 48 ff., 255, n. 3
Barabas, 99, 185
Barcelona, 106, 184
Baron, S. W., 176
Basel, 104
Bavaria, 41, 90
Beard, goat's, 46
Beaumont and Fletcher, 65
Benjamin, tribe of, 52
Benedict fil' Moses, 131
Benedict of York, 225, n. 18
Benedict XII, Pope, 117
Benedict XIV, Pope, 234, n. 1
Berceo, Gonzalo de, 121
Berlin, 86, 114, 240, n. 38, 241, n. 13

Bernard of Clairvaux, 181, 191, 248, n. 11
Bernardin of Siena, 97
Berne, 137, 141
Berthold of Regensburg, 110, 175, 190, 199 f., 203, 227, n. 18
Besançon, Antichrist Play of, 36, 186
Bestiality, crime of, 187
Betraying of Christ, 222, n. 26
Bezaleel, 73
Béziers, Council of (1255), 68, 252, n. 11
Bible, editions of, 38; text of, 15; *see also* Scripture, interpretation of
Binzwangen, 52
Black Death, 102 ff., 145, 214
Black Mass, 205, 212; *see also* Sabbat, witches'
Blasphemy, 68
Blessing, Jewish, 70, 154, 232, n. 35
Blind, Jews born, 50, 151
Blois, 122, 130, 138
Blood accusation, 140 ff., 246 ff.; *see also* Ritual murder
Blood, from host, 111, 113, 116; from image, 120; Jewish need of Christian, 6, 31, 50, 51, 83, 124 ff.; *see also* Blood accusation; Ritual murder; in magic, 140 ff., 214 f.; in medieval Christianity, 247 f., n. 44; in medicine, 141 ff.; in poison, 101; in witchcraft, 212
Boccaccio, 94
Body, human, in magic, 140 ff., 214 f.; in medicine, 141 ff.; in poison, 104
Boer, Nicholas, 187
Bohemia, 97, 113, 185, 237, n. 18, 238, n. 14, 239, n. 17, 248, n. 3
Bolsena, 117
Bonefand of Bedford, 128
Books, Hebrew, burning of, 178 f.
Bordeaux, 184
Bourges, 93; Council of (1236), 165
Brahe, Tycho, 234, n. 52
Braisne (France), 130
Brandenburg, 73, 83, 105
Brant, Sebastian, 38, 92
Bray (France), 127
Breisach, 104
Brenz, Samuel Friedrich, 152
Breslau, 114, 238, n. 14, 254, n. 1; Council of (1267), 100

Brittany, 239, n. 15
Brünn, 164, 211, 254, n. 5
Brussels, 241, n. 16
Buch der Natur, 74
Buda, 67, 185; *see also* Ofen
Bulgaria, 129
Bullets, magic, 72
Bury St. Edmonds, 130
Byzantium, 67, 129

Cagots, 239, n. 15
Cahorsins, 189
Caiaphas, 193
Cainites, 200
Cairo, 15
Calamus Draco, 151
Calixtus II, Pope, 134
Calvin, John, 39
Candia (Crete), 185
Candles, magic, 140
Cannibalism, 128, 138, 139, 214
Canterbury Tales, 244, n. 23
Capet, Hugh, 97
Carloman, 97
Cartaphilus, Joseph, 17; *see also* Jew, Wandering
Cassius, Dio, 128
Castile, 75, 178
Castration, 128
Cat, 213, 218; crucified, 242, n. 29; devil as, 26, 205, 206, 208; Jews turn into, 72; worshiped by Jews, 26
Cathari, 205
Cellini, Benvenuto, 61
Cemetery, 88, 226, n. 19, 229, n. 29
Cercanceaux, 213
Champagne, 160
Characteristics, Jewish, 228, n. 26
Charlemagne, 71, 184
Charles II, Emperor (the Bald), 65, 97
Charles IV, Emperor, 105
Charles IV, King (France), 102
Charles V, Emperor, 80
Chaucer, Geoffrey, 42, 244, n. 23
Chaumont Christmas Play, 23
Childbirth, Christian blood eases, 152
Chillon, 104
China, 227, n. 12, 245, n. 43
Chmelnicki, Bogdan, 75, 80
Christianity, Jewish hatred of, 181 ff.; Jewish refusal to accept, 17 f.

Index

Christianization of Europe, 161 f.
Christians, attend Jewish services, 58; Jews curse, 181, 182 f.
Christmas, 135
Christopher, Duke of Württemberg, 79
Chrysostom of Antioch, 21, 58, 63
Chuetas, 255, n. 3
Church, attitude of, to Jews, 7, 162 ff.; position of, in medieval Europe, 170 ff.; and state, 170, 173
Church Fathers, 15
Church of the Holy Sepulchre, 184
Circumcision, 31, 131, 149 ff., 180
Clement VI, Pope, 103
Clergy, attitude of, to Jews, 159, 164, 166, 168; engaged in usury, 189, 237, n. 2; and ritual murder charge, 124 f., 135
Clovis, 184
Cohn, Ferdinand, 117
Cologne, 107, 218
Comestor, Petrus, 63 f.
Comödie von Nikolaus, 185
Conrad of Marburg, 205
Confessions, Jewish, 83 f., 154
Constantine, Emperor, 20, 65, 142
Constantinople, 66
Constitutio pro Judeis, 134, 165
Conversion, to Christianity, 127; to Judaism, 118
Conversion de St. Paul, 230, n. 11
Conversos, 50, 69, 82, 177, 241, n. 23; see also Marranos
Convert to Christianity, 130, 132, 151, 152, 175, 177, 178, 234, n. 3
Copin, 132, 144
Corpus Christi Day, 117; Pageant, 222, n. 26
Cossack, 75
Council, of Béziers (1255), 68, 252, n. 11; of Bourges (1236), 165; of Breslau (1267), 100; of Elvira (320), 70; of the Four Lands, 80; Fourth Lateran (1215), 109, 110, 116, 211; of Lithuanian Jewry, 79 f.; of Narbonne (589), 58; of Paris (1212), 192; of Polish Jewry, 80; secret, of heretics, 205; of Jews, 6, 130, 131; see also Elders of Zion; of witches, 215; see also Sabbat, witches'; of St. Ruf (1337), 103; of Toledo (694),

184; of Vienna (1267), 44, 100, 113; (1311), 191
Coventry, 212
Crete, 26, 34, 129, 185, 242, n. 29, 243, n. 15
Crispin, Gilbert, 160
Crucifix, desecration of, 118 ff.; in magic, 121
Crucifixion, of boy, 127, 130 ff.; of cat, 242, n. 29; of lamb, 242, n. 29; re-enacted in host desecration, 114; wax image of, 121 f.; see also Blood accusation; Ritual murder
Crusade, Albigensian, 173 f.
Crusade, First, 144, 161, 167 ff., 188
Crusade, Second, 181, 191
Crusades, 11, 159, 170 f., 249, n. 1
Curse, 69, 87, 100, 183
Custom of the Country, 65

Damascus, 138, 230, n. 11
Damhouder, 187
Dan, tribe of, 34, 40, 51, 224, n. 5
Daniel, 64, 73, 233, n. 42
Daniel, Jewish sorcerer, 81
David, 64, 73; Star of, 74
Dauphiné, 69, 103
Day of Atonement, fire on, 90
De judaicis superstitionibus, 68
Deities, horned, 44
Democritus, 126
Demons, in magic, 59, 61, 72, 203, 208; odor of, 227, n. 17
Denmark, 125
Devil, cult of, 199; pact with, 140, 141, 203, 215; source of magic, 60; worship of, by sorcerers, 215; see also Satan
Diall of Princes, 221, n. 1
Dijon, 192
Disease, Jews cause, 106 ff., 214, 238, n. 14, 240, n. 38; see also Plague, Jews cause
Diseases, Jewish, 50 f.
Divination, 140, 144; see also Fortune-telling
Dog, devil as, 84
Dominicans, 141, 178, 179, 180, 211, 250, n. 13
Donaueschinger Passion Play, 222, n. 25
Donin, Nicholas, 178

D'Outremeuse, Jean, 105
Dracoena Draco, 151
Dragon's Blood, 151
Dreams, interpretation of, 57, 72, 93
Drugs, Jews dealers in, 98
Düsseldorf, 138

Easter, 110, 123, 128, 130, 133, 154, 211, 245, n. 30
Eberhard, Archbishop of Treves, 122
Eck, Johann, 93, 121, 146, 182
Edward II, King (England), 95
Egica, King, 184
Egypt, 57, 229, n. 4, 238, n. 14, 246, n. 43
Eighteen Benedictions, 182
Elders of Zion, 3; *see also* Council, of Jews; Protocols of Zion
Elijah, 34, 36, 73
Elisha, 73
Elizabeth, Queen, 98, 238, n. 8
Elvira, Council of (320), 70
Endingen, 149
Endingen Judenspiel, 149 f.
England, 23, 95, 129, 130, 131, 138, 160, 161, 178, 184, 186, 189, 192, 214, 221, n. 1, 244, n. 23, 248, n. 11, 251, n. 1
Enoch, 34, 36, 64
Esplugues, Guillermus Raymundus, 82
Eucharist, 113, 212; *see also* Host; Transubstantiation
Eusebius of Alexandria, 21
Eustratios, 129, 133
Evans, E. P., 187
Evil eye, 70 f., 232, n. 35
Executioner, Jewish, 129
Ezekiel, 64, 73
Ezra, 73

Façan, Jacob, 82
Faust, 23
Feltre, Bernardin da, 245, n. 37
Fertility, human blood promotes, 147, 151
Festivals, Jewish, observed by Christians, 159
Fiorentino, Giovanni, 106
Fire, 89 f.; *see also* Arson
Fischart, Johann, 52, 57
Flagellants, 105
Flud, Thomas, 107

Foetor judaicus, 47 ff., 116; *see also* Odor, of Jews
Folz, Hans, 36
Foods, purchase of, by Jews, 100
Fortalitium fidei, 42
Fortunatus, Venantius, 228, n. 19
Fortunetelling, 71, 76, 93 f., 233, n. 38; *see also* Divination
France, 23, 70, 95, 101, 126, 127, 128, 129, 134, 138, 145, 160, 178, 179, 189, 192, 200, 202, 239, n. 15, 17, 244, n. 24, 27, 248, n. 11, 249, n. 12
Franciscans, 132, 141, 178
Franciscus of Piacenza, 51
Franconia, 82, 101, 107
Frankfort, 37, 90, 94, 105, 141, 250, n. 29
Frankfort Passion Play, 13
Frederick I, King (Prussia), 183
Frederick II, Emperor, 132, 173
Freiburg, 104, 107, 144, 149
Freising, 218
"French disease," 108
Friday, Good, 130, 132
Fulda, 132, 133, 135, 148
Funeral, 88

Gad, tribe of, 51
Galicia, 229, n. 29
Galilee, 35
Garlic, Jews eat, 49, 50
Gemma, Jewish sorceress, 82
Gems, occult powers of, 74
Genghis Khan, 185
Genoa, 247, n. 28
Geoffrey of Meaux, 253, n. 12
Germanus, Moses, 152
Germany, 5, 23, 40, 73, 99, 103, 105, 107, 129, 134, 135, 139, 147, 152, 179, 185, 186, 192, 201, 205, 206, 232, n. 35, 239, n. 17, 243, n. 5, 248, n. 11
Gesta Senoniensis Ecclesiae, 133
Gilles de Rais, 215
Gloucester, 130
Gnostics, 211, 224, n. 2
Goat, and devil, 47, 206, 208, 227, n. 11; and Jews, 46 f., 48
God, attributes of, 59; name of, 65, 69, 230, n. 11
Godeliva of Canterbury, 235, n. 13
Gothe, 74
Gog, 224, n. 2

Golda, Jewish witch, 86 f.
Goldschmidt, Meyer, 125
Golem, 80
Gospels, 11, 19
Gotland, 104
Gottschalk, 168
Granada, 101
Graz, 142
Gregorovius, Ferdinand, 77
Gregory of Tours, 42, 93, 119
Gregory I, Pope, 163
Gregory IX, Pope, 178, 205, 211
Gregory X, Pope, 134, 245, n. 28
Gregory XIII, Pope, 110
Gubbio, Synod of (1303), 115
Gui, Bernard, 211
Guibert, Abbot of Nogent, 66, 205, 213
Gypsies, 71

Hadrian, 229, n. 4
Hair, in poison, 101; red, 83, 107
Halevi, Simuel, 75
Hall (Swabia), 94
Halle, 82, 107
Haman, 127
Hamburg, 71, 141
Hands, washing, 88
Harold of Gloucester, 130
Harrowing of Hell, 19
Hartmann, Bishop of Augsburg, 126
Hat, Jews', 13, 44 ff., 67, 226, n. 2
Head, 137, 138, 150
Heart, 104, 134, 138, 141, 142, 145, 245 f., n. 43
Hebraeorum gens, 226, n. 23
Hebrew, alphabet, 59; language, 15, 61, 230, n. 7
Helbling, Seifried, 48, 244, n. 24, 249, n. 5
Heliodorus, 66
Hemorrhage, 50, 148, 228, n. 27
Hemorrhoid, 50, 148
Henry, Duke of Bavaria, 41
Henry IV, King (England), 95
Henry VII, Emperor, 201
Heresy, 170, 171 ff., 217; death penalty for, 173; and poisoning, 215; and sorcery, 196, 199 ff., 204, 207 ff.; and usury, 191
Heretics, 73, 140; Jews as, 174 ff., 202 f., 249 ff.
Herod, 20

Herzog von Burgund, 36
Hesse, 86, 233, n. 35
Hezekiah, 64
Hilary of Poitiers, 21
Hildegard of Bingen, 32
Historia Scholastica, 64
Hitler, Adolf, 5
Homunculus, 80
Horns, 6, 44 f., 47, 226 f.
Host, bleeding, 117, 152; desecration of, 17, 23, 82, 90, 109 ff., 180, 211 ff., 254, n. 5, 6; effects conversion of Jews, 111; in magic, 115 f., 210, 211 ff.; in poison, 101, 104, 115; *see also* Eucharist; Transubstantiation
Hugh of Lincoln, 131, 143, 244, n. 23
Hugo von Trimberg, 193
Hungary, 138, 151, 153, 186, 228, n. 22
Hussites, 38, 175 f.

Iconoclasts, 120, 175, 211
Iconodules, 120
Image, bleeding, 119; mutilation of, 17, 71, 118 ff., 203, 210 f.; wax, of Christ, 121 f.
Image magic, 122 f.
Inmestar (Syria), 127
Innocent III, Pope, 110, 165, 173, 174
Innocent IV, Pope, 134, 165
Innocent VIII, Pope, 142
Innsbruck, 137
Inquisition, 11, 68, 171, 173, 177 ff., 191, 192, 197, 199, 202, 203 f., 204, 211, 241, n. 23
Inquisition, Spanish, 32, 75, 81
Intermarriage, prohibition of, 103, 187
Isaac ben Moses, 91, 248, n. 3
Isaiah, 73
Islam, 11; *see also* Moslems
Israel, tribes of, 51; lost tribes of, 40, 225, n. 13
Issachar, tribe of, 51
Italy, 76 f., 95, 115, 179, 185, 241, n. 22
Ivan IV (the Terrible), 98 f.

Jacques de Vitry, 92
Jacobs, Joseph, 81
Jerusalem, 34, 35, 126, 184, 236, n. 13
Jesus, coming of, 15; Jews curse, 182 f.; temptation of, 19
"Jew," term of abuse, 12, 221, n. 1

Jew of Malta, 17, 99, 185
Jew badge, 13, 26, 46, 67, 116, 180, 193, 208, 239, n. 15, 242, n. 32, 243, n. 17
Jew, Wandering, 17, 40
Jews, dealers in gems, 74; economic position of, 11; as heretics, 191, 192, 207 ff., 217; persecution of, 42; physical peculiarities of, 44 ff.; position of, in medieval Europe, 161; red, 40; relations with Christians, 159 ff., 168; as sorcerers, 208 ff.; as traitors, 40, 183 ff.; *see also* Attacks on Jews
Joachim II, Elector of Brandenburg, 73, 83, 98, 237, n. 2
Joan of Arc, 215
Job, 64, 73
Johannes, Abbot of Trittenheim, 66
John XXII, Pope, 123, 202
Joseph, 57, 64, 233, n. 42
Joseph, tribe of, 52
Josephus, 71, 92, 132, 229, n. 6
Jourdain, Bernard, 123
Judaism, 12; attitude of Church to, 162, 174 f., 176 f.; goat symbol of, 46; and magic, 58, 67 f.
Judaizing, 181, 191
Judas Iscariot, 22, 193, 222, n. 25, 26, 224, n. 5
Jüdel, 243, n. 5
Juden Badstub, 26, 28 f.
Judenblick, 232, n. 35; *see also* Evil eye
Judenhut, 226, n. 2; *see also* Hat, Jews'
Judenmatz, 147; *see also* Unleavened bread
Judensau, 26, 47, 218
Juden Synagog, 26
Juan I, King (Aragon), 81
Jubilee, 137 f.
Julius III, Pope, 179
Jupiter, 44
Justinian, Emperor, 15, 58
Justin Martyr, 182, 221, n. 8
Juvenal, 57, 76

Kabbalah, 59, 74, 76 ff.
Kabyle, 226, n. 19
Kaisersberg, Geiler von, 252, n. 4
Key, magic, 84
Kidnaping, 82, 128, 131
Kiev, 129, 243, n. 6
King's Peace, 92

Kirchhof, Hans Wilhelm, 153, 228, n. 18
Kisch, Guido, 232, n. 25
Kissingen, 72
Koran, 44
Krems, 137
Kyteler, Lady Alice, 212

Lachrymabilem Judaeorum Alemannie, 134
Lamb, crucified, 242, n. 29
Landi, Ortensio, 77
Langton, Archbishop, 187
Lauder a. d. Tauber, 135
Leo, the Isaurian, 71, 211
Leonast, 93
Leontius of Byzantium, 25
Lepers, 101 f., 239, n. 15
Leprosy, 142, 149, 150, 228, n. 26
Levi, tribe of, 51
Limoges, 122
Lincoln, 131
Lippold, Münzmeister, 73, 83 ff., 98
Lithuania, 99; *see also* Council, of Lithuanian Jewry
Liver, 138
Lombards, 189
Lombardy, 249, n. 9
London, 81, 184, 232, n. 32, 238, n. 6, 244, n. 24
Longinus, the blind Jew, 231, n. 19
Lopez, Rodrigo, 98, 238, n. 4, 8
Lorraine, 143
Louis VII, King (France), 191
Louis IX, King, 68, 95, 252, n. 11
Louis X, King, 179
Louis XIV, King, 214
Löw, Judah, 73
Lowenthal, Marvin, 6
Lublin, 147
Luciferans, 200, 205
Lucius of Samosate, 58
Ludus paschalis, 36
Luther, Martin, 15, 39, 42, 57, 72, 73, 74, 75, 80, 93, 99, 120, 175, 186, 193, 217 ff., 232, n. 24
Lutherans, 186

Madagascar, 245, n. 43
Magdeburg, 242, n. 29
Magic, Christian, 59, 196 ff.; Hellen-

istic, 57, 61; Jewish, 6, 58 f.; Mohammedan, 61; sacred, 198

Magnus, Albertus, 34

Maimonides, Moses, 178

Mainz, 115, 168, 183, 205, 224, n. 2

Malachi, 73

Malcontent, 99

Mallorca, 73, 255, n. 3

Manetho, 238, n. 14

Manicheism, 199, 200

Mannsfeldischen Chronik, 106

Marburg, 87

March, Adam, 132

Margaritha, Antonius, 151, 228, n. 26

Maria the Jewess, 58, 74

Marlowe, Christopher, 17, 99, 185

Marranos, 32, 75, 82, 177; *see also* Conversos

Marston, John, 99

Martial, 47, 227, n. 16

Martin V, Pope, 72, 95, 107, 134

Mary, Virgin, 25 f., 118, 120, 121, 186, 254, n. 7

Massena (New York), 243, n. 6

Mathias of Janow, 39

Matzah, 147, 241, n. 13; *see also* Unleavened bread

Maurienne, 36

Maurus, Rabanus, 224, n. 2

Maximus, Emperor, 199

Medicine, blood in, 147 f.; human flesh in, 141 ff.; Jews in, 92 f.; *see also*, Physicians, Jewish; medieval, 91 f.

Megenberg, Konrad von, 74

Menstruation, 50, 149, 228, n. 27

Mephistopheles, 26

Merchant of Venice, 31

Messiah, 20, 32 ff., 41, 153, 224

Messina, 82

Mezuzah, 91

Michael, archangel, 34, 35

Michelangelo, 44

"Microbe of bleeding hosts," 117

Minorca, 162

Miracle de Théophile, 61

Mirandola, Pico della, 77

Miriam the Jewess, 58

Misanthropy, Jewish, 128

Mohammed, 186, 223, n. 35, 227, n. 17

Molon, 126

Mongols, 40, 185

Montespan, Madame de, 214

Montfort, Simon de, 184

Montpellier, 178

Moors, 183, 184; *see also* Arabs; Saracens

Moravia, 117, 229, n. 30

Moreau, Canon, 41

Morocco, 129

Moses, 44, 58, 64, 73, 133, 229, n. 7

Moses, messianic pretender, 34

Moses of Chorene, 142

Moses ben Yehiel, 88

Moses of Worms, 122

Moslems, 225, n. 17, 227, n. 17; *see also* Islam; Moors; Saracens

Mourning rites, 89

Mouse, 86, 218

Munich, 137

Murder, Jews accused of, 129; *see also* Blood accusation; Ritual murder

Murviedro, 82

Mystère de la Passion, 22, 230, n. 11

Mystère de la Sainte Hostie, 186

Names, mystical, 57, 59, 61, 65, 69, 93; *see also* God, names of

Naphtali, tribe of, 51 f.

Naphtali ben Isaac, 90

Narbonne, 69, 71, 130, 184; Council of (589), 58

National Socialism, 5; *see also* Nazis

Navarre, 69, 178

Nazis, 6, 49, 226, n. 19, 240, n. 38, 243, n. 6, 255, n. 3

Nemirov, 75

Nestorians, 175

New Year, 183

Nicholas V, Pope, 138, 180

Nicodemus, 19

Nietzsche, Friedrich, 4

Nigarelli, David di, 95

Noah, 64

Normans, 184

North, Thomas, 221, n. 1

Northampton, 244, n. 24

Norwich, 125, 130, 131

Novgorod, 73

Nuremberg, 105; 243, n. 6

Oath, Jewish, 67, 69 f., 224, n. 2; taken in synagogue, 58

Oberwesel, 137
Odor, of Jews, 6, 47 ff., 149, 150, 227 f., 247, n. 26; see also Foetor judaicus; of spirits, 48, 227, n. 17; of white men, 227, n. 12
Ofen, 48, 242, n. 29; see also Buda
Ointment, witches', 212, 214
Okes Bogues, Simon, 235, n. 8
Oldenburg, 247, n. 43
Ordeal, 70
Origen, 58, 64, 127, 182, 229, n. 7
Orléans, 205
Ortega y Gasset, Jose, 4
Oxford, 118, 187

Paassen, Pierre van, 57
Palermo, 129
Palestine, 34, 40
Papal States, 76, 226, n. 23
Paracelsus, 80
Paris, 41, 88, 102, 114, 178, 179, 186; Council of (1212), 192
Paris, Matthew, 70, 118, 131, 143, 191
Parkes, James, 127, 163, 175
Passion of Christ, 15, 22, 60
Passover, 31, 89, 124, 129, 130, 133 ff., 154, 245, n. 30; see also Ritual murder
Pastoureaux, 239, n. 16, 17
Paul II, Pope, 198
Paupères, 168
Pecorone, 106
Pedro I, King (Castile), 75
Pedro IV, King (Aragon), 81
Pepin, 71, 184
Persia, 35, 40
Peter II, King (Aragon), 173
Peter of Blois, 224, n. 2
Peter the Hermit, 168
Peter of Luxembourg, 115
Peter the Venerable, 18
Pfefferkorn, Johann (1), 82, 107, 237, n. 2
Pfefferkorn, Johann (2), 179
Pforzheim, 135, 148, 150
Philip II, King (France), 138, 235, n. 22
Philip III, King, 46
Philip IV, King, 68, 179, 180, 202, 250, n. 16

Philip the Good, Duke of Burgundy, 126
Philomena, 71
Phylacteries, 151
Physicians, Jewish, 65 f., 72, 82, 92 ff., 142, 213, 236 f.; see also Medicine, Jews in; women, 236, n. 14
Photios, Patriarch, 66
Pigs, born to Jewess, 52
Pilate, Pontius, 20, 148, 222, n. 21, 228, n. 27
Pius V, Pope, 76, 77, 226, n. 23, 234, n. 1
Plague, Jews cause, 144; see also Disease, Jews cause
Poison, 6, 71, 76, 82, 83, 84, 97 ff., 123, 140, 144, 213 f., 238 ff.; see also Well poisoning
Poland, 80, 98, 147, 152, 223, n. 39, 238, n. 3, 240, n. 38, 244, n. 27, 246, n. 21; see also Council, of Polish Jewry
Polovtzians, 129
Pontoise, 130
Porpoler, Mosse, 81, 202
Portugal, 178, 225, n. 13
Pösing (Hungary), 138, 153
Potions, love, 76 f., 84, 115
Prague, 73, 114, 185, 234, n. 52, 240, n. 37, 244, n. 27, 251, n. 33
Prester John, 225, n. 13
Printing, invention of, 38
Prioresses Tale, 42
Priscillian, 199
Procopius, 58
Prostitute, 77; mother of Antichrist, 34 f.
Protocols of Zion, 224 f., n. 1; see also Elders of Zion
Provence, 69, 89, 103, 107
Prussia, 104, 138, 183
Pterocarpus Draco, 151
Purim, 127, 128, 154

Quinsy, 50
Quod super nonnullis, 202

Raderus, 152
Rain, produced by Jews, 72
Ram, crucified, 242, n. 29
Rameru, 244, n. 24
Rashi, 248, n. 3

Raziel, 64
Reformation, 79, 217
Regensburg, 91, 105, 107, 149
Reineke Fuchs, 74
Reinfrid of Braunschweig, 64
Résurrection du Sauveur, 222, n. 21
Reuben, 64
Reuben, tribe of, 51
Reubeni, David, 225, n. 13
Reuchlin, Johann, 77, 82, 249, n. 13
Revelation, 20
Richard I, King, 70, 142
Richard of Cornwall, 132
Richer of Sens, 133, 143
Rindfleisch, 239, n. 17
Ritual, Jewish, 26, 31, 88, 113
Ritual murder, 17, 124 ff., 242 ff.; *see also* Blood accusation
Rhineland, 91, 98, 201
Robert of Edmondsbury, 131
Romanos IV, Emperor, 129
Romans, 20
Rome, 61, 76, 77, 120, 179, 199, 226, n. 23, 234, n. 3
Roth, Cecil, 18, 128
Rothschild, 226, n. 19
Rudolph II, Emperor, 73
Rumania, 114
Russia, 73, 99, 243, n. 6
Rutebeuf, 61

Saarland, 229, n. 3, 232, n. 35
Sabbat, witches', 205, 206, 210, 212, 214, 215
Sabbath, 210, 243, n. 15; fire on, 90, 123
Sabbato, Elia di, 95
Sacchetti, Franco, 94
Sachs, Hans, 93
Sacrifice, 249, n. 9; human, 126 f., 149, 205, 214
Sachsenspiegel, 92, 202
St. Agatha, 252, n. 4
St. Albans (England), 17
St. Anthony, 252, n. 4
St. Augustine, 148
St. Blaise, 252, n. 4
St. Dié (France), 143
St. Gregory, 242, n. 28
St. Humbrecht, 252, n. 4
St. Jerome, 15, 182
St. John, 20

St. Luke, 20
St. Mary Magdalen, 226, n. 21
St. Nicholas, 17
St. Paul, 230, n. 11
St. Peter, 230, n. 11, 252, n. 4
St. Quentin, 237, n. 2
St. Ruf, Council of (1337), 103
St. Stephen, 48
St. Valentine, 252, n. 4
Salamis, 81
Salzburg, 91
Sampson of Mirabeau, 95
Sanbenito, 203
Sandys, Edwin, 252, n. 15
Santa Clara, Abraham a, 42, 108
Saracens, 101; *see also* Arabs; Moors
Saragossa, 130
Satan, in Christian belief, 19, 59 f., 198 f.; and heresy, 199, 203; and Jews, 6, 11 ff., 19 ff., 32, 41 f., 60; in Jewish belief, 19; as Jewish messiah, 34; pact with, 84, 86; *see also* Devil
Savoy, 103, 135
Saxony, 75
Schudt, Johann Jakob, 57, 71, 74, 79, 80, 86, 90, 106, 108, 115, 228, n. 26
Schwabenspiegel, 202
Scripture, interpretation of, 15, 221, n. 10
Scrofula, 50
Secreta Secretorum, 63
Segovia, 82
Sennacherib, 224, n. 2
Serbia, 129
Servants, Christian, of Jews, 89, 110, 139, 143, 160
Seth, 64
Shakespeare, William, 31, 106
Sheketz, 250, n. 22
Shofar, 183
Shylock, 106
Sicily, 66, 82, 100, 237, n. 27, 242, n. 29
Siete Partidas, 97, 122, 132
Sigismund Augustus, 98
Silesia, 70, 145, 229, n. 30
Simeon, tribe of, 51
Simeon Hasid of Treves, 160
Simon Magus, 231, n. 19
Simon of Trent, 137
Sin (god), 44
Slavetraders, Jewish, 128
Snakes, Jews charm, 229, n. 3

Solomon, King, 25, 63 f., 73, 230, n. 7, 231, n. 16, 18
Sorbonne, 38, 186
Sorcerer, Jew as, 57 ff., 229 ff.
Sorcery, among Christians, 66; a crime, 80; crusade against, 196 ff., 252 ff.
Spaeth, Johann Peter, 152
Spain, 50, 69, 72, 77, 95, 101, 108, 128, 131, 134, 138, 159, 167, 175, 184, 203, 223, n. 35, 226, n. 19, 239, n. 17
Spangenberg, Cyriacus, 106
Sperm, libation of, 213
Spiders, in poison, 104
Spina, Alfonso de, 41, 137
Stapleton, Thomas, 201
Steiermark, 117
Steinschneider, Moritz, 74
Storms, caused by sorcery, 80, 198; Jews tame, 229, n. 3
Strasbourg, 104, 235, n. 14
Summers, Montague, 155
Swabia, 94
Sweden, 104
Sylvester I, Pope, 65
Synagogue, 20, 21, 82, 241, n. 3; building new, 180; buried treasure in, 71; host mutilated in, 113; image of Christ in, 121; of usurers, 192; of witches, 210, 214
Syria, 126, 127

Tabernacles, Feast of, 149, 224, n. 3
Tail, 46
Talavera, Juan de, 82
Talmud, 42, 82, 133, 175, 178 f., 210, 232, n. 32; attack on, 68, 179, 249, n. 12
Tam, Jacob, 244, n. 24
Tartars, 185
Templars, 205
Teruel, 81, 101
Tethel, 74
Theobald of Canterbury, 130, 137
Theodosius II, Emperor, 127
Theophilus, 23 ff., 66, 140, 203
Thomas of Cantimpré, 148
Three Ladies of London, 186
Titus, 92, 236, n. 13
Toad, 26, 101, 115, 206, 212, 241, n. 13
Toledo, 121, 244, n. 27; Council of (694), 184

Toledot Yeshu, 230, n. 11
Tortosa, 69, 224, n. 2
Torture, 84
Toulouse, 123, 184, 191
Tovey, D'blossiers, 49, 118
Trajan, 128
Transubstantiation, 17, 109 f., 114, 211; see also Eucharist; Host
Treasures, buried, 71, 76
Treuga Henrici, 201
Trithemius, John, 64, 239, n. 23
Troyes, 180
Trypho, 221, n. 8
Turks, 38, 40, 129, 183, 185, 186
Typhus, 229, n. 29, 240, n. 38
Tyrnau, 149
Tyrol, 100

Unleavened bread, 147, 149, 245, n. 37; see also Matzah
Urban IV, Pope, 117
Urine, 100, 101, 141
Usury, 67, 68, 138, 188 ff., 202, 233, n. 36, 251 f.

Vaad, Lithuanian, 79 f., 245, n. 30
Valencia, 81, 82, 202, 225, n. 19
Valladolid, Statutes of, 95, 100
Valréas (France), 132
Venceslas II, King, 164
Vengence et destruction du Hierusalem, 22
Venice, 68, 129, 179
Vespasian, 71, 92
Vie de St. Martin, 210
Vienna, 72, 97, 108, 176, 237, n. 17, 238, n. 14; Council of (1267), 44, 100, 113; (1311), 191
Vienne, 165
Villavitis, Hieronymus de, 39
Virgil, 64
Volkmar, 168
Vom Schem Hamphoras, 186
Von den Juden und ihren Lügen, 186, 218
Vulgate, 44

Wagner, Richard, 5
Waldensians, 176, 206
War, Thirty Years', 72
Wartburgkrieg, 64
Warwick, 138

Wedding, blood required at, 31, 147, 153; host mutilated at, 113
Weissenburg, 137
Well poisoning, 101 ff., 144, 238 f.; *see also* Poison
Wendunmuth, 153
Westminster, 160
Wig, red, 222 f., n. 26
William of Auvergne, 197
William of Newbury, 70, 161
William of Norwich, 124 f., 130, 245, n. 30
Wilson, Robert, 186
Winchester, 130
Wine, 91, 245, n. 30
Witchcraft, 38, 47, 59 f., 87, 121, 140, 147, 201, 203 ff., 212 f.
Witch cults, 115, 146, 203 f.
Witches, 47, 90, 108, 198, 208

Witch trials, 81, 86
Worcester, Synod of (1240), 68
Worms, 144
Württemberg, 79
Würzburg, 68

Xanten, 138

Yazid II, Caliph, 241, n. 26
York, 166, 225, n. 18

Zabulon, 65
Zachariah, magician, 73
Zambri, 65
Zebulon, tribe of, 51
Zebulon, magician, 64 f., 231, n. 18
Zechariah, 73
Zedekiah, magician, 65 f., 97